I0818148

Amy Jacques Garvey

AMY JACQUES GARVEY

Selected Writings from the *Negro World*, 1923–1928

Edited by Louis J. Parascandola

THE UNIVERSITY
OF TENNESSEE PRESS
Knoxville

First Edition.

Frontispiece: Mrs. A. Jacques Garvey viewing the bust of Marcus Garvey. Erected Jamaica, B.W.I., November 4, 1956. Courtesy of Photographs and Prints Division, Schomburg Center for Research in Black Culture, The New York Public Library.

Library of Congress Cataloging-in-Publication Data

Names: Garvey, Amy Jacques, author. | Parascandola, Louis J., 1952- editor.
Title: Amy Jacques Garvey : selected writings from the Negro World, 1923-1928 / edited by Louis J. Parascandola.
Other titles: Selected writings from the Negro World, 1923-1928
Description: First edition. | Knoxville : The University of Tennessee Press, [2016] | Includes bibliographical references and index.
Identifiers: LCCN 2015028625 | ISBN 9781621902065 (hardcover)
Subjects: LCSH: Black nationalism—United States—History—20th century—Sources. | African American women—Political activity—History—20th century—Sources. | Feminism—United States—History—20th century—Sources.
Classification: LCC E185.97.G28 A25 2016 | DDC 305.48/896073—dc23
LC record available at http://lccn.loc.gov/2015028625

Contents

Acknowledgments

This volume is the product of almost ten years of labor. During that time, I have been indebted to many people. I would like to thank some of those people below:

My graduate assistants at LIU Mary Walker, Rajul Punjabi, Chris Iverson, Asja Parrish, and Malik Crumpler as well as my former students Tiani Kennedy and Yani Perez for proofreading, collecting pieces, typing, and suggestions.

My editor, Thomas G. Wells; editorial assistant, Emily Huckabay; copyeditor, Kathryn Peck; and the rest of the staff at the University of Tennessee Press for their support and advice.

Dean David Cohen and Vice President Gale Stevens Haynes at LIU, Brooklyn, for their financial support.

Barbara Bair and Ula Yvette Taylor for their encouragement and advice.

My indexer, Jenny Lillich.

Chantel Clark of the Special Collections at Fisk University for help providing materials.

The staffs at the Moorland-Spingarn Research Center at Howard University, the Schomburg Center for Research in Black Culture (NYPL), the Robert W. Woodruff Library at Atlanta University, the James Weldon Johnson Collection at Yale University, and the National Archives of Jamaica in Spanish Town for their help providing materials.

My parents, Ann and Louis Parascandola, my sisters Maryann Barbieri and Judy Bilello, and my sister-in law, Randee Parascandola. I wish you could have all been here to see this.

My brother John and my brothers-in-law Bob and Ben.

The Nero family.

My wife, Shondel Nero, to whom this volume is dedicated with love. I never could have done this without your love and support.

A Note on the Text

The editing in the *Negro World* could be erratic. I have retained the original texts of all the pieces, with a few silent corrections of obvious typographical errors. In a few cases, lengthy subheadings for newspaper articles and speeches have been omitted. Some inconsistencies (e.g., the spelling of "practice" and "practise") have been kept. In a few cases, I have used [*sic*] for odd spellings. Notes on the text are indicated by superscript numbers. If I have omitted material from the original source, the deletion is indicated by an ellipsis in brackets [. . .]. Other ellipses are in the original text.

Introduction

Amy Jacques Garvey (1895–1973) has long been thought of largely in terms of her relationship to her husband, Black nationalist Marcus Garvey, and as the editor of the *Philosophy and Opinions of Marcus Garvey* (1923, 1925). Her importance even then tends to be minimized, as is evidenced by her almost total absence in many of the earlier writings on the Garveyite movement.[1] Study of her life and ideas has slowly begun to take shape over the past thirty years; however, most of her own seminal writing has long remained inaccessible, available only in archives or on incomplete, barely legible microfilm in a handful of research institutions. This neglect continues despite Jacques Garvey's being the most significant female in the Garveyite movement and one of the most prolific women within any Black nationalist group.[2] The current volume seeks to fill this void by making her writings in the *Negro World* widely available for the first time. The *Negro World* proved to be the most consistent and most significant source for Jacques Garvey's writing, particularly between 1924–1927, when she edited a weekly woman's page entitled "Our Women and what They Think." Jacques Garvey concerned herself with a diversity of important and often controversial political and social issues rather than the stereotypical domestic matters expected of most woman's pages. Collectively, her almost 200 editorials and other writings treat not only issues of Black nationalism but also women's struggles globally as well as the resistance of various ethnic groups against colonial oppression. By examining her selected writings in the *Negro World*, one can better understand her powerful contribution not only to Garveyism but also to the growth of Black radical thought, anti-imperialist ideology, and the rights of third-world women, topics that continue to resonate up to the present day.

EARLY LIFE

Since Jacques Garvey remains a relatively little-known figure, I will provide a brief biographical sketch before examining her writings. Amy Euphemia Jacques was born on December 31, 1895[3] in Kingston, Jamaica. She was the eldest of seven children born to middle-class parents, George Samuel Jacques—manager of a tobacco factory—and the mixed-race Charlotte South. Her paternal great-great grandfather had been the first mayor of Kingston. Jacques was educated at several elite Jamaican schools, including Deaconess Home School and Wolmers' Girls' School (*Veiled Garvey* 7–12). Jacques' education was highly unusual, particularly for a girl, since fewer "than 2% of Jamaican youths received a high school education" at that time ([Samuel] Hurwitz and [Edith] Hurwitz 1971, cited in Adler 349). Jacques' father taught her analytical skills from an early age, giving her reading and writing assignments on international affairs. He had plans for her to become a nurse and encouraged her to take courses in shorthand and stenography to help with her note-taking. However, when he died, she followed her own ambition and worked as a clerk and secretary in the law offices of the family attorney. Thus, Jacques learned skills that would prepare her for her future positions as journalist and political administrator as well as teach her the rhetorical skills and independent thinking that would help her challenge Marcus Garvey and the other men in Garvey's organization, the Universal Negro Improvement Association and African Communities League (UNIA).

Jacques moved to New York City in 1917 at the height of Caribbean migration to the United States.[4] She did so against the will of her mother and her Jamaican employer, obtaining a position teaching night school, thus demonstrating early on an "independence of mind, courage, and thirst for knowledge—all of which characterized her for the rest of her life" (Adler 351). She met Marcus Garvey in December 1919. Garvey soon asked her to become his personal secretary, and she served as a bridesmaid at his first wedding, to Amy Ashwood on Christmas Day, 1919. There are debates about how well the two women knew each other and when Amy Jacques began a romantic relationship with Marcus, but in early 1922, Marcus Garvey divorced Amy Ashwood and married Amy Jacques on July 27 of that same year.[5]

GARVEY AND THE UNIA

Marcus Garvey established the UNIA in Jamaica in 1914 and planted it with him when he came to the United States in 1916. By the early 1920s, he had created more than 900 branches in some 40 countries with about 6 million members, which made the UNIA the largest Black mass movement in history (Martin 14–16). The UNIA "was a pro-capitalist, masculinist movement that promoted race pride, Pan African unity, economic self-sufficiency, and the redemption of Africa from European imperial powers" (McDuffie 219). It was a movement that believed in a "biological conception of race" (Goldthree 156), that God had deliberately created the races differently and intended them to be separated; hence, racial mixing was frowned upon. Despite her own racially mixed heritage, Amy endorsed this philosophy. She and Marcus also shared a similar view of Black nationalism and initially founded a relationship based "on mutual respect and admiration" (Adler 352).

Garvey's ideology courted the common man. The UNIA published his weekly newspaper, the *Negro World*, at a price working people could afford, and sections of it were published in Spanish and French in order to appeal to a wider audience. The movement established the Negro Factories Corporation, which managed many Black businesses, including restaurants, laundries, a hotel, a printing press, and a doll factory. The UNIA sold shares (only to Blacks) in his Black Star Steamship Line, a Black-run business that was intended to transport Blacks around the world.

At first, Garvey's movement met with incredible success. The conferences he held were enormous and his "monster" meetings at his Liberty Hall were regularly packed. Soon, however, cracks began to appear. Many of his early supporters questioned his strong-arm tactics and his financial abilities. He came under attack from Black leaders such as W. E. B. Du Bois, who felt that he was crude and that he did not understand the complicated racial situation of American-born Blacks. More radical Black leaders such as A. Philip Randolph and Cyril Briggs balked at his resistance to the growing Marxist movements of the 1920s. Whites were frightened of his separatist views that emphasized Black pride and self-sufficiency. He had, in fact, been under government investigation since 1919 (Kornweibel 100–31). Under fire from all these groups, particularly after Garvey's meeting with the Ku Klux Klan in 1922 to discuss matters of racial separation, the movement began to collapse. Garvey came under indictment on charges of mail fraud involving the Black Star Line stock in 1922, was convicted in 1923, imprisoned in 1925, and was eventually deported in 1927. It was during this turbulent time that Amy Jacques Garvey became involved in the UNIA and the *Negro World* (Grant 396–400).

THE ROLE OF WOMEN IN THE UNIA

As E. Frances White posits, Black nationalist organizations tend to have conflicting progressive and conservative traits.[6] While they often advocate anti-colonial, anti-imperialist discourse, they frequently support utopian images of Africa and dichotomous gender roles (73–82). Despite the presence of several powerful women in the movement, the UNIA generally followed an often chauvinistic, hierarchical model: upholding "with reverence the notion of the woman as the home-maker, culture bearer and as someone who intrinsically carried the memory of the race" (Ford-Smith 76).[7] Lady presidents reported to male presidents and women were largely seen as race mothers. In the female auxiliaries of the UNIA such as the Universal Motor Corps and the Black Cross Nurses, women often had limited roles (Benjamin 75–76). In the ideal UNIA male-female relationship, the woman was seen "not as worker or professional but as helpmate and partner to the man, a moral influence, a charitable volunteer, and an educator of children" (Bair "True Women" 159; Blain 1–10).

Women in the organization often resisted this subordinate role, as manifested at the 1922 UNIA convention, where several female delegates demanded a larger role in the movement. Despite the sexual hierarchy within the UNIA, the movement appealed to many women. Barbadian American novelist Paule Marshall recalls that her mother and other women involved in the organization "attended meetings, marched in parades, and served as members of the nurses' brigade" (84). For many of these women, it was often the first time they were allowed to demonstrate leadership skills in a public place (Watkins-Owens 46). As historian Adam Ewing remarks, "If at times and in places the UNIA sustained existing gender inequalities among African Americans, at others times and in other places it offered a promising vehicle within which women might negotiate better terms" (150). Regardless of women's reasons for membership, many people in the movement thought of them as being "the backbone" of the organization.

Amy's marriage to Marcus Garvey in some ways followed the conflicted role of women in the UNIA. Jacques Garvey stated that in his proposal to her Marcus declared it was imperative for her to marry him for the good of the organization (*Garvey and Garveyism* 89). His proposal summarized the marriage, which was essentially a business proposition: "Marcus Garvey never married me for love. No, sir. That was not the proposal. He needed me. That was all. He needed someone he could trust. It wasn't a personal matter" (Jacques Garvey qtd. in Reed 46).

Jacques Garvey accepted a seemingly secondary role within her marriage because she maintained that a woman's domestic responsibilities were essential to racial advancement ("Negro Women" 105–7). However, she never considered herself to be lesser than her husband; instead, she saw herself as married more to Garvey as he represented the movement than as a man. Jacques Garvey's marriage demonstrates the difficult choices many women, both inside and outside the UNIA, had to negotiate between their public and private lives (Dossett 158–65).

JACQUES GARVEY'S "WOMANIST" BELIEFS AND "COMMUNITY FEMINISM"

The gravestone of Jacques Garvey is inscribed with the epitaph: "The Highest Calling of Womanhood." These words might seem to suggest a woman as having achieved her "ultimate" function in motherhood. In the case of Amy Jacques Garvey, this is only partly true. She was the proud and devoted mother of two sons, Marcus Jr. (born 1930) and Julius Winston (born 1933). However, "her highest calling" was not limited to her role as a mother and homemaker. As a Black nationalist woman, she strove to be useful not only to her family but also to her race and community.

Jacques Garvey did not like being labeled a feminist, saying, "A woman [must have] something that is feminine, something that is gracious, something that is sweet." She believed that "God intended her . . . to help her man and make both of them great" (qtd. in Lewis 68). However, she did have, as Barbara Bair calls it, a "womanist" perspective. "In her analysis of gender relations and the need for improvement of feminine status, she combined the liberal-individualistic premises basic to New Womanhood with older, more collective, social or domestic feminist perspectives" (Bair "Our Women" 103).

Jacques Garvey's views on gender must be considered within the context of her nationalistic beliefs in order to be understood. She was deeply influenced by Black club women such as Mary McLeod Bethune, Nannie Helen Burroughs, and Victoria Earle Matthews. She was inspired by their commitment to racial advancement and admired their stress on morals, hard work, and the doctrine of self-help (Matthews 8). Still, she fashioned "a black nationalist ideology and [spoke] in a black feminist tone that was different and more compelling than that of anyone who preceded her" (Collier-Thomas 248).

Jacques Garvey negotiated a difficult combination of nationalism with a feminist agenda through what Ula Y. Taylor describes as "community feminism," which blends self-determination and feminism. The "activism" of proponents of community feminism "discerns the configuration of oppressive power relations, shatters masculinist claims of women as intellectually inferior and seeks to empower women by expanding their roles and options" (Taylor *Veiled Garvey* 64). The community feminist construct posits that the traditional womanly role as helpmate does not contradict a position of leadership although it challenges the patriarchal agenda, often putting the women in conflict with the men in the organization.

EARLY INVOLVEMENT WITH THE *NEGRO WORLD*

Jacques Garvey's role within the UNIA was considerable. Using the skills instilled in her by her father, Amy read through periodicals to glean information she could supply to Garvey for his speeches and articles (Adler 353; *Garvey and Garveyism* 129–33). She often changed his speeches, softening or taking out more militant statements (Taylor *Veiled Garvey* 46–47).

Jacques Garvey began contributing essays, travel writings, and short sketches to the *Negro World* in 1923, the same year she edited the first volume of *Philosophy and Opinions of Marcus Garvey*.[8] The *Negro World* was launched in 1918 and estimates of its circulation ranged from 60,000 to 200,000 (Dossett 151). The journal significantly impacted the Harlem Renaissance, featuring a number of literary and political figures who would play a seminal role in the movement.[9] Amy had accompanied Marcus on a speaking tour in 1923 where she also gave some short speeches. The public reaction to those speeches and the dispatches she sent back to be published in the *Negro World* convinced Marcus to allow her a regular space in the paper (James 144–45).

Jacques Garvey was introduced to readers in an interview entitled "10 Minutes with Mrs. Marcus Garvey" (March 17, 1923). This was part of a rollout to the membership to establish her as "an able, strong-minded woman equipped in every way to do good work for the nationalist movement" (*Pittsburgh American* July 20, 1923, qtd. in Dossett 160). She wrote two pithy sketches, "Whither Goeth Thou?" (March 31, 1923) and "Who Is to Be Blamed?" (April 28, 1923), that demonstrate her narrative skills. She also penned two biographical pieces: "Tuskegee and Its Founder" (Dec. 1, 1923) on Booker T. Washington and the industrial school he founded, Tuskegee Institute; and "A Black Star" (Dec. 8, 1923) on "Sunshine Sammy" (actor Ernest Morrison) from the *Our Gang* comedies. She demonstrated her political views in a forceful response to a satirical proposal by H. L. Mencken to reinstall, with some tweaking, the peculiar institution in "Will the Negro Be Re-Enslaved" (Dec. 15, 1923). The most substantial writing was an extraordinary six-part travel piece on a cross-country trip (Oct. 27–Nov. 24, 1923). In this nationwide "vacation," Amy turns her keen eye to the inequalities between the races across the span of the nation. All of these works demonstrate different aspects of her nationalistic political beliefs and presage issues that would be reiterated in her editorials.

Shortly after Jacques Garvey became more actively involved in the UNIA, rival groups spread rumors that she was attempting to take over leadership of the movement. *Negro World* editors wrote a denial of these claims in the piece "Look Out for Mud" (July 14, 1923). However, in a letter published on July 21, 1923, "Mrs. Garvey Replies to Article in Negro World," Jacques Garvey railed against being labeled as "innocent and helpless" by her "protectors," claiming to be neither: "I am innocent of the honor of having the UNIA turned over to me by my husband, but I am not innocent of the depths to which colored men can stoop to further their petty schemes even at the expense of a downtrodden race such as ours." Thus, Amy gave notice before her weekly editorials had even begun that she would be a forceful opponent of patriarchy within the UNIA.

JACQUES GARVEY'S WOMAN'S PAGE

Jacques Garvey's woman's page, "Our Women and What They Think," began on February 2, 1924, and ended on April 30, 1927 (though her editorials ran until November 29, 1927, two days after Marcus' release from prison and shortly before his deportation to Jamaica; Broussard 108). As she states in the Nov. 15, 1924 issue, "Usually a Woman's Page in any journal is devoted solely to dress, home hints and love topics, [but] our page is unique, in that it seeks to give out the thoughts of our women on the subject affecting them in particular." The page was multi-lingual, crossed social strata, and was international in scope, "designed to serve as a forum for Garveyite women's thought and opinion, and as a clearinghouse to report women's activities" throughout the many Garveyite divisions around the globe (Bair "Our Women" 105–6). It allowed for "the voices of ordinary female Garveyites" to be heard publicly for the first time (Blain 1).[10] The page, in fact, extended even beyond the Garveyite movement to encompass a politics of "global solidarity," with contributions from women from such locations as Liberia, South Africa, Haiti and Australia (Zackodnik 447–48).

The column, with its emphasis on "social justice and nationalism" (Matthews 4) had a political agenda increasingly at variance with the more conventional woman's page, and it frequently challenged the male agenda of the UNIA. If the "advertisements for dinner sets, women's clothing and hair treatment" signaled a different, somewhat disquieting focus for male readers, the first feature article, "Women's Party Wants Not Only Equal Rights, But Equal Responsibilities With Men" (Feb. 2, 1924), must have been particularly jarring (Benjamin 84–85). Jacques Garvey hoped that through the page "we will be able to command a respectful hearing before the world, and prove that Negro women are great thinkers as well as doers" (Jacques Garvey, "Our Page Is Three Years Old," Feb. 12, 1927). While the most noteworthy aspect of the Woman's Page was Amy's succinct editorials, there were also several other features. These included articles culled by Jacques Garvey from various news venues as well as original pieces and letters from contributors. As Teresa Zackodnik points out, Amy's page, which included previously published articles sent by readers, "was designed to be collaborative" (447).

Articles reprinted from various journals alerted women to topics of interest from a variety of venues and served "as a platform for cultural debates about race pride, new roles and relationships for black men and women, and revised definitions of black manhood and womanhood" (Bair "Our Women" 110). These articles ranged from topics such as women's rights, divorce, labor, nationalism and world politics (Zackodnik 447–49). For example, the September 6, 1926 issue contained a survey on whether men should, like women, wear wedding rings. Another example is an article (June 14, 1924) about how women who are involved in politics affect the home life. This question drew a number of diverse answers from both male and female readers. An article by Hannah Nichols on August 23, 1924 reported on a UNIA "lady delegate" who demanded that boys and girls be raised equally in terms of education and responsibilities. Another article, by Saydee E. Parham (Feb 2, 1924), discussed the New Negro Woman and her place in society. The political, economic, and social achievements of Black women were also stressed in the articles, including those by Lady Vinton Davis on Harriet Tubman (Jan. 3, 1925) and Sojourner Truth (Jan. 17, 1925).

Even the letters, such as one written by Myrtle E. Carter (June 21, 1924) about the age a woman should marry and one written by Eunice Lewis (April 19, 1924) about the role of the Black woman in race leadership, raise important questions (Benjamin 73–74). These, and many other texts, demonstrate that Jacques Garvey's goal to raise the consciousness of women both inside and outside the movement and to build an important dialogue on significant issues achieved some success. This also shows how her work on the page and within the UNIA movement extended to more than just writing her column; her responsibilities involved considerable time working as an editor in reading mail, making grammatical and stylistic corrections, and choosing appropriate pieces from among her readers and from other news sources (Bair "Our Women" 111–122; Benjamin 84–98).

JACQUES GARVEY'S EDITORIALS

Jacques Garvey's editorials combined "her dual political commitment to a Pan-African agenda and to feminist ideas" (Taylor *Veiled Garvey* 64). The "articles asserted that Black women's responsibilities were 'not limited' to homemaking and child care, but included 'tackling the problems that confront the race,' including working with men 'in the office as well as on the platform.' These articles clearly implied a vision of motherhood that entailed community activism as well as private domesticity" (Satter 49). Over the years, her own editorials shifted from issues such as mothering "to more militant editorials on nationalist and anti-colonial topics, political economy, foreign policy, and international affairs" (Bair "Our Women" 110). Although the individual editorials are often too brief to show her true strength as a political and social writer, when examined collectively, they demonstrate the breadth of her nationalist and feminist agenda. As an aggregate, they reveal, as Taylor claims, "an eclectic pattern that hammered home the need for women to work as political agents as well as to perform as helpmates, acknowledging the difficulties related to this nurturing role. Although one might debate the various strategies or most appropriate means of achieving the goal, the goal was the same—empowerment through self-determination and nationhood in Africa" (*Veiled Garvey* 65). Her editor/husband clearly was satisfied with them, saying "Your editorials are all good Miss Vanity, that's why I have said nothing, otherwise you would have heard from me on the subject" (qtd. Dossett 165).

Jacques Garvey's essay topics are permeable, often bleeding into one another. For instance, she argues that the need for readers and thinkers and for better parenting is essential not only for the individual, but, more importantly, these qualities are needed for the race to raise its status. Blacks need to increase their knowledge of business not so much because the race needed individual wealth but because these people could then employ others. In some ways, this belief is similar to W. E. B. Du Bois' idea of a Talented Tenth, a distinguished group of Black leaders who would help uplift the entire race. Though the Garveyite movement is distinguished from the elitist structure of Du Bois' NAACP by its more egalitarian nature geared towards the Black masses, Jacques Garvey often appeals to those in the race who are educated enough to write lucidly on topical issues and with grammatical correctness. The plea to Blacks to populate Africa was not directed to the rank-and-file job-seekers but to doctors as well as those with trade skills, such as shipbuilders and land surveyors. This emphasis on the Black elite is not surprising since in many ways Amy's middle-class upbringing was closer to Du Bois' than it was to Garvey's.

The structure of Jacques Garvey's editorials often follows a general pattern, starting with a broad topic before narrowing to a more specific focus. She frequently supports her point by using a fairly lengthy excerpt from a recent publication, demonstrating the extensive range of her reading. While there can sometimes be a shift in focus, the essay ultimately takes a final shape—sometimes based on what was suggested in the title and/or opening paragraph, but sometimes something entirely different. However, the seeming disparateness of the topics is always connected by the theme of Black nationalism and the need for justice and fairness throughout the world. Everything, no matter how trivial or disconnected it might seem, ultimately revolves around that theme. It is the essence of all of Amy's writing and of her life, and it is what compelled her to stay with Garvey despite the personal differences that sometimes surfaced between them.

The style of the essays is often similar to the style of her husband and of the Black preacher tradition. There are frequent biblical allusions, and she uses such devices as repetition, inversion, and parallelism. A particularly common device in her writing is the Homeric simile, which begins with a clause that uses "like" or "as" and ends with another clause that uses "so." This device, common in epic poetry, is appropriate for the seriousness with which Jacques Garvey takes her subject. It is also reflective of the heroic struggle that she sees the race as undertaking. She often poses questions, attempting to challenge her readers into considering solutions for the problems she raises. Her essays inevitably end on a note of optimism, indicating the hope for victory in the struggle. Whatever the problems posed by the essay, Amy ends with at least the possibility of overcoming them through racial unity behind Garvey and his message. It is, of course, propaganda, which Jacques Garvey would be the first to admit. To her, propaganda was not seen negatively, but as a way to enlighten people to the truth, a means of spreading the gospel of Garveyism, which is often linked to Christianity, with Garvey serving as a substitute Messiah.

Jacques Garvey's work on the page often took a tremendous toll on her health. She stated that producing the page "certainly [was] a hardship" since it was necessary "to put in eighteen hours of work daily," and she continued on to say that she "sometimes [got] only three hours of sleep" (Bair "Negro Women" 120). She suffered from eye trouble, lost weight, and at times was unable to continue, being confined to her home due to ill health. However, true to her credo, she continued her work in the belief that the overall good of the race was more important than the individual.

The pieces from Jacques Garvey's woman's page collected in this anthology are grouped under ten fairly broad subject headings:

INTERNATIONAL AFFAIRS/WHITE EXPLOITATION OF DARKER PEOPLES: Jacques Garvey often spoke out on issues affecting people around the world, in places including Egypt, India, China and sub-Saharan Africa. In her writing, she condemns White exploitation of those she labeled as "darker peoples" both in their homelands and abroad, and she supports the desire of the native peoples for self-government and independence.

GENDER ISSUES: Although Jacques Garvey often advocates traditionally assigned gender roles, with women as caring, nurturing supporters of men, she simultaneously praises the fact that women worldwide are demanding more rights in both domestic matters and political affairs. She generally condemns Black men for their lack of leadership and virility and for not being supportive enough of their women.

PARENTING/CHILDREN AND YOUTHS: Child-rearing, often left largely up to the mother, was an important role in the uplifting of the race according to Jacques Garvey. She believed that mothers, though sometimes underappreciated, were essential in lifting racial awareness and raising self-sufficient and productive members of the race. In her writing, she asserts that men need to accept their responsibility in parenting.

AN EXAMINATION OF THE RACE: ADVICE AND CRITICISM: Jacques Garvey advised Blacks on how to improve their lives, thereby raising the overall health of the race and criticizing those who held the race down. Her advice includes taking pleasure in making others happy, in saving money, and in being tactful. Jacques Garvey often took Blacks, including those in the UNIA, to task for their lack of will and devotion to the cause and their selfishness, laziness, and hypocrisy.

CALL FOR CONTRIBUTIONS TO THE WOMAN'S PAGE: In her requests for contributions to the Woman's Page, Jacques Garvey urges all Black women, regardless of affiliation or educational background, to express their views in English, Spanish, or French. She asserts that this will "demonstrate to other races of the world the progress [Blacks] have made since emancipation," pointing out that if women don't do their duty, the Woman's Page may cease to exist ("Have A Heart," the *Negro World* Aug. 2, 1924).

RELIGION: Jacques Garvey was a believer in Christ and his teachings even though the UNIA did not advance a particular religious doctrine. However, she condemned the hypocritical Christianity preached by many Whites, who did not practice goodwill toward all men. Jacques Garvey had mixed feelings about Jews, admiring their willingness to fight for a Jewish state. On the other hand, she believed Jews, despite their similarities to Blacks as persecuted groups, often were not supportive of Black concerns.

READING AND LEARNING BUSINESS AND TECHNICAL SKILLS: Jacques Garvey believed in the necessity for practicality. In her editorials, she maintains that Blacks need to dedicate themselves to business and technology in order to earn money and respect and advance the race. She also asserts that reading and critical thinking are key to advancing the race and, states that "[n]ations hold other people in subjection by enslaving their minds." She believed that reading must be a large part of the New Negro and was a tool for the liberation of Blacks.

BLACK NATIONALISM/AFRICAN REDEMPTION: The liberation of Africa from colonization was at the core of the Garvey message. Jacques Garvey posits that all Blacks need not return to the homeland, but they must be unrelenting in their struggle to make Africa a homeland for Blacks, and that for this to be a reality, they must prepare themselves with the necessary skills before undertaking the endeavor.

GARVEY AS A LEADER WHILE IMPRISONED: During the time Jacques Garvey's column ran from 1924–1927, Marcus was either under indictment or in jail. She constantly reminded the readers of Garvey's indomitable spirit while he was imprisoned, and she kept the leader and his message at the fore. He was seen as a martyr to the cause and his release from prison was awaited in messianic terms.

RACE PRIDE AND RACIAL PROPAGANDA: One of the chief goals of the UNIA was to remind Blacks of their proud heritage and to show them the beauty in their Black bodies. Although many today would question her belief in the separation of races (or that there is even such a biological construct as race), Jacques Garvey steadfastly maintained the necessity of racial "purity." She believed that propaganda, "advertisement on a large scale," was essential to advancing one's racial group and that Garvey was a master of it. Whites controlled the image of Blacks by using "the poison of movie propaganda" as well as religion, the educational system, and other means. Blacks, according to Jacques Garvey, needed to fight back with propaganda of their own.

POST-WOMAN'S PAGE MATERIAL

The Woman's Page ceased on April 30, 1927. The reasons for its demise were probably twofold: 1) the column had become increasingly burdensome to Amy, and 2) her editorials, particularly ones criticizing the men of the movement, became more controversial and polarizing. She did not, however, stop writing editorials. Over the next several months, Jacques Garvey wrote on topics that had long been issues for her: the burden of motherhood, the lack of available good men as husbands, White oppression, the need for Black nationalism. Relieving Amy of the pressure of editing a weekly column allowed her to devote more time and space to these later editorials.

Jacques Garvey was a frequent speaker at UNIA gatherings as well. However, she was usually allowed no more than fifteen minutes to speak and few of her speeches were written down. This anthology provides a glimpse into her role as a speechmaker by providing three examples of her talks. The first, from 1925, was given at Liberty Hall in New York and embodies several of the themes of her editorials; further, it makes a pointed plea for Blacks to make the sacrifices needed to achieve the UNIA's goals. The second, from 1928, was given to a group of White women in London after the Garveys had departed from the United States. The speech deftly blends criticism of Whites for their treatment of Blacks while simultaneously appealing to the audience on the common ground of gender. After his deportation, Garvey was not allowed to return to the United States. He did, however, visit Canada and other nearby countries. In "Mrs. Amy Jacques-Garvey at Bermuda," from 1928, Jacques Garvey also delicately treads a tightrope, visiting a colonial territory and subtly calling for its independence—all under the watchful eye of suspicious British officials.

POST-NEGRO WORLD LIFE

Jacques Garvey's *Negro World* articles ended shortly before Garvey was deported to Jamaica in 1927. In 1935 he moved to England, where he remained until his death in 1940. Except for a brief period from 1937 to 1938, Jacques Garvey lived in Jamaica raising their two sons. She did not, of course, stop writing after leaving the United States, but continued to pen occasional pieces for the *Negro World* and in Garvey's *New Jamaican*. She also wrote for the Harlem-based periodical *The African* and *West African Pilot* in the 1940s. She continued to write sporadically, even contributing a piece in praise of the Black Panthers and Angela Davis in *Massachusetts Review* in 1973. This was consistent with her lifelong involvement in Black nationalist movements. However, never did she write as consistently as she had for the *Negro World* from 1924–1927.

In addition to her journalism, Jacques Garvey wrote several other important pieces including "The Atlantic Charter and British West Africa, Memorandum on Post-War Reconstruction of the Colonies and Protectorates of British West Africa" (1943) and contributed groundbreaking work to the Garveyite movement in *Garvey and Garveyism* (1963), *Black Power in America* (1968), and *More Philosophy and Opinions of Marcus Garvey* (1977). She remained a mentor to Black nationalists and a valuable resource to scholars of Garveyism until her death in Jamaica on July 25, 1973. She was buried in Saint Andrews Parish Churchyard in Kingston.

CONCLUSION

Some of Jacques Garvey's predictions never came to pass, and some of her ideas may now seem outdated. The grand homeland in Africa never occurred, and the possible unity of "the darker people" of the world against Whites has not (at least to this point) happened. However, her writings did accurately embody the radical Black politics of the era, and she did correctly gauge the rise of nationalist movements, many of which were in their infancy, against the forces of imperialism. And she did foresee an Africa ruled eventually by Africans.

Her views of Africa itself may now be seen as somewhat simplistic. She, like many of her contemporaries, did not always have the foresight to recognize the vast differences between the different cultures, languages, and political structures of the peoples of Africa that would make it difficult to unite them (let alone Black peoples of the Caribbean, the United States, and elsewhere) simply along racial lines. Nor did she consider whether enough skilled Negroes from around the globe would be willing to put in the work to return and develop the homeland even if it were freed from European control. It is, however, easy to imagine why Amy and other Black nationalists dreamed of a unity among the millions of Africa and their diasporic brethren. In that way, the race could gain the power, wealth, and stature it so desperately desired. These dreams of nationhood did not originate with Garvey but went back to Black nationalists at least a hundred years earlier. The views espoused by Jacques Garvey and the leadership of the UNIA tapped into this desire and were perhaps better organized and formulated than these earlier movements. As a result the UNIA was able to galvanize the largest Black mass movement in history.[11]

Jacques Garvey's ideas of distinct racial categories have also largely been discounted. However, we must remember that such racial categorization was created by Europeans in the 19th century and perpetuated by its scientists during Amy's lifetime. In addition, even if the notion of race is no longer considered biologically sound, it remains a powerful social construct today and far into the foreseeable future.

Since people, whether correctly or incorrectly, have been assigned these various racial categories, Jacques Garvey maintained that Blacks should rightly be proud of their ancestry.[12]

Jacques Garvey did correctly anticipate many of the racial problems that do still exist in the world. This includes not only the obvious income disparities between races that remain and the biases that still hamper so many people, but also the less obvious problems such as immigration quotas limiting peoples of colors in industrialized nations, the relative overrepresentation of Blacks in some professions such as law and preaching, and the exclusion of Blacks in other necessary trades and professions.

Jacques Garvey has left a powerful legacy through her writings. Jacques Garvey's work was at the center of the largest Black nationalist movement in history. It instilled racial pride in hundreds of thousands of people and continues to resonate for many today. It contributed to the growing nationalist movements and advocated for the rights of women inside and outside the UNIA. However, her writings and other achievements, partly due to her own actions, have rarely received the attention they deserve. Although a very forceful person, she often deflected attention from herself to her husband and the UNIA which is evident in her words, "I thank God for the opportunity to serve my people, by standing besideor [*sic*] him [Garvey], and since his passing, by standing up for him" (qtd. in Collier-Thomas, 247). Nevertheless, she played a "crucial role in shaping the ideological framework of Garveyism—a strain of black nationalism and the basis of Pan-Africanism" (Taylor *Veiled Garvey* 234). Her work is a constant assault on racism, sexism, colonialism, and imperialism. No matter what her position in relationship with her husband, Amy Jacques Garvey left a legacy of her own in her writings—particularly in her work published in the *Negro World*—and it is a legacy that continues in movements involving radical politics, Black nationalism, and women's rights.

PART I
EARLY WRITINGS

Interview/Editorial Reply

The interview with Jacques Garvey, "10 Minutes with Mrs. Marcus Garvey," introduced her to the *Negro World* readers. Though the unnamed interviewer is often condescending to her, asking innocuous questions about fashion and women's beauty, Jacques Garvey makes it clear that she is interested in more substantial issues. While she is portrayed as "a good wife" who helps her husband with his work, her own feisty personality is apparent as she frequently challenges the interviewer's comments.

In "Mrs. Marcus Garvey Replies to Article in Negro World," Jacques Garvey forcefully defends herself against charges that she is trying to take control of the UNIA, leveled by Cyril Briggs' Crusader news service. Briggs did sense the disunity within the UNIA at this time, in part caused by some male members' opposition to Jacques Garvey's influence within the movement (James 146). However, Amy targets particularly her UNIA "defenders" who attempt to protect her as an "innocent" and "helpless" woman, saying that she does not need their assistance. In doing so, she demonstrates that she is more than capable of handling the patriarchy of the UNIA.

"10 MINUTES WITH MRS. MARCUS GARVEY," MARCH 17, 1923

Interviewing ladies is the most pleasant task that could be assigned me, as I have always prided myself on knowing something about their pet subjects—theatres, music, cosmetics and dress! Armed with this stock of knowledge, I wended my way to West 129th street[1] to see the wife of the most talked of Negro.

"Just my luck!" I thought on entering the building to find a notice posted on the elevator, "Car not running." "So this is no better than other colored folks' homes." Step by step, climbing higher and higher, I landed on the sixth floor and rang the doorbell. On[c]e, twice, thrice. No sound. That also was not ringing. So I applied my knuckles as vigorously as my panting breath would allow.

The door opened. "Is Mrs. Marcus Garvey in?" I asked, as a petite feminine figure with a wealth of dark brown hair and two braids hanging down her back stood in the doorway. Her small black eyes blinked facetiously as she replied all in one breath: "I am Mrs. Garvey. What can I do for you?" With difficulty, I suppressed my astonishment, and after using the name of The Negro World as my sesame password, I was ushered into the apartment.

Certainly it was not the usual Harlem "parlor." Instead of a three-piece parlor suite and a player piano, I saw tall Egyptian vases, pots with palms, jardinieres of flowers, curious looking African baskets and ornaments. The mellow sunlight streaming through an open window on a sheet of music, "Cavalleria Rusticana,"[2] resting on an open piano. Did I hear the "swash" of the oars of a gondola?

"Please be seated," said a soft voice, and, feeling ashamed at being caught staring around the room, I blurted out, "What do you think of the Tut's[3] creations this season, Mrs. Garvey?" and nestled in the nearest chair.

"They are indeed very beautiful and apart from being ornamental to the Negro woman, they are historical in value and make her hopeful indeed of a full revival of her ancient history; but gowns do not help very much in making a beautiful woman."

"No, her face is her beauty," I added, eager to show my knowledge.

"No, I do not quite agree with you," she replied. "Her face only helps to reflect the beauty of her soul. The truly beautiful woman is one who is able to permeate her surroundings with the light of a beautiful soul, and creates beautiful surroundings out of the most sordid material.

What if you mar the gown or the face? But can you mar the soul—the higher self? It rises supreme above the material obstacles and is truly permanently beautiful."

Here was a new kind of reasoning, and from such a little woman, too. Her small eyes lit up with intelligence and almost challenged me to further argument, although she had stopped speaking. "Well," I said, "most people would like to know just what you are thinking about."

"About my husband," she replied roguishly.

"And his work?" I queried.

"His work," she echoed, "is his whole existence. Take away his work and you take away his life. Knowing this, I endeavor to be conversant with subjects that would help in his career, and try to make home a haven of rest and comfort for him."

"I understand you have edited a book—"

"Oh, yes," she interrupted, settling back more easily in her chair and resting her hands on the arms of the chair, at the same time displaying a plain gold circlet on the third finger of her left hand. I noticed that there was no other ornament on her arms or fingers. "I compiled some of my husband's prophetic sayings for my personal record, and on reading them over one day the idea occurred to me to enlarge on them and give the public an opportunity of reading some of his thoughts written in simple and condensed style. I named the volume **"The Philosophy and Opinions of Marcus Garvey."** It will be off the press in a week or so, and you will observe on reading my preface[4] that my greatest wish is that this small volume will help to counteract many of the misquoted statements attributed to my husband, and the colorful and misleading newspaper and magazine articles written against him for financial gain by members of my race."

The clock struck, perhaps as a gentle reminder that my time was up. After thanking her for the time allotted me, I left with a different stock of knowledge added to that which I had before I entered the apartment, and with these thoughts uppermost in my mind: Here was a woman, a member of my race, helping a man to make the present and future of Negroes secure and happy; doing her full share as a good wife and helping him to accomplish his task as a Negro leader. Here, indeed, was the better half of Marcus Garvey!

"MRS. MARCUS GARVEY REPLIES TO ARTICLE IN NEGRO WORLD," JULY 21, 1923

Editor The Negro World:
Please be good enough to publish the following re your editorial "Look Out for Mud,"[5] which appeared in last week's issue of The Negro World.

In referring to a news item circulated by the Crusader Service[6] in several Negro newspapers to the effect that my husband "had turned over the organization" to me, you stated that "it is beneath the dignity of common decency to attempt to drag the name of an innocent and helpless woman into an arena where she cannot properly defend herself."

I desire to state that the article was shown to me, but, knowing that every division, branch and chapter of the Universal Negro Improvement Association in the world had been officially notified of the appointment of a Committee of Management to direct the affairs of the organization with the advice and instructions of my husband (such committee comprising Messrs. Sherrill, Poston and Bourne,[7] officers of the organization), and that your paper carries a half-page notice to that effect, I ignored the article, because the news in itself is such a clumsy, unvarnished lie that it is worthy of the source from which it came, and did not in the least disturb the divisions, branches and chapters of the Universal Negro Improvement Association, I was certainly surprised to see your valuable paper giving such news almost a column of editorial space.

You have characterized me as "innocent and helpless." I am innocent of the honor of having the Universal Negro Improvement Association "turned over" to me by my husband, but I am not innocent of the depths to which colored men can stoop to further their petty personal schemes, even at the expense of a downtrodden race such as ours.

I am not "innocent" of the tactics employed by men of my race to get easy money from alien individuals, groups and sometimes nations.

I am not "innocent" of the undermining influences used by local individuals and rival organizations to destroy my husband and the Universal Negro Improvement Association; because such individuals and rival organizations fear the power and strength of our organization and have not the ability to create anything like unto it.

I am not "innocent" of all this, and, more, I am not "innocent" of individual psychology, and know how, when and where to treat with some men. My four and a half years of active service in the Universal Negro Improvement Association under the personal direction of Marcus Garvey has given me a fair knowledge of men and the methods they employ in the organization and out of it.

With my unusual general knowledge and experiences for a young woman, may I not ask if the word "helpless" is not misapplied?

If the editorial was written in my defense, I have to thank you for same, and hope that if ever I am in need of a protector (not to draw his sword in my defense, but to flash his quill), you, sir, will as on this occasion, unsolicited, spill as much ink as will prove my "innocence" and protect me as a "helpless" woman.

I beg to remain,
Yours truly,

AMY JACQUES-GARVEY
July 16, 1923

Sketches

In "Whither Goest Thou?" and "Who Is to Be Blamed?" Jacques Garvey tries her hand at creative writing. In doing so, she keeps with the UNIA credo that artistic work should be used for propaganda to advance the movement's agenda. The poignant "Whither Goest Thou?" shows that in the Jim Crow era, prejudice against Blacks extended beyond the South but also to the northern United States. The cruder "Who Is to Be Blamed?" features stereotypically cunning, money-hungry Jewish merchants who victimize a consumer. The sketch opens with a lyrical description of Black Harlem. The idyllic mood quickly changes with the introduction of other "spiderlike" ethnicities into the scene. The title of the sketch is ironic. On the one hand, the Jewish merchants are at fault for selling shoddy products, but the subtler message may be that Blacks share the blame by not patronizing their own merchants.

"WHITHER GOEST THOU?" MARCH 31, 1923

"I stole these things. For God's sake, send me away where I can get food to eat and a warm place to rest my head. Send me to Atlanta—anywhere," cried a Negro to the police lieutenant at a West Side precinct in New York city, at the same time depositing two packages on the lieutenant's desk.

Bill Jones, formerly of the South, now of nowhere, stood shivering in a suit of homespun tweed, a cap drawn tightly over his head. Surely Shakespeare must have pictured such a man when he penned these lines.

Famine is in thy cheeks,
Need and oppression stareth in thy eyes.
Contempt and beggary hangeth upon thy back:
The world is not thy friend, nor the world's law.[8]

But let us hear his tale. It runs thus:

"Two years ago I was a care-free and happy young man, working on a farm in Winona, Miss., where I was born. One Sunday night my pal and I, on leaving church, were attacked by a white mob. A white man pointed my pal out as having been seen with a white woman, and we were taken into the woods. My pal was lynched and burned and I was beaten into unconsciousness.

"When I regained consciousness, I found myself on a train and a colored man bending over me. He read aloud a note pinned to my coat: 'Nigger, don't set foot back in Mississippi or you'll be a dead man.'

"'Never mind,' said the man, 'I will help you all I can.' He did. He took me to his home in Eldorado,[9] Ark., and cared for me.

"After I got well I found work and for more than a year I tried to forget that horrible night.

"Passing through the main street of the town one night I saw quite a few colored folks gathered together; some crying, some talking excitedly. One old woman was on her knees praying aloud. 'What's the matter?' I asked, and someone said: 'Read,' pointing to a notice stuck up on the outer wall of a little shop: 'Niggers, clear out of town in 24 hours or else you will be as good as dead.'[10]

"Not one of our group had expected such a thing. No trouble had ever occurred between the whites and the blacks in that town. Of course, quite a number of whites had come in and Negroes had become more prosperous since the war. I myself had hoped to be able to buy a home and settle down. What now? Stay and be tortured to death? A thousand times no! Whither, then? Anywhere.

"Next evening found me on a train bound for an Eastern city. Arriving in New York city with a little money I soon found lodgings, after which I set out to find work. I scanned the 'want' columns of the newspapers daily, made several applications for positions, but I was always greeted with the same answers: 'No colored help wanted,' or 'you must have experience.'

"One week passed without success and the second week I tried the employment agencies, but I was asked for recommendations. Should I have waited in Eldorado for recommendations? I tried to explain to an agency clerk why I had no recommendation. 'Why didn't you stay South from the start?' the impatient clerk asked.

"'Man,' I cried, unable to bear it any longer, 'have you ever seen one of your kind being roasted alive by a white mob? Have you ever smelled burning human flesh and heard the dying groans of your best pal? Have you ever been beaten almost to death and thrown into a dirty Jim Crow car? Man, go South.'

"Out in the street again. Back to my lodgings, only to meet an irate landlady at the door demanding either her rent or her room. She wanted rent and I wanted food.

"I retracted my steps downstairs to the street and, as the keen winter air struck my cheeks, I buttoned up my overcoat and plunged my bare hands deep down in my pockets. My right hand touched something cold. I pulled it out—a nickel! My last nickel.

"I walked on for blocks until I came to the subway. I could at least think if I were warm, so I purchased my ticket and boarded the first train.

"Thoughts, countless thoughts, chased through my brain, but at the terminal I was in the same position, penniless and hungry. All my possessions—a couple of suits of underwear, shirts and socks—were in my suitcase at the room; the balance was on my back.

"I changed my coach for the return trip, and kept riding up and down for about two hours until a conductor found me out and ordered me off the train and a guard saw me to the street.

"My mouth felt hot and dry inside; my stomach almost kissed my back. Unable to bear it any longer, I went into the nearest pawn shop and left my overcoat. I came out, fifty cents in hand, and darted into a restaurant.

"Satisfying my hunger to the extent of fifty cents, I was again on the street. It was eight p.m. by the nearest clock; the snow commenced to fall. I dodged in and out of hallways until 12 o'clock, when they were all closed.

"I walked up and down for a couple of hours until my body was almost rigid with cold; my brain was on fire. I backed up against a shop door—visions of that last night in Winona, Mississippi, came before me. At intervals I heard the haunting cry of my dying pal—a mail wagon came—I felt the heavy lash of the whip—my stiff hands felt something—two mail bags."

The police lieutenant looked at Jones. "Hem," he said, "this is a federal case," and instructed his assistant to lock him up and trace the owners of the bags.

The owners of the bags were found, but refused to prosecute Jones once their property was returned. A detective at the station finally made a charge against him, and he was taken before a magistrate, who promptly dismissed the case.

Jones, summoning what little strength he had, appealed to the magistrate to send him to prison, but the police with a "This way out," led him toward the door. "Officer," said Jones, "you are sending me out into the streets again hungry and cold. I am going to commit one of the most fiendish robberies, for by hook or by crook I must have food and warm clothes."

The door closed behind him and the blizzard raged before him.

Negro, whither goest thou?

"WHO IS TO BE BLAMED?" APRIL 28, 1923

Spring had come at last. Dark Harlem fluttered out like erstwhile caged birds to enjoy the noon-day sun. Mothers with perambulators bedecked in pink and blue vied with each other in a slow motion carriage race. Children just let out of school made the air re-echo with their play and laughter. Little ladies and big ladies tripping backwards and forwards on pleasure or business bent, would stop occasionally to greet some well-groomed gents. Gray-haired men and women with measured steps and radiant faces reflected as it were the warmth and energy pulsating around them. And such a riot of complexions! Ranging from a dark ebony to light maple. Eyes! Like night in all its stages, to the breaking of dawn. Hair! Large waves, small waves, straight sailing, and shades as changeable as the tropical seas.

This slow moving mass of Africa's lost sons and daughters are to be found on Lenox Avenue, the Main Street of Harlem. But Africa does not hold the monopoly of this Harlem thoroughfare, although it does by majority. Palestine, Italy, Greece and Germany are represented in the control of the shops and stores. Some of these commercial representatives are outside their establishments. Taking the air? No, not exactly, spiderlike looking for trade.

There is Al, the Grocer, known as Mr. A Mosckowitz, resident of the Bronx.

Tony, the iceman, otherwise Sr. Antonio Vermecelli, brother-in-law to Kuiseppe [*sic*] Bacardi, prosperous Fruiterer of No...... Lenox Avenue. X. Zenophen of the hat cleaning and shoe shine establishment, and Jake the Butcher! A beardless Shylock,[11] with deep set eagle eyes, hands down in his pockets underneath his blood-stained apron, his eyes looking furtively up and down the avenue. He has focused his eyes on something. Let's see. A colored lady, who could easily tip the scale at two hundred. She is coming at top speed, panting and blowing.

"Jake," she bawled, advancing towards him, shaking her right hand in his face, and her left supporting, her hip, "I want to know what you mean by giving me that cow hide for steak yesterday?" with a stamp of her right foot in emphasis, her breath almost gone from the effort.

"Oh, Lady, Lady," pleaded Jake, "don't get excited, come inside," and backed into the shop behind the counter.

"Get excited nothing," she shouted, recovering her breath, "I have to work d——n hard to lose my money——"

"You lose money in mine shop," interrupted Jake. "Honest to Gott I——"

"Say, listen man," she cried pounding the glass counter with her clenched fist, and with an emphasis on each word, "you give me steak no good. I give you money, money good. You get me?"

"O-h!" said Jake, drawing a long breath. "You say my steak no good, how is it that you say my steak no good. I got the best meat, fresh killed. Don't you see the sign in my window. All fresh, every day, fresh——"

"I don't care about your window. I am talking about the steak."

But ignoring the interruption, Jake continued his recitation. "Such lovely, juicy meat. Every day I get from my Cousin Moe, fresh, Kosher meat. Mine gracious Lady look at this piece of sirloin. I bet you anytig [*sic*] you can't beat that any place else."

"I am talking about the piece yesterday," corrected the customer.

"Yesterday, today. What's the difference? Always fresh," remarked Jake with a Yiddish shrug of his shoulders. "I had some of the same steak for supper yesterday."

"YOU?" queried the Lady.

"I should live so," said Jake solemnly, looking up to the ceiling of the store.

"I don't believe one——"

"Wait a minute Lady," interrupted Jake, laying a detaining arm on her shoulder.

"O-h—— Beckie!!!"

Jake's connubial half appeared in the rear doorway of the shop, a faint smile on her face, perhaps because of the conversation she had overheard; or was it the day-dream of an expectant mother that provoked the fleeting smile?—- "Beckie, darling, tell the customer about the wonderful steak we had for supper yesterday," said Jake, hurriedly with a knowing wink to her, and moved off to serve four of yesterday's fresh pork chops; taking good care to weigh his fingers along with the chops and wrapping paper; also to impress on the customer that the very bones of the chops were tender.

After finishing this very satisfactory task, he turned his attention to Beckie in her defence of the tender sirloin. "And when I took it out of the pan, Gee! You should smell that steak, mine husband, he comes into the kitchen right away and wants to eat."

"And when I put my steak in the pan, you should see that thing shrivel up like an old hag."

"The pan was no good," exclaimed Beckie, eager to make a point.

"Sure the pan was no good," echoed Jake, backing up the defence.

"They sell some rotten stuff now-a-days, I tell you. I had the same trouble. One night I had company, everything was burnt; so in comes in the kitchen mine sister's brother's wife, says she [']how much did you give for that pan [']. [']I says 98 cents at Hearn's['],[12] [']Don't you know['], says she, [']that a big firm has got to pay so much rent, clerks, delivery wagon, and all that so they charge up all that to the customer. Mine father always says, patronize the little man." Beckie paused for breath while Jake seized the opportunity to join in the defense. "I says the same thing. The little man has got to make a living."

Beckie recovering her breath determined to have the last word, continued: "Now, I buy everything up here—dishes, pans; I buy from mine brother-in-law, 'cross the street. He is in the hardware business. Such bargains he has! I couldn't believe myself—no car-fare to pay—just 'cross the street. Come, I introduce you to mine brother-in-law."

"But I haven't got any money."

"Money! That's nothing. Such a good customer you are, I tell mine brother-in-law. He let you have everything. Come!"

"Well, I will see what he has."

Marcus Garvey had been a supporter of much of Booker T. Washington's agenda after reading his autobiography *Up from Slavery* (1901). Although their solutions to the so-called Negro Problem in the United States differed greatly, both leaders appealed to the Black masses and emphasized the need for Black economic self-sufficiency. Garvey had even come to the United States, in part, to meet Washington and discuss organizing the UNIA in this country; however, Washington died before any such meeting could take place. Therefore, it is not surprising that Jacques Garvey in "Tuskegee and Its Founder" presents a laudatory portrait of Washington and the institution he founded.[13]

Jacques Garvey took a strong interest in Hollywood, which she believed often perpetuated negative images of Blacks. In the essay "A Black Star," she discusses two of the young Black stars in the popular Hal Roach *Our Gang* comedies: "Sunshine Sammy" (Ernest Morrison) and Farina (Allen Hoskins), who were virtually the only Blacks seen in Hollywood films at the time. Thus, Jacques Garvey provides a unique Black perspective on the early years of Hollywood.

The *Smart Set* magazine, edited by H. L. Mencken and George Jean Nathan, was among the most influential and widely respected periodicals in America in the 1920s. Mencken was considered one of the great intellects of the time, so when the publication's December 1923 issue featured an article titled "The Crime of January 1, 1863" that raised the question, somewhat tongue-in-cheek, of reintroducing slavery, many people were shocked. Jacques Garvey, not fully recognizing Mencken's satire of the South, warned in her provocative essay "Will the Negro be Re-Enslaved?" that the "brutally frank" views expressed by Mencken and Nathan were consistent with those of many White Americans.

"TUSKEGEE AND ITS FOUNDER," DEC. 1, 1923

To many Tuskegee signifies only an industrial school, where young Negro men and women are taught manual labor. To the few who are acquainted with the work of Tuskegee it means an educational center where the youth of the race are taught to use their hands as well as their heads and thoroughly fitted for service to themselves and to their race, along educational and industrial lines.

The students are taught and disciplined by Negroes, thereby learning the great principle of honoring and respecting their own. A principle that this baby race of ours needs to help it stand on its own legs and eventually step independently, free from the guidance and control of the other race. [. . .]

Most of the buildings are built of brick and were put up by student labor. Bricks are made on the premises by students. All the food consumed on the place is grown by the students.

The government has established a department of the Reserve Officers' Training Corps, and the boys are trained in military tactics by the officer in charge and his staff. This has greatly assisted the discipline of the institution, as the officer in charge works in co-operation with the Commandant of the Institute.

This is the kind of institution that I saw on my visit to Tuskegee—modern, sanitary, up-to-date buildings—occupied by teachers and students, who seemed to work in perfect harmony, making school life not a drudgery, but a pleasant duty, where the one imparts and the other receives, both determined to give to the world the best in them; 1,800 students are enrolled and more than 2,000 applicants have been turned away, because of lack of space and accommodations.

The teachers are painstaking and thorough in their methods and fit the boy or girl for his or her particular trade or line of study as carefully as a workman turns out a fine garment. Special training is given students who show promise to become managers and foremen, or those who desire to engage in business of their own. [. . .]

With this kind of training and a little capital a young man can soon become a captain of industry and be able to give employment to members of his race. [. . .]

I spent a day and a half at the institute, and were I to write of all that I saw and learned in that short time I would use many columns of The Negro World for many weeks and yet, perhaps, omit some important information of interest. The principal, Dr. R. R. Moton,[14] is a simple, genial man, who has made many improvements since his incumbency in office, and followed the policy laid down by the founder.

Tuskegee was built on a foundation of inspiration. The inspired vision of a man whose only capital was inspiration, backed by courage and perseverance, and helped by his faith in his God and in his race; inch by inch and foot by foot, he struggled against hardships and criticisms and proved [sic] what is today the greatest educational centre in the world for Negroes—a thing of beauty, because its loveliness has increased with the years; it is a lasting joy[15] to those who enter its gates, whether as student or visitor, and a living monument to the memory of the late Booker T. Washington, its founder.

The first place I asked to be shown on my arrival at Tuskegee was his grave, and as I stood with bowed head before that ivy-covered mound, paying my respects to him who is no more, involuntarily the words burst from my lips, "Washington! thou shouldst be living at this hour. Africa hath need of such as thee!"

I walked around the chapel on the other side of which is the monument [. . .] erected to his memory by Negroes. The base is of granite and the statues are of bronze. The standing figure represents Dr. Washington lifting the veil from the face of the kneeling figure. Below the statues are inscribed these words:

Booker T. Washington
1856–1915
"He lifted the veil of ignorance
from his people and pointed the
way to progress, through education and industry."

Around the base at the monument are inscribed quotations from his writings, such as:

"There is no defense or security for any of us, except in the highest intelligence and development of all."[16]

"I will let no man drag me down so low as to make me hate him."[17]

Such are the noble thoughts of a noble soul, who saw the light of day on a slave plantation in West Virginia. Though shackled in body, yet he was unfettered in soul. He soared to the heights of progress and achievement, and unselfishly worked and sacrificed to lift his people to his level. He had no beaten path to follow; he was the pioneer; he blazed the trail for others. [. . .]

That is the kind of start Dr. Washington had, and Tuskegee of today is what he produced out of that dilapidated shanty. Yet this genius has been ruthlessly criticized by members of his race; criticized because he sought to make real men in the race and not overeducated monkeys; criticized because he dared to show them how to use their hands as well as their heads. Why criticize? Is not industry the backbone of all peoples, of all nations? Close down your industries and what becomes of your Latin and Greek scholars? Drive your industrial captains from your communities, and your lawyers, doctors and professors starve.

I am not advocating that all present-day Negroes should become industrialists; we need a few professionals, but quite a number of industrialists—real men who build for others, who provide employment for the teaming masses.

Negro men who criticized Dr. Washington failed to take into consideration the time in which he labored. He started work at a time when the Negro in America had just emerged from slavery—slavery that had left its imprint of ignorance and crudities. The question then was "How best can I train this uncouth mind, this poor illiterate being, to be a useful man to his race and a good citizen in the nation?" The answer was "Tuskegee."

It is true that at that time the whites had experimented with a few Negroes along higher educational lines, and they had mastered Greek and Latin, but these men were the proteges of white people, specimens used in the higher educational experiments.[18] But what of the poor, destitute masses? Teach them Latin or Greek, or teach them to write the only language they knew, to earn a living and to live clean, healthy lives?

A man or race cannot evolve upside down. Evolution is a slow process. Man evolves by stages, and the evolution of the Negro from slavery to full manhood (comparable to the standard of the white man) must come by stages. No baby is born with a man's head. It would be topheavy. All the different parts of the body must be developed in equal proportions. As of the stages of development in the life of a child, so of the stages and phases of development in the life of a race or people.

Dr. Washington's critics also failed to take into consideration the fact that the race was too poor to give him much financial assistance in his work, and he, perforce, had to appeal to the white philanthropists to help him. Knowing this, he was guarded in his utterances and never said anything that would hurt the racial feeling of the white people who aided his work financially.

Oh! how Dr. Washington must have suffered at times when goaded on by his critics to make public utterances which his finer sense of gratitude prevented him from doing. And who were his critics? Negro men who had been used by the whites in the higher educational experiment. Negro men who have never done anything for the race, and who are still alive, still criticizing, and still proteges of white people.

Dr. Washington had not only the idea of establishing the educational center, but a city. He started to develop a community adjoining Tuskegee called Greenwood, for the purpose of giving an opportunity to the graduates of the school to start out in business, and with the determination that one day the community would grow into a city, where a Black man would be Mayor, and with a staff of Negroes control the City of Negroes, and thereby demonstrate to the world the Negro's capability to govern himself. But Washington died before this, his second ideal, could be realized, and Greenwood remains a community. Leaders are not made, but born and inspired by God Almighty.

When Dr. Washington heard the call of his people he could have said, "I am called to preach." No, he did not select the easiest way. He said: "I am called to serve my race." Not to prepare their souls for the great beyond, but to train their minds to be partakers of this earthly paradise. When men's bodies are cared for and their minds trained they will burst forth into praise to their Creator and glorify God; but when a man is in ignorance and poverty he wails against his Creator and blames either his fellow man or his God for his condition.

By the death of Dr. Washington the Negro race has lost, not only a leader, but an educator, a diplomat, a man who served humanity for humanity's cause, a Negro who lived for his race, that they also might live and enjoy life more abundantly.

"A BLACK STAR," DEC. 8, 1923

"Master Morrison would like to see you at the studio today."

"Is that a command or a request? Who is the kid?"

"Why, he is our colored star. Don't you know 'Sunshine Sammy'?"[19]

There! I had been caught tripping in my history of stardom, but quickly recovered myself, and added, "Yes, of course, I will be delighted to see him. Arrange an hour convenient to him."

I drove over to Hal Roach's Studio[20] in Culver City at the appointed time to see this child genius. He was shooting pictures. Acting the part of a pirate. Something had gone wrong with the engine of his ship, and as the child worked feverishly to get the engine righted, his director, Mr. McGowan,[21] looked at him admiringly and said to me, "He is a perfect wonder. Not merely an imitator, as most children are, but he has creative genius. If an accident happens to his setting he will go right on with the scene and fit in his own little part."

The whistle blew for lunch; the click, click of the camera ceased, and the pirate left his ship and was formally introduced to me as "Master Frederick Ernest Morrison—the star of Hal Roach's 'Our Gang Comedies.'" He is known on the screen as "Sunshine Sammy."

"What is the name of the picture you are making?" I asked, by way of starting a conversation, while the young gallant looked me over.

"I don't know yet. Most of our pictures are named after they are made, and if they are named before they are made, the names are sometimes changed." His attention was immediately attracted to a man rigged out in a cowboy's outfit, their eyes met and they smiled, knowingly. Seeing my inquiring look, he exclaimed, "That's Will Rogers,[22] the comedian."

"And who is that?" I inquired, pointing to a little colored child about three years old, rolling over on the grass.

"Oh, that's All[e]n Hoskins.[23] He plays a girl's part and is called Farina."

That was another one on me. I had seen Little Farina on the screen with her long braids and cute smile, but had no idea that "she" was a "he."

Sammy ran off to get dressed and I became better acquainted with Farina. He is three and one-half years old and has been playing in the movies for two years. He was discovered by Sammy's father and trained by him. Farina is a young star, or starlet, in the movie constellation and well deserves his pay envelope.

We next had some pictures made with Sammy in the leading role, and as the lunch hour had nearly expired he very graciously invited me to his bungalow the following day to meet his sisters.

He is called "Ernie" at home, and is the eldest of five children, and the only boy. His sisters are Florence, Vera, Dorothy, and Ethel. Florence plays his double any time, while I was there she mischievously dressed up in his clothes and I could hardly tell the difference between them. Vera plays the piano and accompanies Ernie, who plays the violin.

Dorothy used to play as Little Farina, but some of the parts were too rough, so her father trained All[e]n Hoskins for her part. Even baby Ethel, who is not a year old yet, can make goo-goo eyes.

"How can you account for this talented family?" I asked Mr. Morrison, the father.

"Well," he said, modestly, "I used to do vaudeville work in New Orleans." "And my sister was an actress," chipped in Mrs. Morrison, determined to prove maternal heredity. "I was crazy about dancing and won the prize four times for cake-walking."[24]

"Then, you are not Californians?"

"No, we are both from New Orleans. Ernie was born there. I brought him to California when he was one and one-half years old.

"How did you get him in the movies?" I asked, getting more interested.

"It just happened as most things in life. I worked in Hollywood, and one day Bill Bertram,[25] a director, asked me if I could get him a little boy to work with Baby Marie Osborne.[26] I told him I had a little boy at home and would bring him in for the test. So Ernie entered the movies, working two days; then two weeks, and at the end of that time I signed his first contract with the Rowland Film Company[27] for $50 per week. This amount increased after the first year, but, two and a half years later he joined the Hal Roach Company. Now he is ten years old and earns $500 per week."

Not much, I thought. Norma Talmadge[28] gets $10,000, Gloria Swanson[29] $6,500, etc. If colored movie fans would demand colored pictures from their local theatres, the three or four colored stars could demand better pay, and hundreds of other colored actors and actresses of the legitimate stage would be given a chance on the silver screen to show their natural ability and earn a good living. It is a question of demand and supply. Demand a colored "sheik"[30] and rave over him. Rave over some one who looks like you. Demand a colored Norma—- But I am moralizing, and must get back to Ernie, our star, the black star.

He had become very friendly and was leaning on the arm of my chair.

"Do you go to school?" I asked.

"No, my tutor goes to the studio with me and I have my lessons in between the scenes when I am not working. I like to read fairy tales." His large black eyes opened wide and he leaned closer to me, as he continued: "I like to read the ones where the pretty girl gets under the spell of a witch and a prince comes along and rescues her. Gee, I would love to be the prince."

The age of chivalry, I thought, is not gone. Black knights are budding forth and in the coming generation knighthood will be in flower.

Mr. Morrison is a business man and has big plans for his children. He owns a candy factory and considerable real estate. The family leads a simple wholesome life and, with such natural gifts, the children are bound to become great artists.

"WILL THE NEGRO BE RE-ENSLAVED?" DEC. 15, 1923

I have heard of many solutions to what is commonly called the race problems, but the most malicious one, as coming from white men, is the re-enslaving of Negroes in America.

About a year ago my husband (Marcus Garvey), in a public address, warned his hearers that if the Negro race did not make plans for its future existence, the day was not far distant when the white man would make efforts to re-enslave Negroes. Some of the "professional critics" laughed at him, and said it was hot air talk; no white man would even dare to think that way in this present civilization, this highly developed period. But here are two white thinkers, Messrs. [H. L.] Mencken[31] and [George Jean] Nathan,[32] the retiring editor of the Smart Set Magazine,[33] advocating the re-enslaving of the Negro, as a relief from the ills he now suffers as a citizen.

The Smart Set is called the aristocrat among magazines, therefore, it is well for all of us to know the kind of propaganda that is being disseminated among the class of white people who read this monthly aristocrat. The following appears in the December issue under the caption "The Crime of January 1, 1863."

"The present parlous condition of the late Confederate States, with the native blackamoors emigrating to the rolling mills, illicit distilleries and jazz-palaces of the North by the hundred thousand, will probably give some pause to the surviving proponents of the old doctrine that chattel slavery was economically sound. Was it, indeed! Then try to imagine Georgia under chattel slavery, getting into the appalling economic condition that it labors under today. One of the leading bankers of the State is authority for the estimate that the departure of field-hands will cost its cotton growers $20,000,000 this year. Certainly they never suffered any such staggering loss under slavery. The slave may have been an indifferent workman, but he at least did some work.

The truth is that the plan of remedying the acknowledged evils of slavery by abolishing it altogether was as extravagant and imprudent as the plan of cutting off a man's head to cure his headache. As a matter of historical fact, it was not adopted with any such nonsensical intention; it was adopted simply as a device for harassing and punishing the confederates. Unluckily, it set a precedent which still harasses and punishes all of us. . . .

If, as was widely held at the time, chattel slavery was full of defects, then the obvious remedy was to search them out and remove them[,] [. . .] for example, the custom which allowed a slave-owner to separate a slave family. A few simple reforms of that sort, most of which would have been supported by the overwhelming majority of Southerners, and the slaves would have ceased to fret under the bondage. As everyone knows, the complete freedom that was so suddenly thrust upon them demoralized them almost unanimously, and brought upon them a host of woes. Before ten years had come and gone, the white Southerners, in self-defense, had to take their liberty away from them again by extra legal devices—this setting another evil precedent. In most parts of rural Georgia today the black field-hands is [*sic*] almost as much a slave as his grandfather was on December 31, 1862. He is not allowed to exercise any of the common rights of citizenship. [. . .] The free Aframerican is thus worse off than [Roman slaves] were. [. . .] These blackamoors shiver when they hear the word SLAVERY, though the thing itself would unquestionably rescue them from most of their current troubles. They'd rather be 'Free' chained to an upright rail with a pyre of fat pine-knots burning under them, than 'slaves' in a comfortable cabin, with plenty of hog-meat in the smoke house and no tax bills to pay."

This statement is brutally frank, but any one who knows anything about H. L. Mencken knows that he is one of the keenest minds of America, and one of the most outspoken of his group.

Here are two editors, Messrs. Mencken and Nathan, stating in plain language that the abolition of slavery was an extravagant and imprudent act, and that the defects of slavery should have been remedied rather than have the institution abolished, and, finally, that if Negroes were re-enslaved it would rescue them from their present troubles.

Perhaps these white men do not know that there are leaders in the Negro race today who are not paid by the white folks to do their bidding, but leaders who are supported by the race to think and act for the race, and to the interest of the race, and that these leaders are determined to so work and plan that Negroes will not become so economically bankrupt that they will have to submit to enslavement in order to exist.

The idea is now to squeeze the Negroes out of jobs and fill those jobs with white immigrants from Europe. The Negro, after a few years, will find starvation staring him in the face; then slavery, in a modified form (modified to suit present-day civilization), will be offered to him as a relief for his condition. He will either have to accept this offer or starve and die. This is one of the plans of the thinking white people to deal with the Negro, and sometimes an outspoken member of the white race spills the beans and shows us in what direction the wind is blowing.

These white men are figuring without their host, they are thinking and planning for the Negro of fifty years ago; not for the Negro of 1914–1918 and of today. The Negro of fifty years ago might have been satisfied with a cabin and plenty of hog-meat, but this New Negro[34] wants everything that the civilized, progressive white man wants. The New Negro wants nice homes, and the means to protect them. He wants the biggest industrial and political jobs in a nation. And since this New Negro knows the white man has only such luxuries as a cabin and hog meat to offer him, he is planning and working toward establishing a government and a nation of his own, where he can satisfy his needs and ambitions as a MAN. If any re-enslaving is to be done, it won't be done to this progressive, forward-looking New Negro.

Unfortunately a few of our writers are wickedly blind, and in the face of the attitude of the white man toward the race, they tell us of a better future, and sit with folded hands waiting for the day to dawn.

I came across a Negro newspaper published in a mid-western city in which a Negro writer states:

"The white man has made many concessions that it was thought he would not make. What is needed is to teach the Negro to measure up to meriting the concessions he demands."

What concessions in the name of God, could the white man make [to] the Negro that he did not merit? Can you imagine a Negro writing such nonsense? Are we in America [a] set of uncivilized barbarians? Or are we as civilized and Christianized as the white man in his western hemisphere? I hate to think that the weakling who would write such puny rot is a member of this noble race of ours, and that he contaminates others with such apologetical statements. I would like to know that the writers of the race, in fact, that all Negro men are MEN. Men that we women can feel proud of; men that can protect us and plan for us; not men that we have to apologize for, not men that suffer from curvature of the spine and shaking knees! In other words, "Marse boss good niggers."[35] Please, Lord, straighten out their back bones, and strengthen their shaking knees, so that they will all be real men.

Travels

Jacques Garvey's six-part travel journal "On a Trip from Coast to Coast" is her most extensive piece in the *Negro World*. She describes the trip as a "vacation," but it was more of a barnstorming tour as well as a sort of delayed honeymoon. It "was mainly initiated to attract new members and strengthen the cohesion within the organization" (Wiegmann 94). Her journal is much more than a description of the places she and Marcus visited. Instead, it is clearly "a political text," a trenchant examination of the prejudice that still existed in many parts of the country, including St. Louis; Portland, Oregon; Indiana; and the Southern states (Wiegmann 104). California, too, did not escape her caustic gaze: "Los Angeles and its surroundings would be a real Eden to Negroes if it were not for that viper, race prejudice, with its fangs of hate ever ready to strike and kill the rising ambitions and hope of Negroes." The whole nature of travel, particularly for vacation, challenged the class and race boundaries imposed on Blacks, who were perhaps at their most vulnerable in the often hostile and unknown places to which they ventured (Wiegmann 100–102). The trip across the United States seemed to make her even more certain that the future of the Negro was not in this country but in Africa. In her reports she touched on all of the major topics that she would later discuss in her editorials. The writing seemed to convince Marcus and the other UNIA leaders that Amy was ready to undertake a weekly woman's page in the *Negro World*.[36]

"ON A TRIP FROM COAST TO COAST: IMPRESSIONS OF MRS. AMY JACQUES GARVEY, WIFE OF PRESIDENT-GENERAL, ON VACATION," OCT. 20–NOV. 24. 1923

(FIRST ARTICLE) OCT. 20, 1923

To the Editor of The Negro World:

In keeping with my promise to send you a weekly letter of my impressions while on my vacation, I send you the following, as I am unable to write my numerous friends and well-wishers who would like to hear from me.

Sunday night, September 30. After an impressive and enthusiastic meeting at Liberty Hall, New York, we dashed off for the Pennsylvania Station, just in time to hear the familiar shout, "All aboard." It was midnight, and although we tried to observe the rules of the sleeper by being "Quiet, Quiet," our porter could not help breaking same on recognizing my husband, by exclaiming, "Mr. Garvey, himself—My, my. I never thought I would have seen you again. Yes indeed, the folks in Pittsburgh are looking out for you."

After being rocked in the cradle of a Pullman berth[37] for half a night I woke up to see if I was all there, and, if not, to pull myself together. No sooner had I made my toilet and sat by the window to enjoy the feeble morning sun in its effort to penetrate the mist, than a waiter came along with dignified steps, and, as it were, chanting these words: "Last call for breakfast! Dining car in the rear."

We went into the dining car and after having breakfasted, I said to myself the meal was worthy of that syncopated chant. Colored porters and waiters have certainly built up a reputation for Pullman cars. At about 10.30 we reached Pittsburgh. As usual Pittsburgh had all her furnaces lit, and her chimneys smoking, some belching forth flames. The smoke hung thick and low in the skies like rain clouds. This town controls the coal and steel mines of the outlying districts; it refines and moulds steel articles for local consumption and more particularly for export to all parts of the world. Negro laborers get from fifty to sixty cents per hour, working eight hour shifts. Some of the large plants employ [N]egro foremen. The influx of immigrants from the South has not affected the labor market, but it has affected to a great extent the housing conditions. Driving from the station, I noticed large placards, with the inscription, "Prepare for the Ku Klux Klan." On enquiring, I learned that the Klan was expected any night to parade through the city.[38]

In the afternoon the Local Division had a large parade, which was well attended by the uniformed ranks of the Organization, and members in automobiles and on foot.

At 8.30 we arrived at "The People's Tabernacle," where 2,000 people crowded the building, with hundreds on the outside who could not get in. [. . .]

My husband spoke for more than an hour. He described the two schools of thought in the race, and showed how the New Negro had evolved a philosophy of his own and refused to apply white men's philosophy to the needs, yearnings and ambitions of black men. He drew a vivid and realistic picture of two competitive races (black and white) living side by side in this country, and showed that the future boded ill for the weaker of the two if no provision is made now, as the weak and unprepared race is bound to starve and die, through economic pressure. In closing, he expressed his deep gratitude and appreciation to the members of the division, who in conjunction with the other members of the organization throughout the world made it possible for him to be released,[39] by their splendid example of loyalty and devotion. Such conduct, he said, has caused the world to have a new estimate of the awakened spirit of the Negro, and made them realize that we are a force to be reckoned with in the future.

I was deeply impressed with the earnestness and devotion of the members and added my thanks to those of my husband's on introduction by the chairman. [. . .]

Two thirty p.m. found us boarding the train for Youngstown, Ohio. Arriving there at 4.55 p.m., we were met at the station by Mr. W. Vaughn,[40] the president of the local division, from whom I inquired the reason for the newspaper reports to the effect that the mayor of the city would prevent my husband from speaking there, and had called on the police to enforce his order. "Why," said Mr. Vaughn, smiling, "we got some cheap publicity. A preacher and some of his congregation, being jealous of our success, made representations to the mayor[41] that Mr. Garvey was coming here to stir up race hatred and strife. When the mayor told them that he was present at the meeting at which Mr. Garvey spoke the last time he was in the city, and welcomed him to Youngstown, the preacher, without the least hesitation, told the mayor that it was not the same Garvey coming this time; it was another man. The mayor, to satisfy himself, sent for me, and when I explained it all to him, he was surprised at the hypocrisy practiced on him and readily agreed to attend our meeting."

We had two hours to rest and eat supper, and then off to the meeting at the Oak Hill Auditorium. I learned that it was the first time that Negroes had held a meeting there. On our arrival the musical part of the program was gone through, and my husband was called on to speak. There were many white persons in the audience, and by the change of emotion on their faces one could easily see that they were deeply impressed with the seriousness of our program, and were perhaps a little surprised at the unvarnished truths leveled at them during my husband's speech. He made them see themselves as they really were in their contact with us, and exposed their future plan of slow extermination and further subjugation of our race. Then he pointed them to a true solution to the vexing problem of the races, to be achieved through following the divine apportionment of the earth: that is, each race to its native habitat—Europe for the Europeans, Asia for Asiatics, America for the white Americans, and Africa for the black peoples of the world. He felt sure that America, the greatest democracy in the world, would be large-minded enough to help us establish a national home of our own in Africa, even as we labored and worked in this country for over 300 years to help them build up this republic and make it what it is today.

"Yours truly," was next introduced and I got off lightly with a few remarks, as we had to leave immediately for Farrell, Pa. [. . .]

(SECOND ARTICLE) OCT. 27, 1923

In my last letter to you I closed just as we boarded on our way to Gary, Ind., on the morning of October 3. [. . .]

My attention was attracted to a colored man who looked as if he had made the station his temporary headquarters. He walked around so leisurely that I was convinced that he belonged to the I.W.W.C. (I Won't Work Club) and must have been highly recommended on examination by "Dr. Eat More and Work Less." The gentleman looked me over, then my bagga[g]e, and finally said something to the approaching station master, who also surveyed me and my outfit. I moved nearer to them, and was just in time to hear the station master say, "Why, those are Africans traveling." I chuckled to myself at the tact of that white man. If we were traveling with bundles and had the air of "scared to death" folks running from the South, we would have been called "Niggers," but being well-clad, independent-looking people traveling first class, we were "Africans." That white man tried to impress the colored man that, because we were not in the same position in life as he was, we were a different people to him. And that colored man looked so strangely at me afterwards that I am sure he must have gone into town to tell the folks that he had seem "live Africans" without tails. [. . .]

Our train was one of those local express trains that start out at high speed and limp in on the home stretch; so we were an hour late arriving in Gary at 8.15 p.m., just in time to rest our baggage at the hotel and go over to the hall. And such a scene met our gaze. One thousand people packed in a place that could only seat 600; one thousand eager and enthusiastic persons, some of whom had come all the way from Chicago, Milwaukee and sections of Indiana. The pity was that some could only crowd the sidewalks and have a peep at my husband, as the hall was overcrowded from 7 o'clock that evening. The devotion of those people almost moved me to tears. One old lady said to me after the meeting: "Honey, while the young folks were clapping and shouting I was giving thanks to God for his (my husband's) deliverance, just as He took Daniel out of the lion's den."[42]

Mr. McHurst of Chicago introduced my husband, but the hall was so warm I could not retain all that was said. And Heaven's to tell how he was able to speak for an hour and fifteen minutes. The very platform was so crowded that there wasn't even enough space for me to stretch out my feet, and two children, lulled by the music and exhausted from the heat, cushioned their heads in my coat on the back of my chair and fell asleep standing up. The meeting came to a close, and after the usual shaking of hands and enthusiastic embraces we went back to the hotel. Although the room was cold I was quickly carried away in the arms of Morpheus[43] and dreamed I was in Africa, out in the fields picking mangoes, and as I reached up to get a nice, yellow, juicy one I woke up to find my husband holding tight to my nostrils in order to awaken me, to find out the time. I won't tell you what I did to him for making me lose that juicy mango. [. . .]

The K.K.K. is strongly organized in the State of Indiana;[44] its voters are said to number between 300,000 to 400,000 in the entire State. It is said that the organization defeated several candidates in the 1922 election. It has grown considerably since and dominates affairs in rural Indiana. They are organized in Gary, but have not made any public demonstrations. They were recommended by the town officials to parade outside the city limits, as the inhabitants are of mixed nationalities. [. . .]

We received quite a number of callers, and at midday my husband took me to see Mrs. [Zenobia] Bagby,[45] who is, unfortunately, confined to her bed at the Mercy Hospital. She is a refined, cultured woman and one of the pioneering women of our race in big business. She, along with her other two sisters, own the "Gary Sun," a weekly newspaper, with an up to date printing plant.

I inquired of her if the newspaper was printed in her plant, and she said, "No, I am almost afraid to risk it just now, as our people are so unreliable. When I do succeed in getting a competent man he works for a while and then quits without notice."

I said, "Amen," softly, because that is the complaint of all colored people who place members of their own race in positions of trust and responsibility. Colored employe[e]s seem to delight in making colored business men and women look ridiculous in the eyes of the public, by their neglect of duty and being untrustworthy. The public only sees the failures and attributes them to the owners or controllers, but it invariably comes about through the unpreparedness of the colored employee; not in the particular line of work in which he is engaged, but his unpreparedness to realize that he is a member of the race, and his employer's failure is his, and that his employer's rise in the business world lifts the race one rung higher in the ladder of human achievements, and fits the individuals for the standard by which men are measured in this highly developed civilization. [. . .]

We had so many callers at the hotel that the proprietor, shrewd business man as he is, charged us $5 per night for our room, which was a regular ice box, and caused my husband to get an attack of asthma. So I left Gary the night of the 4th with anger in my heart against that son of a g—I mean that wily son of Ham.[46]

The sun rose early in the morning of the 5th and I arose with the sun, as its naughty rays stole through the shades of the window and by the motion of the train played hide and seek on my face. I made a hurried toilet, regular "dry cleaning." Had my bed made up day time style and sat by the window to view the wonders of nature, preserved and improved on by the white man for his own satisfaction and comfort, even to the exclusion of others. I gazed in admiration.

My thoughts wandered on. I questioned within myself, "Should we not as a people be partakers of some of these earthly bounties? Why should we be satisfied with the crumbs that fall from the white man's table? Yea! the very husks of the land. Are we not made of the same flesh and blood, with the same longing for this world's goods, and all that goes to make life comfortable and happy? Friends, let us awake; let us become dissatisfied with ourselves and our lethargy; let us be up and doing; let us bestir ourselves and get from the world an equal share of wealth and happiness with the other races; so that our children may not look on us as a set of cringing, crawling beggars, a set of parasites, but let them look back at us with pride and love, as a people, who in our generation worked and fought to secure for ourselves and for them a place in this world apportioned by God Almighty as the earthly abode of all humanity. [. . .]

My husband soon awoke, feeling much better from his attack of asthma. The train pulled into St. Louis at about 8:30 a.m. Mr. S. R. Wheat,[47] the president of the local division, along with some of the Legion, came to meet us, so we did not have to encounter those weak looking, lazy white porters at the station, who, by the way, are not called porters, but ushers. Here is where labor is dignified even by a name. [. . .]

(THIRD ARTICLE) NOV. 3, 1923

As stated in my previous letter we arrived in St. Louis on the morning of the fifth and were taken to a hotel. I made sure that the room was warm before taking it. After breakfast we went to the telegraph station. On our way back, within a block of the hotel, my husband became thirsty and we stopped at a drug store. The soda fountain clerk said he had no ice. A peculiar thing I thought, a soft drink counter without ice.

We crossed the street to an ice cream parlor, and a Polish-looking clerk, in answer to our query, said: "We have no ginger ale." "But," said I, pointing to a bottle [of] coca-cola, "that will do as well." The man looked puzzled, and spoke to a Greek standing near by. The latter leaned over the counter and almost whispered the strange news to my husband: "Sorry, but we don't serve colored people here." I was stunned, and repeated the words audibly. I looked around the place. Seated at two tables were four common-place looking white girls, talking and laughing at the top of their voices. A colored man was being served at a patent medicine counter. Seeing my surprise, perhaps, the Greek, apologetically, said: "If you want to take the bottle home"—we did not wait to hear the rest, but walked out in disgust.

We met the proprietor of the hotel where we stayed and told him of the incident. "That's the way the Greek is," he explained. "I remember the time when he had a peanut stand at the same corner. When he made his pile out of colored folks he opened up that ice cream parlor and now they dare not go in and get a glass of anything." That sums up a condition that obtains in many more cities besides St. Louis. Negroes still patronize the Greek, even though they could not get a drink of water in his store to save their lives.

I may mention that the ice cream parlor is situated in Congressman [Leonidas] Dyer's[48] district. That worthy white gentleman who is making so much noise about passing a law to punish lynching—I speak of the anti-lynching bill. Friends! Think of it, passing a law to punish lynching! Passing a law to stop an angry white mob of 500 from lynching a lone black man! What law or ordinance in the world can or will stop the vicious brutal spirit of a white mob? Pass the law if you can, but who will dare to put it into execution?

There is no law which says that a colored man cannot get a cold drink in an ice cream parlor in St. Louis. But the fact remains that because of the spirit of the white majority a black man is denied their right of being served.

Pardon me. I am digressing from my tale. We were directed to a colored drug store about three blocks away. We were well served. I bought postal cards and wrote on them. We spent about twenty minutes there, and not a single customer came in during our stay. Do you wonder why the race is listed by others in the dependent, helpless class? Why cannot Negroes learn the lesson of patronizing their own?

Since the migration from the South it is estimated that there are 100,000 Negroes in St. Louis. People with warm blood in their veins, and, yet, as unconcerned to the progress of others, and the dire needs of themselves as Pharaoh's mummies. Sometimes I think it will take more than lynching, burning, flogging, etc. to awaken some of our people to racial consciousness and co-operation.

At 8.30 p.m. we attended the meeting at Douglass Hall. As usual, the crowd was immense. Someone said to me that he was afraid the fire department would come down on them for overcrowding. "Why didn't you get a large church," said I. "Not one of the big preachers would rent us their churches" said the man. "We have some of the finest churches in the country—still building more—and yet we have hundreds of our folks right here who are starving." This is the Christianity as practiced by some of our colored preachers. We are being overfed with heavenly promises while we starve for some of this earth's goods.

I really was too upset from the incident in the day to take an active part in the meeting, but my husband, after drinking about five glasses of ice water, was evidently cooled off and spoke for over an hour. He touched on conditions among them and pointed them to the dangers in the future [if] they did not prepare now. From the enthusiasm in the audience I felt sure that every one in that hall was a disciple going forth to preach the gospel of preparedness of the race. Mr. Wheat is to be complimented on his good work in this city in the cause of the Universal Negro Improvement Association.

On the morning of the sixth we had many callers. Among them was an old lady who said she just wanted to shake my husband's hand. He inquired of her health, etc. In reply she said, "Well, son, I had to run from Bam (Alabama) a couple of years ago and I guess I will soon have to leave St. Louis. My next place will be New York. You see, child, I am getting nearer and nearer the sea." These are the pathetic tales that one hears all over the country. Where are Negroes going? Where are they wanted?

In the afternoon my husband, seeing that I was depressed, took me for a drive. He ordered the taxi driver to drive through the rich white section of the city. And such a scene was there—beautiful homes, from the cozy bungalow to the majestic looking stone and brick mansions, artistically surrounded with flower gardens and lawns. Everything suggested comfort, happiness and prosperity. But who enjoyed all this luxury? Black men and women? No. White m[e]n and women. They are the lords of those homes, and black men and women are but their servants. We left the boulevard and entered the park. I saw lines of automobiles, which, of course, were occupied by white men and women. Others were playing golf and visiting the zoo. They looked curiously at us, as much as if to say, "Why have you dared to enter on our preserves?" I went back to the hotel in a brown study[49] and wondered, "How long, oh! Lord, how long?"

Some one gave me a copy of "The Patriot," a weekly newspaper, published by the Ku Klux Klan in St. Louis. The editors are Rev. C. C. Crawford and F. R. Barkhurst. Their motto is, "One Country, One Flag, One Language." I understand there are more than one hundred such organs of the K.K.K. all over the country.[50]

We bade adieu to our friends in St. Louis at 11.35 p.m. and left for Kansas City, Kan. [. . .]

Sunday afternoon at 3:30 we attended the meeting at the Summer School Auditorium, in Kansas City, Kansas. The building was packed with people, the crowd outside being almost as great as the crowd inside. Mr. W. W. Gordon,[51] the Mayor of the city gave the welcome address. [. . .]

My husband, in thanking the Mayor for his welcome address, said among other things:

"I was so pleased to hear the good Mayor of your city speak in the language of human brotherhood. Searching the universe over, I am convinced that if there were more humanitarians like good Mayor Gordon we would have a better world, but it is unfortunate that there are so few, and that is why there are so many wars and conflicts in the world today. Because we have but very few humanitarians, very few men of broad minds and souls, who regard us as one family and children of one common father. But things are so mixed up that is why we have first to bring back [man] to his sober senses, before we can teach that larger brotherhood.

"I am not going to speak of city and municipal rights because we know where we are. No two communities are alike. There is good fellowship in Kansas and a bad spirit in St. Louis. We are looking forward to a universal condition, and we are hoping to have some more like Kansas; but, in the meanwhile, the Universal Negro Improvement Association has searched the world over and discovered that because of our disorganization and our weakness other peoples and nations trample upon and rob us of our rights. We are endeavoring, therefore, to bring this great scattered mass of people together without committing any outrage, without disturbing the peace of the world, for the purpose of founding and establishing a nation and a government of our own in Africa[.][. . .] All of us are not going to Africa to build that government, [. . .] but you can remain right here and support it morally and financially.

"I am not preaching a doctrine of injustice. I am preaching a doctrine of justice and love to all humanity. We believe in human rights. We believe in an equitable division of the things of the earth for all mankind—yellow, white and black. [. . .] Some of us are unreasonable to expect too much of white people. Some of us expect that the white people are Christs and are going to give up to us the best of everything. [. . .] We will never be able to realize our ambitions in this country. We live under a constitution that guarantees the greatest good for the greatest number, and you don't want me to tell you who is in the majority." [. . .]

That is why the Universal Negro Improvement Association, with a deep souled desire[,] is endeavoring to build for the Negro a country of his own in Africa, so that he can rise to the highest in government, without coming in contact and competition with the other fellow. That is the only solution to the vexed question of races." [. . .]

In the afternoon of the 8th we had a delightful drive of 26 miles through the country to Leavenworth. Unfortunately, we had to catch the train at 6:15 p.m. and could only get as far as the State Prison, the Federal Prison[52] being fourteen miles further. However, my husband was well pleased with the place and its surroundings and showed me a nice little three room bungalow that I will have to call home in case he is forced to spend five years' vacation in the pen. [. . .]

(FOURTH ARTICLE) NOV. 10, 1923

On the 8th of October we left Kansas City, Mo., for Portland, Ore., by the Union Pacific railway route, passing through the States of Kansas, Colorado, Wyoming, Idaho and Oregon. For three days I viewed the grandeur of the West—miles and miles of grazing pastures in Kansas, fields of corn and vegetables, and stacks of hay. In Idaho I saw several hot springs, and for almost a day the scenery was confined to a plateau land with stubby growth—trees only two feet in height; but everywhere that vegetation could thrive was well cultivated, and scientifically, too. [. . .]

A town or city cannot exist on nothing. Its backbone is either the minerals of the earth or the vegetation of the fields. Either manufacturing or farming, and in both cases handling and distribution play an important part. In cases of seaport towns and big railroad centers, distribution of goods of all kinds is an industry in itself. This is the white man's method of providing for his own people. It is sound, it is practical, and he is not making any provision for Negroes in any part of this country. From the producer to the consumer he is keeping it all in the big white family. A few industrial magnates may employ Negroes, but that is only when they cannot get white men to fill the jobs, and they pay the Negroes less than the white man. If Negroes don't like any mistreatment and unfairness they receive in such menial jobs, then they can quit and starve, for beggars must not be choosers. Where are our big industrial magnates to give us good jobs? Where are our producers and distributors? Where are our big thinkers who are laying an industrial foundation to save us from economic starvation? We have none.[53] [. . .]

Friends! Let us step lively. Let us get together and have our own manufacturing plants and our mills. Let us employ ourselves. Everywhere I go and ask about labor conditions, I hear the same old wail, "The white folks are tightening down on us, we can hardly get work now." What on earth will we do if white folks close their industrial doors on us altogether[?] Just suppose for argument sake that we woke up one morning and read a proclamation that all white people had decided to stop employing Negroes. How long do you think it would take before we would all be boarding in heaven and feasting on milk and honey?[54] It may sound like a joke, but it is not impossible. It may happen, and, perhaps, sooner than we expect.

These and other thoughts chased through my brain while viewing the great industries of the Western States, built up and run exclusively for white people, whether they be native Americans or poor European emigrants. All are welcome to enjoy the benefits of this great country as long as they are members of the white race.

October 11 we arrived in Portland, Ore. About 1,500 Negroes live there. There is no black belt in the city, as the Negro population is so small; but Negroes are not allowed to live in certain sections. If they happen to get in by some means or other they have an exciting time living there. A prominent wealthy lady of the race told us that she lived in a very fine white neighborhood, but she had to sleep with two guns near her pillow, in expectation of the white mob, I admire her courage, but certainly fear her environment. The majority of our people own their own homes. The men are employed mainly by the Pullman company as porters and waiters on the trains; a few of them are tradesmen. Lumber, wheat, fish and fruit are the chief products. Much of the lumber and wheat is shipped to Japan and China. [. . .]

An old Oregonian told me that the "black laws"[55] are still on the statute books, whereby no Negroes can own land or vote. By the Fourteenth and Fifteenth Amendments[56] to the Constitution these laws are null and void, but the white people have refused to strike them from the statute books. They have no civil rights bill, either, in the State to protect Negroes.

The Ku Klux Klan is very strong in politics in Oregon and Washington.[57] [. . .]

You may ask why do I pay so much attention to the Klan? I am interested in their activities, because I agree with Mr. Garvey when he says that this organization is the hidden spirit of America.[58] After traveling for three weeks through this country and seeing the political machinery of the nation in the hands of this Invisible Empire, I believe that all Negroes should know more about it and make an effort to PERPETUATE THE BLACK RACE for who knows what methods the Klan may use to attain their main object, that of "WHITE SUPREMACY." God to tell what will happen to Negroes when the Kayseys (Knights of Columbus) and the Abies (Jews) settle their differences over the power of the Vatican, and who should carry the money bag and get together on the principle that is so dear to all of them be they sons of Abraham or sons of Rome—that of WHITE SUPREMACY? Friends! I leave this question with you. Think it over. [. . .]

Even Klansmen have a sense of humor, and here is an example of it:

"The newly organized Klan, having held its first parade, was now in session behind closed doors for the purpose of conferring the secret work upon a batch of aliens. A stranger tried to shove his way into the hall. The Klexter shooed him away. Presently the persistent intruder returned.

"Say, look here," said the warden, "you don't belong in here." He took a closer look at the stranger. "I'm sure of it. Aren't you Jewish?"

"Sure, I'm Jewish," answered the other, with an ingratiating smile.

"Well, don't you know the Klan won't let Jews join it?"

"I don't vant to join."

"Well, what do you want then?"

"I vant to see the fellow vot puys de bedsheetings." [. . .]

(FIFTH ARTICLE) NOV. 17, 1923

We reached Los Angeles on the morning of the 15th of October. At the station hundreds of colored people had gathered from 6:30 awaiting our coming, they fairly took charge of the station, and we were almost carried to the automobiles in their arms. The white people were amazed and had to stand aside until we were in our cars before they could come or go. I was amused to see a white newsboy waving his paper in the air and shouting, "Garvey in Town—G-A-R-V-E-E."

At 8:30 p.m. the local division of the Universal Negro Improvement Association held a big meeting at Rev. J. Brown's Baptist Church. The edifice was packed with people, who not only resided in Los Angeles, but had come from all the nearby sections, journeying by trucks and automobiles to hear the program of the organization explained to them—the message of hope to a suffering, down-trodden people. Wealthy Negroes and poor Negroes were there. Old and young—even the crippled had to be wheeled in on chairs. Hundreds were content to stand in the aisles and at the doors. Such is the enthusiasm of Los Angeles for the Universal Negro Improvement Association—the cause of an emancipated Negro race, and a redeemed Africa.

I will not attempt to report the meeting, as the secretary of the division sent in his report already, but I was very much impressed with the juveniles (boys and girls) from the Watts division, under the leadership of Mrs. W. A. Corbin. The little girls were all dressed in spotless white, with nurses' veils on their heads and black crosses on the fold of the veils that rested on their foreheads. Charming little tots and intelligent-looking, who were being trained at a tender age to be good citizens in the community in which they lived, and to be the future presidents, senators, congressmen, financial magnates, professionals and ladies of the African republic to be. [. . .]

The population [of Los Angeles] is comprised of many nationalities and races, besides native born, of which there are about 45,000 to 50,000 Negroes. The Negro population has increased considerably within the last year, due to the fact that Negroes with a little money leave the South and even the Middle West and settle there. The Negroes do all kinds of work for a living. Of course keeping within the limit prescribed for him by the white man who is ever watchful, ever on guard, saying, "Nigger, thus far shalt thou rise and no farther." Friends! Members of my race, I would not advise you (as some of the "big Negroes"[59] have done) to try and break down those barriers, or to pray and hope for a brighter day—a day when that same white man will voluntarily let down the barriers, because to resist the white man in this country is like a bird beating its head against the bars of its cage in order to get freedom. It is hopeless to obtain industrial, economic and political freedom in this manner, when we are in the minority and the white majority rules without mercy. And as for praying and hoping that the white man will have a change of heart, and as a Christian say "Welcome, brother," why, that's a joke. [. . .]

Men and women! Let us not knock our heads to smithereens against this high thick wall of "white supremacy." Let us not kick our heels against the pricks and hurt ourselves, but let us turn our eyes in the other direction and look toward Mother Africa, where we will be able to rise to the heights of true manhood and womanhood and live in happiness and prosperity with our brothers and sisters over there.

To return to my subject, let me say that I spent six days in California and had a delightful time, enjoying the warmth of the climate and the warm hearts of the people. [. . .]

The anti-Japanese feeling has subsided somewhat since the terrible catastrophe in Japan.[60] I do not believe this has come about because of any real sympathy of the whites towards the Japanese, but due to the fact that the Americans are the greatest bidders for re-construction work in Japan and most of the material used in such work is imported from America. So these shrewd business men are smart enough to let their people know that they must not at this particular time do anything that would hurt the feeling of the yellow men in this country, as the stream of yellow gold may stop flowing from Japan to America and be diverted somewhere else. [. . .]

Pasadena is charmingly situated in the San Gabriel valley. It is the famous residential center for rich people. One can ride for over an hour and view the splendor and luxury of the palaces occupied by white people who revel in all the comforts that this western civilization affords.

One of the most picturesque boulevards is nicknamed "Millionaires' Row," bordered by trees, whose branches interlap overhead. I saw the magnificent home of [William] Wrigley[61]—the man who made his millions out of chewing gum. Think of it. Chewing gum made from chicle. Chicle runs wild in Africa, and some black men say, "They have lost nothing in Africa." Wake up, fools! If you can't mine for gold, diamonds and other minerals in Africa, go find chicle and become black millionaires.

I saw the big estate of [August] Busch,[62] the man who made his millions from beer. Yes, beer, that some of us Negroes could not do without before prohibition,[63] and would spend our last dollar on. Well

Busch, the white man, got it, and he is a millionaire today. What fools we Negroes be.[64]

I saw the mansions of pork-packers, miners, manufacturers—all in Millionaires' Row. Men who had started out in life penniless and worked their way up to be controllers of industries, and then—millionaires. [. . .]

We also had many callers. People came from San Diego, Riverside, and even from Arizona to see my husband. Our old friend, Mr. Noah D. Thompson,[65] the former president of the Los Angeles Division, of the Universal Negro Improvement Association, called on us. He seemed in the best of health and was warm in his greeting. He said that he had been very much misunderstood in his recent attitude toward the Universal Negro Improvement Association, that he is a friend of the organization, as he has always been, in so much that the owner and publisher of the leading "Negro yellow sheet"[66] induced him to give evidence against Marcus Garvey in the recent case in the Federal Court, and offered him ten dollars per day for his time in court, and a bonus if Garvey was convicted, besides having his expenses paid, and yet he turned down this magnificent offer on principle, because he was a friend of the organization and a Negro like Marcus Garvey.

I have heard many similar tales told of the easy money offered to anyone who would testify against my husband in the court. I can spot many a man that waxed fat after his conviction—men who had risen to prominence through the organization. Men who had come pleading distress and want, and were given jobs (and lucrative jobs too) by my husband. Men to whom he had stretched out the helping hand and dragged them out of the mire of want. But the mills of the gods grind slowly, but exceedingly fine, and as they have sown so shall they reap, and many shall, like Judas, throw away the thirty pieces of silver and go out and hang themselves.[67] [. . .]

Los Angeles and its surroundings would be a real Eden to Negroes if it were not for that viper, race prejudice, with its fangs of hate ever ready to strike and kill the rising ambitions and hopes of Negroes. [. . .]

(SIXTH ARTICLE) NOV. 24, 1923

We did not leave Los Angeles without bouncing into the camera. Our arrival and departure scenes were filmed, fishing expeditions, etc. Our director was loud in his praise of my husband's easy grace before the camera. One of the local papers gave him a head-liner. Oh! Vaselino,[68] watch your step! The African Star is a dangerous one and may forsake politics for a movie career.

We said good-bye to Los Angeles and Pasadena (Paso de Eden—the threshold of Eden) and journeyed up to Oakland. Arriving there in the morning, October 22, we were greeted at the station by Mr. T. E. Smith, president of the local division of the Universal Negro Improvement Association, and the Lady President, who presented us with two beautiful bouquets of roses. We were driven over to Berkeley, where we stayed. At night the Local Division staged a monster meeting at the City Auditorium, in Oakland, which was packed. The concerted program was excellent, one of the best I had listened to for a long time. "Yours truly" was called upon to speak and being fully wound up could not stop under half an hour. However, I was rewarded with a large bouquet of flowers. [. . .]

We continued our drive through what was once the exclusive residential section [of Berkeley], now a mass of ruins, with the exception of six or eight houses, that miraculously escaped the ravages of fire of a few months ago. I learned that just after a city ordinance had been passed preventing Negroes from owning homes in that section, during the day, a fire started and swept over the entire section for blocks and blocks. Men who had gone to business, women who had gone to their clubs and visiting, returned to find their "Exclusive District" a mass of flames. Some Negroes think it was the wrath of God. Thousands of homes were burnt and millions of dollars lost in the conflagration. [. . .]

On the 24th we crossed the Bay by ferry boat to San Francisco. It is a cosmopolitan city, picturesquely built upon many hills. [. . .]

There are about 1,500 Negroes living in this city. About three times as many work there, but on account of the bad housing conditions for them, the majority live in Oakland but work in Frisco. Many of the light colored Negroes "pass" as Cubans, Filipinos, etc. crossing the racial border. Sometimes they get lost over the border and sometimes they come back penniless and penitent. I heard of a light-colored man who, on coming to Frisco and learning of conditions, discarded his dark wife and went to another part of the city to "pass" as white. But sickness took him. He was put out of his job and his white friends forsook him; so hungry and ill he came back home to "Meely," and confessed that it was not such a wonderful thing to be a poor sick white man among white people. Oh, for the patience of Negro women with some of our white-black and black-white men! [. . .]

On the night of the 25th we bade adieu to the golden State of California and turned our faces Eastward. Journeying through the States of Nevada, Utah, Wyoming, Nebraska, Iowa and Illinois until Sunday afternoon, the 28th, we reached Chicago, changed trains and turned southward through Indiana, Kentucky and Tennessee, until we reached Birmingham, Ala., on the 29th. Ye gods, what a difference in the people, the surroundings. Even the atmosphere is different to that of the Golden West.

Birmingham has become a thriving center because of her mineral wealth—coal and iron—in abundance. [. . .] There are about 70,000 Negroes in this city and about 100,000 whites. The north side of the city produces coal and the south side iron. The Negroes get good pay in these plants, as they do the more laborious work. They seem to invest their money in real estate, because they cannot go to the big theatres and other places of amusement that require the spending of it, as the Southern white man says in plain language: "Nigger, you go this way and I go that way; don't cross my track or I will swing you up!" [. . .]

I asked about the Southern sport [of lynching] among the white gentry and was told that they had not indulged in it for a long time in Jefferson county, as the last game had cost them hundreds of lives. The story goes that a white man murdered his wife and children and was arrested and taken to jail. The white sports from all around gathered and decided to take the law into their hands. The sheriff warned them that he would open fire on any mob that tried to take the life of his prisoner. But the spirit of the game ran away with reason; the thirst for human blood could not be satiated by mere appeal to conscience; their nostrils dilated with the expectancy of smelling burning human flesh, and the mob charged the jail to get their prey. But the sheriff, true to his word, fired and fired. When the smoke cleared only groans were heard. When the morning dawned lawyers were missing from the courts, doctors from their offices, merchants from their stores, and preachers from their parsonages. Swollen, disfigured corpses, strewn around the city, were all that was left of them. The lynching game played well by both sides ends in a "dead draw."

On reading one of the leading white newspapers I noticed that on the front page inset was an article showing that for the week there were seven murders committed by colored people on members of their race, and only one committed by a white man. Strange, on arriving in New York I noticed in a Sunday paper a full page article with pictures of three different types of colored men, and across the top of the page was a huge axe clutched by a black hand on which was written, "Mystery of the twenty axe murders." In the article the writer described the twenty murders committed on white people, with harrowing details, and attributed them to a colored person, or persons, stating that not one of them had been caught and punished. He ended by saying, "Who will be the next, and how many more victims will he destroy, are the questions the helpless police themselves are pondering?" This is the kind of propaganda that helps mobilize the white mob; this is the kind of fuel that is used to blaze the fire of hate and revenge. Birmingham Negroes are making almost as much money as the whites, and a means is being sought to get Negroes out of Birmingham. Half of the stories of murder and rape are untrue, but propaganda distorts truth and even swallows it up when convenient. I hate to predict it, but Negroes in Birmingham, look out and prepare! You may not have a lynching in Jefferson county, but a race war. [. . .]

On the 3rd we went to the railroad station to get a train for Louisville, Kentucky, and were escorted to the special waiting room for the exclusive use of colored people, and saw there a mass of our people huddled together with bundles, bags and babies. Bah! I can't describe any more of it. My soul was sick. I hate to see my people living—no, not living, just breathing, merely existing, under such conditions. The train pulls in and we follow this heartsore and hopeless mass of itinerates to our jimcrow car—specialty de luxe, next to the engine. Why? If you don't like it, walk. If you want to enjoy the comforts of driving, then, "there is your car, Nigger. This is the South!" I enter. Dirt, smoke, not only smoke, but dust. The porter is sweeping the floor. Oh, horrors! He is sweeping the muck on my new dressing case. Help! I am suffocating with the foul odors. Some one opens the window and I hang my head out to breathe once more God's fresh air.

That night we found out that we had to change trains. By the way, a Negro is not given any information by the white railroad clerks. He has just to find out. It was pouring rain, and I had some experience with a white conductor at the station gate. I asked him on what track was the Louisville train, and that son of the soil refused to answer me, so I stamped and bawled at him, and he snarled back at me, until my husband, not seeing me return, came up and made that man know that there were other Negroes in the world besides "good Dixie niggers." That cracker[69] loosened up his tongue after that and directed us to the train, saying, "I have been showing you all the time and you couldn't see." It takes from 500 to 1,000 "southern braves" to lynch one lone black man. [. . .]

Traveling through the sections of the South that I have already named, I saw neglected farms, forest land, deserted homes and shacks. These places looked as if a blight had struck them. A terrible comparison to the other parts of the country! I asked my husband his opinion of the Negro migration north. He said he believed that there was a skillfully organized scheme among some northern white men and Southern thinkers to intimidate Negroes through the K.K.K. and other agencies, to compel them to leave the South. The Southern white farmer, deprived of his colored laborer will, perforce, open his section of the country to white European laborers that are being dumped into

America; in a few years the South will throw off its colored laborers and the problem of races will be gradually solved there. That's his opinion.[70]

The Negroes coming North in such large numbers will not only be a problem to the white employer, but a problem to themselves, for their economic existence, and Southern conditions will spring up all over the country if this wholesale migration keeps up. I noticed that the migration is like a relay race. Negroes from Georgia move up to Kentucky, while Negroes from Kentucky move up to Ohio. Negroes from Louisiana move up to Missouri, and Negroes from Missouri move to Michigan, and so the moving continues. Negroes are trying to find bread and butter and a place of safety—these poor lost sons and daughters of Africa! Talk of the wandering Jew.[71] That is past history. Look and pity the poor wandering Ethiopian. Oh, philanthropic white men, don't be ungrateful. Remember the Negro has helped you build up America. Help him now "find" Africa, and he will not be a parasite on your economic and industrial life.

The Virginia farm lands look much more prosperous than other parts of the South, and the white people in the cities are not so savage looking. Naturally, the colored people, as a whole, are of a higher type.

In the South one will notice that as the white man is, so is the Negro. Where the former is ignorant, so is the Negro. Through no fault of his own he indicates his erstwhile master. There is nothing else for him to copy. [. . .]

I will bring to your attention a point made by one of the speakers—Mr. H. J. Ward,[72] president of the Westmundon Division. He said that a white grocer tried to induce him to buy a new brand of tea by showing him a beautiful white woman with long hair down her neck, which was in the package, and told him he could take it home and hang it on his wall. He said, "I can't use it." "Why?" the grocer asked in surprise. "Well," replied he, "that is just what you white men have been lynching us for all these years." Continuing, the speaker shouted: "Negro women, tear down these pictures of white women from your walls, for your children will grow up to worship them and later on they will want what they worship. Put up in their stead the pictures of black men and women, and your children will grow up to respect and appreciate their own." [. . .]

We left immediately after the meeting for New York, which is called home. On the whole my trip has been a wonderful experience. I observed my people all along the journey and, although conditions differ in different sections of this great country, yet the whole problem boils itself down to a question of a good job, the means whereby to get bread, and protection to life and property. The North is fast becoming like the South, and if we are not being hounded by the mob and run out of town, we are being turned out of jobs and left to starve. Wake up, folks, and think for yourselves. Look for the future. If you don't live to feel it, your children will. Think of them and for them. Those of you who are hale and hearty, get the pioneering spirit and go look for Mother Africa. Build her up. Help her so that she can help you. Find your natural and national home and hold it against all intruders and exploiters. And I am sure that white American philanthropists will help you make men of yourselves. And who can tell that America may not revive her spirit of democracy as far as the Negro is concerned, and stretch out a helping hand to the brave African pioneers? Surely, America has not forgotten the Pilgrim Fathers, who made America what she is today, and surely she will not be ungrateful to the noble sons of Ham, who suffered side by side in the struggle for American nationhood. [. . .]

With best wishes to you all,

Yours truly,

Amy Jacques-Garvey

PART 2
EDITORIALS FOR THE WOMAN'S PAGE

International Affairs/White Exploitation of Darker Peoples

Jacques Garvey showed a broad knowledge of global affairs in her editorials. Rather than focusing only on areas largely populated by Blacks, she supported nationalist movements around the world and condemned the stifling effects of colonization. In "The New Premier of Egypt" she supports Zaghloul Pasha in his struggle to obtain autonomy for his people "against British oppression and greed." The leader's desire for independence augurs well for the rest of Africa. Jacques Garvey also praises India's Mahatma Gandhi in "Can Gandhi's Fasting Unite Moslems and Hindus?" for his efforts to unite all Indians, regardless of religion or caste, "for an India governed by Indians." She likens the Indian cause to that of "scattered" Africans, and she compares India's "saintly" leader with Marcus Garvey. In "The Tidal Wave of Oppressed Peoples Beats against the Color Line," Amy awaits a unity of Black Moslems and Black Christians. Similarly, in "The Cause of the Chinese Trouble," she supports the Chinese in their attempts to throw off the yoke of colonialism and, in turn, she expects "them to be in sympathy with us in our struggle to redeem Africa." The need to unite what she called the "darker peoples" of the world against their White oppressors is one of the most frequent themes in Jacques Garvey's writings.

The articles "Black Emigration and White France" and "British Negros in England Rated as Aliens—Why?" are especially topical today in terms of the tight immigration quotas for people of color in the United States and Europe. Amy may have also been thinking about the Johnson-Reed Immigration Act of 1924, which sharply reduced immigration of peoples not of Northern European stock to the United States.

Jacques Garvey, of course, is especially concerned with the plight of sub-Saharan Africa. She condemns American and British greed and the treachery of Liberian statesmen for selling Liberia for "thirty pieces of silver" in "Liberia, the Savior of American Rubber Manufacturers—At What Price?" The condemnation of Whites in Africa is reiterated in the editorials "Why White Men Want Africa" and "Minerals and Raw Products Attract White Exploitation." These writings inevitably call for Blacks to unite behind Garvey and the UNIA and "to take charge of their destinies and seek to create opportunities in Africa and worldwide" (Broussard 110). In a revolutionary tone, she states that Black demands must be made "in the white man's language—FORCE."

"THE NEW PREMIER OF EGYPT," FEB. 9, 1924

Said Zaghloul Pasha[1] has won his first fight against the British. He is now Premier of Egypt, as also Minister of the Interior.

It will be remembered that during the World War Zaghloul was a thorn in the flesh of the British, by his persistent demands for complete independence for Egypt and the Soudan. He headed a delegation to the Versailles Peace Conference to plead the cause of his people, but was not admitted to the Conference, and later seized by the British and taken to Malta. Owing to the persistent agitation of his followers he was released and the British tried to make terms with him, but he refused all compromise. In December, 1921, he was again seized and sent to Suez. Before he left Cairo he issued a manifesto, which reads in part:

> "Britain has always toyed with us. After the occupation she promised evacuation; after the protectorate she promised to recognize our independence. She is now throwing aside the mask, declares that Egypt is indispensible to

her common interests and demands that we must form part of the British Empire. [. . .] You are sworn to live free or die. Do not let history say that you were unfaithful to your oath. Let us go forward; whether to gather the palms of martyrdom or the flowers of liberty."

Zaghloul Pasha has been called the "Gandhi of Egypt," but unlike Gandhi, he is an active politician and an aggressive forceful character; while Gandhi is primarily a spiritual leader. Major Barnes, an Englishman who visited Egypt, referred to him as the "Lloyd George of Egypt."[2] Like the great Welshman he is a born statesman, and can match wits with English intrigue and diplomacy.

In accepting the Premiership he made it quite plain that he remains President of the Nationalist party, and that the policy of the party—that of complete independence for Egypt and the Soudan—will be the policy of his cabinet.

With a man of such determination and patriotism as Premier, we feel sure that the Nile Valley will once more be independent. On the whole it is a healthy sign for Africa. Egypt is waging her fight against British oppression and greed. Will all Africa unite to make the alien disgorge?

"BLACK EMIGRATION AND WHITE FRANCE," SEPT. 27, 1924

Powerful white nations, who stalk through the world exploiting and robbing weaker peoples of their lands, adopt certain methods and policies in subjugating and controlling the victims of their conquest. Their respective policies differ according to the location of the territory and the disposition of the inhabitants to be exploited.

France is such a past master in the game of foreign aggression that she has fooled even her oppressed into believing her to be the most liberal member among the gang of exploiters.[3] Her treatment of Negro subjects in the West Indies differs to that meted out to those on the west coast of Africa, and the treatment of both differ to that accorded her black citizens in the Republic of France.

The low birth rate in this republic for years compelled her to put into training camps hundreds of thousands of black men during the great World War. These men, having learned the art of modern warfare, have become a problem. Since the armistice was signed black uniformed men in France have been most courteously treated. Those that were not kept in the ranks were allowed to live in France as citizens, not as subjects. All this was done in order to make them feel so satisfied that they would not be disposed to return to their native homes en masse. French diplomacy saw the danger to their colonies in allowing thousands of valiant black men, who had won glory in battle for France, to return home as subjects in their own native land. On this account also she stood the ridicule of other nations in keeping black soldiers on the Rhine.

Five years have rolled by since peace was declared and black ex-soldiers in France have sent for their families, and increased considerably the black population, while France has now become aroused and the republic faces a race problem that needs new adjustment. White labor demands that the government stop the black emigration to France. Jobs are scarce, hungry whites must be fed before blacks. This is the contention of labor and as white men they feel that unrestricted influx of blacks of prolific stock in contrast to the low birth rate of whites, would in a short time produce an equal population of the two races and a high percentage of mulattoes.

White Frenchmen politely advance the economic reason for demanding drastic emigration restrictions for blacks, but the racial feeling has much to do with their demand. M. Herriot[4] and his government are faced with the difficult task of pleasing white labor as well as black colonials. At the same time taking into consideration these facts—that white labor, if not satisfied, can tie up the republic with strikes and agitations and further weaken its finances; and, on the other hand, if black citizens are subjected to drastic restrictions and humiliations one cannot tell to what extremes they may go in retaliation; now that they have been adjudged the best fighters of the last war, it is interesting to see what French diplomacy will do to bring harmony to both parties.

Meanwhile, fallen Germany looks on in grim amusement and secretly drinks "To the day!"

"CAN GANDHI'S FASTING UNITE MOSLEMS AND HINDUS?" OCT. 4, 1924

Mahatma Gandhi, the spokesman for India, is fasting for twenty-one days to atone for the recent clashes between Moslems and Gandhis [*sic*]. The question which arises in the minds of men and women of this Western Hemisphere is, "Can Gandhi's Fasting Unite Moslems and Hindus?"

The caste system of India has been the most helpful agency of the British in maintaining control of this vast empire. Indians are all of one race, yet their religious beliefs have kept them apart socially and politically, divided their country into rival factions and thus make it easy for the alien invader to maintain its yoke of oppression on a people and country so divided.

Mahatma Gandhi is the first leader who has endeavored to unite all Indians politically for the purpose of working toward self-government. His task is a difficult one, for Eastern people on the whole are fanatics in their religious beliefs and customs, and will allow neither love of relatives nor country to interfere in the ordering of their religious lives. Unlike the people of this hemisphere, who are distinctly material in the performance of their religious beliefs, the Eastern people are distinctly spiritual and idealistic. Gandhi, knowing his people so well, appealed to them spiritually, although seeking a material object—that of political emancipation. His saintly manner and silent personal suffering has done more to unite his countrymen than propaganda, literature and fiery speeches could have accomplished. More than that, it has caused even his enemies to respect him, and created friends for the cause of India throughout the world.

About three years ago he was sentenced to prison by the British because of his activities as non-co-operationist leader. His manly behavior at his trial; his appeal to his people not to resort to violence on his behalf, have won the admiration and sympathy of many. He bore imprisonment nobly, while the cause for which he fought continued to spread throughout India. Soon after the Labor party of England came into power he was released before completing his sentence. Emaciated in body and broken in health, he was compelled to take a rest cure for several months, while England wondered what would be the next step of this saintly leader. Minor clashes occurred between Moslems and Hindus (as will be expected between people of such different spiritual beliefs), the soul of Gandhi burned within him, and he started a twenty-one days' fast. Already a conference of the representatives of all religious communities of India have met at Delhi and sent a resolution to him expressing the country's deep sorrow at his suffering, condemning the recent clashes, assuring him that the country would do its utmost to enforce his principles, and entreating him to discontinue his fast. So much has this saintly leader accomplished already by his personal sacrifice.

A people so profoundly religious can only be stirred by such methods. Western ideas cannot work effectively on Eastern minds. In the course of years all India will be united politically and we of the Negro race hope that Gandhi will be strengthened to continue his fight of self-government for India, and send the alien intruder back to his own country, thereby weakening our common oppressor and strengthening the prestige of one of the members of the family of darker peoples of the world in the field of achievement and world power. The methods this saintly scholar and leader adopts may seem strange to us, but the ends to be served are similar to ours, and as Moslems and Hindus unite for an India governed by Indians, so are we Africans, scattered all over the world, forgetting our sectional and tribal differences and uniting on the great objective of "Africa for the Africans, those at home and those abroad."

"WHY WHITE MEN WANT AFRICA," APRIL 18, 1925

It is conceded by those who study world affairs that nations lay claim to territories mainly for either of these reasons:

1. To find an outlet for their surplus populations.
2. To use as a war base certain strategic points. [*sic*]
3. Lastly, and chiefly, to exploit the raw products and minerals of those territories for their home consumption and comfort.

Nations, whose desire for colonial expansion warps their Christian ethics and preachments, adopt all sorts of subterfuges in order to make entry into the seized regions they covet. The white missionary is used to spy out the land, as also the big game hunter, who bluffs the world by having his picture taken with the butt of his rifle on the carcass of a lion or tiger which some fearless native had killed, while he, the white hunter, was at a safe distance. Sometimes it is an erratic explorer who happens to get certain information from natives who do not know the value of their minerals. The biggest game that constitutes the object of the wanderings of these adventurers is GOLD AND DIAMONDS. These men are the forerunners of machine guns, battleships and aeroplanes, which are used to oust the natives and make them powerless in the face of exploitation and robbery of their property. In an article on "The World's Gold," by Josiah Spurr,[5] in Foreign Affairs for this month, [he] says: "The most spectacular flood of gold in the history of the world has been that which, between 1900 and the present moment, has flowed from the British dominions in South Africa, principally the Transvaal." [. . .]

This is the reason why England wants to keep a stranglehold on as much of Africa as she can. It is the cry for gold, the basis of the currency of nations. Take away from England the African gold mines, and her pound would be on a par value with the German mark. France, Spain, Italy, Belgium and Portugal all are holding on to slices of Africa. Why? Just to boast that they control the natives? For the purpose of civilizing and [C]hristianizing them? No. Their sole purpose is to draw from Africa all of her raw products and mineral wealth, so as to replenish their bankrupt treasuries, and to prop up their boasted white supremacy, which is toppling fast, with the awakened consciousness of the darker peoples of the world. The new Negro who belongs to this awakened group, envisions mother Africa stretching out her bleeding hands to her scattered sons and daughters, bidding them to return home, and also realizes that if we, as a race must survive, we must get power, and the quickest way to obtain this it to acquire wealth.

The old-time Negro who had swallowed the white man's malicious propaganda about Africa and in belching it up, used to say, "I haven't lost anything in Africa, and I am not going there for the cannibals to eat me," has now changed his talk, and is saying, "I lost the richest continent on the globe, when I lost Africa, and by the help of God I am going back there to find wealth and happiness."

The Negro has served well his apprenticeship in this Western Hemisphere, and through the guidance of the Universal Negro Improvement Association he has learned to accept the good and reject the bad elements of this civilization, and has sworn to work and act so that the redemption of Africa for the Negro people of the world will soon be a possibility.

Why should the gold of Africa be used to rehabilitate bankrupt Europe, when this poverty stricken race of ours needs it? It is ours by divine apportionment. If diamonds and other precious stones are taken from Africa to adorn the throats and arms of white women, why should black women use glass beads or go without? Wake up, Mr. Blackman, and go up and possess the land! Your women are tired of menial jobs and being abused by men of other races; your children want care and provision made for their future if they are to live. Your race wants a first class rating according to present day standards. Your country calls. Will you answer these appeals, Mr. Blackman?

"THE TIDAL WAVE OF OPPRESSED PEOPLES BEATS AGAINST THE COLOR LINE," JULY 18, 1925

The thoughtful of the white race are alive to the fact that the darker peoples of the world are taking the much discussed war pronouncement of the late Woodrow Wilson seriously, namely, "the principle of self-determination."[6] This phrase has been echoing and re-echoing round the globe since it was uttered, the practical application of which would usher in a new era of political and economic freedom for the darker peoples, and peace to the world; but the avaricious, selfish white man sees in it a menace to the exploitation of the labor of his darker brother, a menace to his land grabbing activities in the East, and a menace to his overlordship.

The Eastern Giant is awakened, and in his consciousness he listens to the Christian teaching of the white missionary. "Do unto others, as ye would that they should do unto you."[7] He watches them put this into practice, and he realizes that they preach what they do not, and never intend to, practice. He unmasks him, and behold! He sees a common land thief, whose sole purpose is to exploit and rule. The phrase, "the principle of self-determination" coming from the lips of the white man is applicable only to members of his race; but when it is spoken to men of other races it loses its original form, and in its application resembles "the principle of exploitation." The Eastern Giant is now exercising his muscles, and we notice a quiver in China, and an expansion in Morocco, but the day is fast approaching when he will have corralled all the strength of his scattered nerve power and stalk forth to sovereignty and to power.

The white man is too innately selfish to yield one inch of his ill-gotten power to another race. He refuses to be just and fair in his dealings with the other portion of humanity that does not look like him. Hence the Mohammedan has learned this—that as the white Christian preaches, "Thou shalt not kill," and yet he does, even so the Mohammedan teaches, "Thou shalt not kill," yet he must, or be wiped off the face of the globe by the white Christian.

Many white missionaries today are changing their tactics in the East, and instead of forcing the Bible and the rum bottle on the natives, are urging their religious home offices and nations to cooperate with them in an effort to apply a larger measure of fair play in their contact with the natives. They who are on the spot can better appreciate the necessity for this change of attitude, before the avenging hand of the Eastern Giant strikes his fatal blow at "white superiority." [. . .]

The groans and entreaties of our forebears have gone up to high Heaven, and our supplications have been heard, and in God's good time he will bring to pass that happiness on earth that all downtrodden peoples pray for. Whether we be black Mohammedans or black Christians, we all believe in the same God, the Father of all. Our forms of worship may differ, but the basic principles are the same. We worship in spirit and in truth. Our racial interests are identical. We are all struggling under the same yoke, and by the help of God, Allah, the First Cause,[8] or the omnipotent, we will join forces, and throw off the common oppressor, and live up the to high calling of our Creator, and in obedience to His injunction—"YE ARE THE LORDS OF CREATION."[9]

"THE CAUSE OF THE CHINESE TROUBLE," SEPT. 5, 1925

As Morocco is holding her own against aggression and oppression, even so China is waging a similar fight for freedom of action in her own country. The most powerful nations of Europe have gone through the world plundering the lands of the darker peoples, but these weak peoples are gathering strength through organization and enlightenment through education and racial contact; therefore the European marauder is having a hot time at his old time game and in a few years will be driven back into his own territory, leaving Africa and Asia to work out their own destiny.

Col. Alexander Powell,[10] a traveler of wide experience in Asia, sums up the attitude of the European powers toward China, in his book "Asia at the Crossroads," as follows:

> [. . .] The story of the pillage of China is saturated with intrigue and corruption, deceit and trickery, selfishness and greed. It forms one of the most shameful and depressing chapters in the history of our times and makes a mockery of Europe's sanctimonious championship of justice and fair dealing.

It is said that once in the parks of Shanghai, the Europeans displayed signs such as this, "Chinese and Dogs Are Not Admitted." This reminds of the Southern States of this country where the same brutal and unfair motives cause the white man to post this sign: "Niggers and Dogs

Not Allowed Here." The white European is the same at heart racially as the American white man, although at times the exigencies of the moment demand that they show their prejudices in slightly different ways. But the time has come when yellow, black and brown races are determined to measure up to the high calling of the Creator, and for this purpose they unite, feeling that God made them higher than the animals; in fact he made all mankind alike. The white man has stepped ahead within the last few centuries, but he has done so by foul means, and the Almighty Umpire has disqualified him. We see that exemplified in the crumbling of empires, and in his decaying civilization. It remains to be seen whether black, yellow or brown will take the lead and guide the world righteously and well.

The Chinese are now conscious of their potentialities. As the Chinaman see [*sic*] it, "the Occident[11] would cajole them with the Bible in one hand and threaten them with the gun in the other—not to save China's soul but to fill an imperial purse." Therefore having unmasked the white hypocrite he is determined to throw him out as China should be governed by Chinese, and we, the Negroes of the world, are in sympathy with the Chinese, as we expect them to be in sympathy with us in our struggle to redeem Africa.

"LIBERIA,[12] THE SAVIOR OF AMERICAN RUBBER MANUFACTURERS—AT WHAT PRICE?" SEPT. 12, 1925

So many persons use manufactured products in their homes and at business, yet never give a thought as to how they are made, and from whence the raw material came. Rubber, for instance, is universally used, and made into products used by young and old, by the small boy romping in his sneaks, mother in the kitchen with her rubber apron and gloves, Auntie sick in bed with a hot water bag, to dad at the wheel of his auto pondering over the prices of balloon tires,[13] all enjoy the various uses of rubber.

The story of the early discovery of rubber by the white man goes, that an Englishman went to Brazil, collected some rubber seeds, and smuggled them to England, where they were planted in Kew Gardens. In 1877 young trees were sent to Singapore, later to Borneo and Malaya. Forty years later the English controlled 75 per cent. of the world's rubber. So much for the daring of that Englishman who stole the first rubber seeds from Brazil, and succeeding others who exploit the labor of the Asiatics to produce rubber, which is as precious as gold today.

In 1921 the cost of rubber was 19 cents per pound, in 1922 it dropped to 14 cents, then certain agreements were reached between the English producer and the American consumer, which culminated in the Colonial Restriction Act,[14] thereby regulating the exportation until the stocks on hand could be stabilized. Due to the Englishman's longheadedness and the increase in demand for rubber goods in America, the price per pound today is $1.25, and still it soars. We have a sneaky feeling that there is something deeper behind the sudden inflation in price than just supply and demand. England owes America billions of dollars which she can't or won't pay. England's unemployed is rated at over a million today. [. . .] America demands a repayment of the war loan. England retaliates by a sudden rise in the price of rubber of over 150 per cent. John Bull[15] seems to think that if he is forced to repay what he borrowed during the "bloody sport" of 1914–18, then he will maneuver so that American greenbacks will come into his coffers by trade, and be paid out again to America in reduction of his little I.O.U. How does the American rubber manufacturer take it? is the query.

Mr. Sherman Rogers, in an article in Success Magazine answers the question partly when he states:

> They are not asleep, but the public and the American manufacturer must remember one thing. Regardless of all talk, we cannot grow rubber commercially in large quantities in Mexico, and compete with the East Indies. We cannot grow it in South America and compete with British and Dutch owners. [. . .]
>
> Sumatra, the most fertile section of the tropics for rubber cultivation, is only a short distance from Java,[16] a country smaller than the State of Texas that contains 35,000,000 people, who are deeply concerned in making enough money to keep body and soul together.

> And all of the British East Indian possessions lie in close proximity to the 400,000,000 people of India, and the hordes of coolie labor in China. Therefore, they will always be in a position to command tremendous supplies of extremely cheap labor, labor that only demands a fraction of the amount of wages commanded by people of any section of either Central or South America, where rubber can be produced.

But the American rubber manufacturer did not despair. He turned his eyes toward Africa, in particular to the little black Republic of Liberia. He saw rubber trees growing wild, without proper cultivation, and yet able to produce an appreciable amount of rubber. Mr. Harvey Firestone[17] discovered this nugget and entered into negotiations with the Liberian government for a concession of one million acres or more to be exploited for rubber or "any other development" on conditions similar to the American occupation of what was once Panamanian territory—now called the Canal Zone.

Marcus Garvey protested, as he foresaw the danger to Liberian autonomy consequent on a ratification of such proposals. In vain. The concessions granted the Universal Negro Improvement Association were revoked, and Garvey was barred from Liberia. Three weeks ago Edwin Barclay,[18] secretary of state of Liberia, arrived in America, and after a two-day conference with Harvey Firestone closed the deal. In an interview with the press, Mr. Barclay stated that "Labor is very cheap in Liberia and strong, healthy men work for 25 cents a day. . . . Neither Garvey nor any of those identified with him would be received in Liberia."

The American rubber man has got what he wanted, rubber lands and all the minerals under the ground, also cheap labor. All at the expense of poor black natives in Liberia, who will be compelled to toil for white American capitalists for a mere pittance.

Liberia owes America money, and if Liberian statesmen were honest about the betterment of the republic, they would have kept their word with the Universal Negro Improvement Association and allowed this organization of black men to enter into and cultivate rubber plantations and participate in other development of the country, which, in a few years, would bring into the country enough revenue to repay America and create a healthy treasury for the republic. Liberia could have cornered the rubber market through the U.N.I.A. and restore[d] her finances to par; her native sons would be on equal terms with the blacks from America, and their wages standardized to allow them to live like men and not like peons. Barclay does not want Garvey or Garveyites in Liberia because had they been there, these things would not have happened.

Poor Liberia has been bartered away. Who has received the thirty pieces of silver? is the query from black America.

"BRITISH NEGROES IN ENGLAND RATED AS ALIENS—WHY?" JAN. 30, 1926

Since the beginning of last year the English government has found it expedient to make stringent restrictions in its immigration measure and today we find the alien entering the shores of England subject to the following conditions:

> "Every alien entering Britain today must declare the purpose of his visit, satisfy the immigration authorities that he will not become a public charge, and must also guarantee that he is not in search of employment.
>
> "Every alien staying beyond two months must register with the police, and possess a police book containing his photograph and address; nor may the latter be changed without notifying the police."

We concede to every country the right to protect its subjects or citizens from unemployment and bad housing conditions by drastic immigration measures, but what puzzled us for some time was the fact that Negroes from any part of the British Commonwealth of Nations, being born under the British Union Jack, should have been rated as "aliens" in England. This is quite as paradoxical as the case of Australia and New Zealand (both dominions of the British Commonwealth) barring Negroes from the British West Indies and British controlled Africa, in their effort to keep Australia and New Zealand white.

Several months ago we examined the "alien" passport of a seaman born in Sierra Leone, but domiciled in England for many years, and we were surprised, then amused to note that under the heading "nationality" a pen stroke was placed by the clerk who had filled out the particulars of the passport. So, according to John Bull's new strategy, his black subjects in England have no nationality. It is to laugh and ask what next?

Recently in conversation with a gentleman who had just returned from a visit to England, the question of passports came up, and he being an American citizen was at first puzzled to see British Negroes carrying alien passports and reporting to the police in England. He asked a police commissioner, who feigned ignorance, but in the course of his walks around London he was given the following information in answer to his query: That the Moroccan war[19] had opened their eyes to certain dangers in the future, that it was unsafe to rely on British Negroes as soldiers to quell any uprising by members of the darker races, hence they were listed as "aliens" so that in case of war and they did not join the side of England voluntarily they could be interned and in general treated as enemies of His Majesty's government.

When we, as members of the Universal Negro Improvement Association, talk about a government of our own in Africa, a flag of our own and a national anthem of our own, some Negroes laugh at us, but we have only pity for them, as they know not what they do.[20] When Uncle Sam lynches her black boys with her uniform on their back, and John Bull calls her ex-soldiers aliens who helped her in the Ashanti and Zulu wars[21] to take big slices of Africa, then it is high time for some dull, apathetic Negroes to think in terms of nationhood.

The majority of Negroes all over the world since the close of hostilities in 1918 have determined that they will not shoulder the white man's gun and under his command go out and kill our brothers, so as to enable the white man to take their lands. We have been taught by him that the divine law is, "Man, love thy brother." Our lawful brother is any other Negro in any part of the world he may be found. Although he may have wandered far from home is no reason why we should disown him, and take up arms against him for our half-brothers, the white or yellow man.

British agents may persecute Marcus Garvey and try to get him out of the way, but Garveyism has reached the utmost parts of the world, and the persecution of Garvey but invigorates his followers, and may have far-reaching effects.

We Negroes of the western world believe that it is our duty to protect from invasion the countries in which we are domiciled, but as no country in the world affords full citizenship to Negroes on an equal footing with its white nationals, then we feel more than justified in our most righteous endeavor to create an African citizenship that white and yellow nations may respect. We refuse to be called citizens, without rights and subjects without protection. We are Africans by blood, and Ethiopians with a glorious ancient history, which we are striving to revive, God being our Helper and Guide, and Marcus Garvey being our leader and trail blazer. It is God's will and it will be done.

"MINERALS AND RAW PRODUCTS ATTRACT WHITE EXPLOITATION," SEPT. 11, 1926

This is an age of activity—a feverish activity on the part of the white race to hold the darker peoples of the world in subjection, so that they may monopolize this world's goods, and a labored activity by the oppressed to free themselves from serviture and enjoy some of the blessings of creation. It is a grim struggle that is taking place daily and is evidenced in every walk of life, when the two opposite races come in contact with each other.

In order to retain its leadership, the white race pillages the countries of other peoples, and subjects the latter to the most inhuman treatment, thereby existing off the loot and free-booty. Honesty and brotherly love are not practiced by this "superior race" who have long since forgotten how to speak the truth, or to play fair with the "poor benighted heathens," to whom they would gladly give all of Jesus, while they grab the world and all therein. But the colored races are beginning to realize that man cannot live off religion; that man stalks the earth looking for wealth and territories to provide a continuous supply of food; and that man experiments in his laboratories and manufactures all sorts of man-killing machines in order to protect that which he acquires; therein is man superior, according to present day standards, when he is able to get that which he covets, and to hold [it] against all others. He who would survive in this materialistic struggle must learn the art of taking and keeping.

Years ago many people thought that if they lived in remote countries, and were not aggressors, they would be immune from invasion; but that's a foolish thought today, when ships and aeroplanes have conquered distance, the earth has become man's footstool. Abyssinia[22] remained in seclusion for centuries, having no ambassadors or representatives in foreign countries, being completely shut off from modern progress, Italy tried to scale her mountains, twenty-five years ago, and was defeated; but with the connivance of England she is making another try without firing a shot. The world of anxious, but unprepared, black men are looking on to see whether the Switzerland of Africa will be divided up between England and Italy, or whether the international freebooters will squabble among themselves and save Abyssinia.

Irak [*sic*] with her oil gushers, the Philippines with rubber trees, Liberia with rubber and gold, South Africa with diamonds, are places that white men will fight to get, and hold, because they abound with products and minerals that they want. Prayerful petitions and tearful appeals are a waste of time and energy, when you make your demands in the white man's language—FORCE—he will readily yield or feel your heavy hand; but appeal to his conscience and he will think you too stupid to live, since you cannot interpret the spirit of the age, and will feel justified in exterminating you, so as to make room for people who are better able to appreciate and participate in modern progress, caring not how unethical it is.

Africa, the treasure-house of the world, has been partitioned by every white nation. Not for the fun of taking the black man's country did they do it, but because that vast continent has on its surface and in its bowels every conceivable product that man could use for his comfort and happiness. The Africans at home had no means of protecting the country, while the Africans abroad being steeped with white propaganda, pitifully babbled "We haven't lost anything in Africa." The result has been a general European scramble to take what the foolish Negro did not even know he had lost.

Through nine years of hard labor and terrible sacrifices, Marcus Garvey has awakened in millions of Negroes an appreciation of material values, to the extent that the redemption of Africa from white exploitation is their sworn duty. When all Negroes place the right value on Africa, then its redemption will be accomplished hastily, and the race lifted up to a place of respect and honor among others.

Gender Issues

Jacques Garvey's view of gender roles is tied in directly to her nationalistic beliefs. She has no problem if Black men can lead the race and protect their women; however, she feels that they generally do not fulfill this role. As a result, Black women are often underappreciated by their men and are forced to take on a disproportionate burden. In editorials such as "The Larger Usefulness of Women," "Our Women Getting into the Larger Life," "Women and World Peace," "Women as Leaders Nationally and Racially" and "Women's Function in Life," Jacques Garvey praises the leadership role women of all races (but especially Black women and in particular the women of the UNIA) have undertaken in recent years in all spheres of life. They are frequently at the center of advancements in business, politics and in the home. Today's woman "is not afraid of hard work, and by being independent she gets more out of the present day husband than her grandmother did in the good old days." She resists the notion of women being considered "human incubators and slaves to do the bidding of their husbands." Jacques Garvey claims, "The doll-baby type of woman is a thing of the past and the wide-awake woman is forging ahead, prepared for all emergencies, and ready to answer any call, even if it be to face the cannons on the battlefield."

Jacques Garvey is frequently hard on the men of her race, increasingly so through the course of her tenure as editor of the Woman's Page. For example, in "For You and Your Sons," she chastises Black men for not assuming the responsibility that men of other races have in "protecting their women, and providing for their offspring." She states that "[u]ntil you can fulfill these and other manly duties, you cannot expect to be rated as a man, and a race cannot progress, nor can a nation be built with weaklings." Jacques Garvey defends women's dress in "Scanty Clothes Make Hardy Women," then proceeds to await the day when women rule the world, which she predicts will be better than the "pretty mess" created by men. The editorial "Listen Women!" undoubtedly is her most vitriolic attack. In it, she calls most Negro men "parasites" who have "no love for [their women]." They are inherently indolent "and the race is that much poorer because of [their] slothfulness." Remarkably, she even defends the exploitations of Whites, because they have done their misdeeds so that their "women may live in comfort and luxury." Winston James feels that the anger and frustration expressed in such editorials is in part due to the increasing demands placed on women as male members began to desert the UNIA in large numbers after 1925 (James 154). While this is true, as Barbara Bair states, Amy grew increasingly "frustrated with the sexism of men who refused to let women enter the ranks of leadership or pay attention to what they had to say, who failed as breadwinners, and who did not have the gumption to keep up the militancy of the UNIA program" (Bair "Our Women," 120).

"THE LARGER USEFULNESS OF WOMEN," MARCH 22, 1924

There is nothing more significant in the life of mankind than the gradual emancipation of woman from utter dependence upon man and the giving to her a decisive voice in her relations to man in the family, the Church and the State. In the United States and Great Britain she has been given the right of the franchise,[23] a citizenship which carries with it all of the rights, privileges and immunities so long monopolized by man. The Young Turks[24] have virtually abolished the harem, under the leadership of Mustapha Kemal, a reformer with a vision, and Madame Kemal[25] who has a good English education, is working for a larger freedom and usefulness of all Turkish women. The Turkish movement for a more honorable place for women in the life of mankind is bound to affect the 350,000 Mohammedan people[26] of Asia and Africa and affect them for their good.

The part that woman has played in building up the Christian Church and furthering all reforms for the betterment of mankind, such as the abolition of slavery in the United States and the British colonies, and in bringing the temperance question to the high point of success it has reached in the United States and is reaching in Great Britain and some of the Continental States, notably Russia,[27] has been a part of heroic self-sacrifice, devotion and brilliancy. In the politics of Great Britain woman has begun to play a conspicuous part, her members of Parliament standing out bravely and intelligently for reform in the treatment of wage-earning women and children; while in the United States she has just begun to make her influence felt upon questions with which politics has to do, and this influence will grow and have its influence, as her influence has been felt for half a century in all uplift movements and in the work of the home, the school room and the Church.

In the life of the Negro, in the United States, in the West Indies, in Africa, as well as in the Latin American States, and her larger use done—[sic] a heroic work during the past fifty years, and her larger usefulness has been shown in the advantage she has taken of every opportunity to help make the home and the church and school room the proper places they should be for the training of the childhood of the race for the work of service which awaits them as grown-ups.

Whatever should the Universal Negro Improvement Association have done in its gradual growth from small beginnings to worldwide influence and helpfulness but for the loyalty, devotion and sacrifice of the Negro woman? At every advance she has sustained the efforts of the men, deeming no service too great, no demand too exacting, when made upon her. And her work in the Association has just begun, especially in far off Africa, where her voice has begun to be heard in defense of her sisters who are outraged and degraded by the white man's soulless rule. It was Napoleon, we believe, who declared that "the hand that rocks the cradle rules the world."[28] Right now that is more largely true of the woman of the African than of any other race, and we are sure she will make the most and not the least of the larger usefulness which has been opened to her, as to other women, for service.

"OUR WOMEN GETTING INTO THE LARGER LIFE," JULY 12, 1924

The world wide movement for the enlargement of woman's sphere of usefulness is one of the most remarkable of the ages. In all countries and in all ages men have arrogated to themselves the prerogative of regulating not only the domestic but the civic and economic life of women. In many countries women were subject entirely to the whims and legislation of men. It is that way now in most Asiatic countries and among some of the tribes of Africa.

The recent upheaval in Turkey has carried with it condemnation of the harem relations and the sanction of the family life as it has developed in Christian countries. Madam Kemal is the leader of the Turkish women for larger freedom in the ordering of their lives, but the innovation, which is bound to work for the betterment of men as well as women, as the harem life is a blight on womanhood which degrades manhood as well, could only have been accomplished by the separation of Church and State, the Sultanate and the Caliphate, which amounts to negating the hitherto predominating influence of the Mohammedan religion in the affairs of State as of Church. However far the innovation will extend to other Moslem countries, and what influence, if any, it will have on the domestic life of the people of Asia and Africa, where the Mohammedan religion is strong, remains to be seen.

In Europe average womanhood has been held at a very low valuation until it got into the recently developed currents of modern innovation, and the average still remains low, peasant life for the man and the woman and their children being of the lowest and hardest. Only in Great Britain has the movement for the larger and better life for women, by allowing them reasonable voice in making and enforcing the laws, made any appreciable headway.

The United States has gone further than any other nation in giving woman a share in making and enforcing the laws and in regulating her economic life to her advantage and not entirely to the advantage of man. She is now given an equal part in political matters, and she is allowed a freedom in earning and controlling her earnings which is a great improvement upon the former of old things. In social and personal matters the American woman has attained to an independence and freedom which it will take centuries for the women of other nations to attain to.

Negro women of the United States share equally in the larger life which has come to women, of other race groups, and she has met every test in the home, in bread winning, in church and social upbuilding, in charitable uplift work, and in the school room which could have been expected of her reasonably. She has yet to develop as active interest in political affairs as the women of other race groups, but she is bound to grow in this as in other matters in which her interests are involved.

The women of the Universal Negro Improvement Association have shown an interest and a helpfulness so far flung as to make it doubtful if the organization could have reached the high point of strength and effectiveness it has without them. To take woman and her sympathies and work out of the association would be like taking the wife out of the home of the husband. The women of the association are a tower of strength. They know it and glory in the fact, and their men are proud of them, and justly. The success of the Negro race thus far has been largely due to the sympathy and support which our women have given to the cause.

Our women are getting into the larger life which has the womanhood of the world in its sweep. We are sure they will be equal to all of the demands made upon them in the future as in the past, and the demands are going to increase in volume and importance as we go along. It stands to reason.

"WOMEN AND WORLD PEACE," JAN. 31, 1925

With the entry of women into politics and big business the next important factor that is engaging her attention is the problem of war. Should she bring children into the world, train them to the best of her ability, and when they arrive at an age of usefulness see them snatched from her and used as can[n]on-fodder or munition workers? The woman of today rebels against this ancient custom that robs her of her most precious gift—her children—and yet debars her from questioning the "whys and wherefores" or the justice or injustice of wars.

In some countries politics has given the sex a voice in the affairs of government which enables her to decide nationally the important question, "To war or not to war?" But her voice in politics in these countries is still young, therefore weak, while in others it is inaudible. Consequently she has divided her attention between politics and educating public opinion toward world peace. [. . .]

"War," said a famous lecturer, "is the outgrowth of a state of mind."[29] The state of mind of the powerful nations of the world is made up largely of selfishness, greed and avarice. They have no regard for the rights of weak peoples, and wage war on defenseless groups to fill the coffers of their treasuries, to expand their national boundaries, and to find an outlet for their surplus population. What matter if a few thousand Negroes are killed yearly mining diamonds to adorn the bodies of white women? Who cares if sixteen million Negroes are maimed and slaughtered in seven years in order to produce rubber for the Belgians? Does it matter at all if all the general wealth of Africa and India is robbed and exploited by the powerful white nations of the world to satisfy their greed? Is the small, wee voice of conscience stilled in the breasts of statesmen who administer the affair of those big nations? This is the age of force and power. "Might is right," is their cry, and who dares dispute their claim must fight it out or submit to oppression and exploitation.

Some organizations are agitating for international peace, but we believe that such an era will never dawn until nations learn to respect the rights and privileges of unorganized peoples. The same spirit of avarice that prompts the exploitation of weak peoples will cause strong nations to fight each other for the spoils of their pillage. There can be no peace among nations until there is peace in the whole world, and oppressed peoples everywhere, of every creed and race, are determined to get freedom and independence or die fighting for it. Powerful nations will always be kept busy stemming the tide of liberty and democracy, until they practice it among all humanity.

Women are playing a very important part in bringing about humane legislations, and it is hoped that they will use their influence and educate international opinion to the tenets of true [C]hristianity—which they profess—and which is embodied in these two scriptural injunctions, "Man, love thy brother,"[30] and, "Do unto others as you would that they should do to you."

"WOMEN AS LEADERS NATIONALLY AND RACIALLY," OCT. 24, 1925

The exigencies of this present age require that women take their places beside their men. White women are rallying all their forces and uniting regardless of national boundaries to save their race from destruction and preserve its ideals for posterity. We see them in the law courts pleading as advocates; they preside as judges and administer laws; while in less numbers, yet they are to be seen in parliaments, congresses and council chambers legislating for their people. White men have begun to realize that as women are the backbone of the home, so can they, by their economic experience and their aptitude for details participate effectively in guiding the destiny of nation and race.

No line of endeavor remains closed for long to the modern woman. She agitates for equal opportunities and gets them; she makes good on the job and gains the respect of men who heretofore opposed her. She prefers to be a bread-winner than a half-starved wife. She is not afraid of hard work, and by being independent she gets more out of the present day husband than her grandmother did in the good old days.

The women of the East, both yellow and black, are slowly but surely imitating the women of the Western world, and as the white women are bolstering up a decaying white civilization, even so women of the darker races are sallying forth to help their men establish a civilization according to their own standards, and to strive for world leadership.

Women of all climes and races have as great a part to play in the development of their particular group as the men. Some readers may not agree with us on this issue, but do they not mould the minds of their children—the future men and women? Even before birth a mother can so direct her thought and conduct as to bring into the world either a genius or an idiot. Imagine the early years of contact between mother and child, when she directs his form of speech, and is responsible for his conduct and deportment. Many a man has risen from the depths of poverty and obscurity and made his mark in life because of the advices and councils of a good mother whose influence guided his footsteps throughout his life.

Women therefore are extending this holy influence outside the realms of the home, softening the ills of the world by their gracious and kindly contact.

Some men may argue that the home will be broken up and women will become coarse and lose their gentle appeal. We do not think so because everything can be done with moderation. Some women are good cooks, yet because of the call to other duties they rarely ever cook a meal, but when the necessity presents itself they know how. Others are good business women, yet they would not neglect their children and homes to attend business with their husbands, but if hubby dies or becomes incapacitated, they can fit in his place and save a situation. The doll-baby type of woman is a thing of the past and the wide-awake woman is forging ahead, prepared for all emergencies, and ready to answer any call, even if it be to face the cannons on the battlefields.

New York has a woman as secretary of state.[31] Two States have women governors,[32] and we would not be surprised if within the next ten years a woman graces the White House in Washington, D.C. Women are also filling diplomatic positions, and from time immemorial women have been used as spies to get information for their country.

White women have greater opportunities to display their ability because of the standing of both races, and due to the fact that black men are less appreciative of their women than white men. The former will more readily sing the praises of white women than their own, and who is more deserving of admiration than the black woman, she who has borne the rigors of slavery, the deprivations consequent in a pauperized race and the indignities heaped upon a weak and defenseless people? Yet she has suffered all with fortitude, and stands ever ready to help in the onward march to freedom and power.

Be not discouraged black women of the world, but push forward, regardless of the lack of appreciation shown you. A race must be saved, a country must be redeemed, and unless you strengthen the leadership of vacillating Negro men, we will remain marking time until the yellow race gains the leadership of the world, and we be forced to subserviency under them, or extermination.

We are tired of hearing Negro men say, "There is a better day coming," while they do nothing to usher in the day. We are becoming so impatient that we are getting in the front ranks and serve notice to the world that we will brush aside the halting, cowardly Negro leaders, and with prayer on our lips and arms prepared for any fray, we will press on and on until victory is ours.

Africa must be for Africans, and Negroes everywhere must be independent, God being our helper and guide. Mr. Black Man, watch your step! Ethiopia's queens will reign again, and her Amazons protect her shores and people. Strengthen your shaking knees and move forward, or we will displace you and lead on to victory and glory.

"WOMAN'S FUNCTION IN LIFE," DEC. 19, 1925

Quite frequently we hear the question debated as to whether woman's place is in the home, in business, in politics or in industry. Countries differ as to woman's status; but present day events convince us that woman, lovely woman, if you please, is making her presence felt in every walk of life.

Some men are slow to admit that the woman of today has a place in nearly all phases of man's life, and when such a place is not yet properly established, her voice is heard in that regard, yet these men are the ones who more readily fall under the influence of mere woman.

The women of the East are fast being emancipated and educated to the point where they no longer consider themselves human incubators and slaves to do the bidding of their husbands, but intelligent, independent human beings to assert and maintain their rights in copartnership with their men.

Recently Mustapha Kemal Pasha, one of the westernized leaders of the East, while addressing some students at the Girls' Training School at Smyrna, was asked the question, "What must Turkish women be?" And he replied as follows:

> Turkish women must have the best cultivated minds, and must be the most virtuous and the most serious ladies in the world. The duties of Turkish women ought to be to prepare future generations who will be able to protect their country mentally, morally and physically. Women being the source of the nation and the basis of human society, they can only fulfill their duty when they are virtuous.

This splendid answer should serve as a guide for Negro women the world over. They must realize that they are indeed the basis of human society, and that the race cannot achieve nationhood and world power unless the women are prepared to wield the proper influence over the men, and exact from them service to race and love for country.

Eastern women are taking an active part in all movements for the liberation of their people. Whether they be in India, Egypt or Turkey the new woman is making her impress on the world. Who knows but because of the softening, conscientious effect of woman's entry into politics and big conferences, that the world will be better off and will in the future more readily concede to every race and nation its moral rights. Women are supposed to be tender-hearted. Well, if they can succeed in putting a little more heart in this sordid selfish world, they will be able to lessen wars and racial conflicts.

Woman's function in life is to soften the ills of this wicked old world and to draw man nearer his Creator, in the practice of his beliefs and in his mode of living. If in the carrying out of this most noble task any new departure has to be undertaken it is the duty of noble woman to rise to the exigencies of the demand and continue upon her destined course, "blessing and blessed where'er she goes."[33]

Women of the Negro race! If you have not yet hearkened to the call to duty, do it now, and fall in line with the women of the Universal Negro Improvement Association who feel that their place is alongside of the men, in the thick of the battle, if need be, but always serving the cause of their oppressed race, in the endeavor to redeem Africa, and to lift the race to the level of progress and respect enjoyed by other peoples. Think ye that this is woman's most perfect function in life? Then join our band, and make your contribution, while you are young and full of hope. Mother Africa needs the assistance of her scattered daughters, and surely she shall not call in vain.

"FOR YOU AND YOUR SONS," NOV. 13, 1926

When man takes no thought of the morrow and makes no provision for his children, he has failed in his duty to his fellow man. The builders of races and nations are men and women who give self the least thought, and spend their lives forecasting events, and working to make present and future secure. It is the lack of this idealism that aggravates the backwardness of the Negro. He can see no farther than his immediate surroundings, and he firmly believes that "the good Lord will take care of the future,["] so why should he worry. As for his children it is their hard luck if they don't look out for themselves; he didn't have as many opportunities as they have today. This selfish[,] mean feeling is a blight on the race. Father has no love for his own children. They come by accident and they exist by chance. The mother that brings them into the world, quite often, has all the responsibility for their care, while she, poor soul, has no protection, as she can be mistreated and ravaged by the white man at will.

Men of other races assume the responsibility of protecting their women, and providing for their offspring, hence they are ambitious—always striving after something whether it be new territories for surplus populations, rubber, gold, oil, diamonds or building great industries to employ their own people, they are ever on the go, restless, determined and untiring in their efforts to have and to hold.

The exploitation of the tropics by white men is an example of the risks they have run to bring wealth and prosperity to their families and incidentally to their race. Look at the map of Europe, locate the little scrap of land called England. Now consider this, if Englishmen had been as lazy as Negro men, and remained in England eking out an existence, with a surplus population, what position would they hold in world affairs today? But, they are energetic people, their fathers before them were, and they left their winter homes, and braved the heat of Africa, Asia and other tropical and semi-tropical countries to conquer man, subdue nature and satisfy their own desire for wealth and glory. Thus a great British empire was formed.

Notwithstanding England's wealth, yet her sons and daughters are not satisfied to bask in the glory of their fathers. No, they are busy preparing for future generations, still annexing new territory, exploiting the wealth of such territory, and finding outlets for their surplus populations. The following is an advertisement which appeared in an English paper recently:

> For You and Your Sons—Settlement in Southern Rhodesia provides real opportunities in a young self-governing, British colony, where Taxation is Light, Good Land is Cheap. Genial climatic and social conditions prevail, and Great Agricultural and mineral wealth await development.

This inducement is for Englishmen and their sons, to go to Africa and settle. It may be remembered that Rhodesia is named after Cecil Rhodes,[34] the white man who founded the colony.

Now Mr. Negro the women of your race would like to know what provisions are you making for yourself and your sons? When will you be able to protect your women and provide for them? Until you can fulfill these and other manly duties, you cannot expect to be rated as a man on equal footing with yellow and white men. You are merely an apology for a man, and a race cannot progress, nor can a nation be built with weaklings. Wake up men! Women are advancing. What are you doing?

"SCANTY CLOTHES MAKE HARDY WOMEN,"[35] NOV. 27, 1926

The activities of modern women have caused them to abandon their bustles, hoops, stays[36] and long skirts, and the trend is to wear less and less clothes each year. Modest man at first became alarmed at the brazen display of limbs, but common sense dictated that bustles and long skirts could not be worn in factories, or in base hospitals, without great inconvenience, so male eyes have become familiar with the exposed limbs of women, and they rub shoulders in business without stopping to gasp and stare. The exigencies of the war period hastened the change, and now medical men realize the good derived from the scanty attire of women. Professor Leonard E. Hill,[37] London physiologist, in a lecture on dress to an audience of women stated:

> I have no objection to low necks and bare or silk stockinged legs as long as they are reasonable. Talk of 'pneumonia blouses' is all nonsense. No girl ever caught pneumonia wearing a low blouse. It hardens her and helps her to resist such diseases. [. . .] With modern methods of education and constant exposure women seem to be becoming he hardier sex. Some day we may all be ruled by women.

It is interesting to note that the men and women of Africa and other tropical and semi-tropical countries of Asia wear very little clothing, and this accounts for their healthy bodies and wonderful strength, as they live in the open air mostly, and get the full benefit of the sun's rays. A white writer in describing the natives of a remote country facetiously said all they wore was beads of perspiration and a smile. While this may seem terrible to westernized Negroes, yet those people don't know what tuberculosis, pneumonia or cancer is, and their women are pure.

Scantily clad women need not be vulgar. They can be modest and innocent looking even in an abbreviated garment, while fully clad women can be suggestively vulgar.

As to the last statement of Professor Hill that some day women may rule men, we agree with the prediction, and feel sure that the world will then be a better place in which to live: for women have a conscience, while men have not, and even-handed justice will more likely be meted out. We want to make it clear that we would not for a moment try to feminize men, nor desire to see them so, but their own efforts to shift responsibility on women, causes the latter to become more capable daily, in all walks of life. Next, they will be trying their hands at mastery and control. Why blame them, men? You had your day at the helm of the world, and a pretty mess you have made of it, fighting, oppression, massacres, debauchery and disease are dominant, and perhaps women's rule will usher in the era of real brotherhood, when national and racial lines will disappear, leaving mankind in peace and harmony one with another. Who knows?

"LISTEN WOMEN!" APRIL 9, 1927

Negro women are the acknowledged burden bearers of their race. Whether this is due to the innate laziness of Negro men, or to their lack of appreciation for their noble women, we are not quite sure. Perhaps both these reasons are contributing factors, yet the results are the same—an overburdened womanhood, and a backward race. We hope some of our male readers will in defense of their sex supply us with a plausible excuse; that is, if they can summon enough energy to do so.[38]

With Negro women in this important, yet unenviable position, she should be careful in keeping pace with daily events and training her mind to cope with situations and problems. Her tasks become greater as the cycle of civilization shifts nearer to Africa, and nationalism and self-determination the rallying cry of the East.

One of the great dangers that face us is that the majority of us cannot realize that ours is a young, virile race, while the white race is slowly decaying; therefore it is disastrous for us to imitate the old fellow who indulges in excesses, knowing that he will soon depart. This birth control suits them, not us; it is our duty to bear children, and care for those children, so that our race may have good men and women through whom it can achieve honor and power.[39] Their night life and "good times" act like opiates on their jaded nerves and guilty consciences. Your recreation must be wholesome and clean, you are in the position of the young child who should be kept away from places of debauchery; with the old man it is different—he has already made his mark. Let him indulge.

Our men are our greatest concern. They lack faith in themselves. Therefore they must be driven to accomplish anything. Perhaps this state of mind has been caused by the oppression of slavery, which has dulled their initiative. The achievement of any Negro man can always be traced to the push and perseverance of a good woman. White men, on the other hand, idolize their women and for them they will dare anything in order to merit their look of admiration. They have braved the tropical jungles, slain black men, in order to get gold and diamonds with which to adorn their women; they have ventured forth into the Arctic regions so that she may have beautiful furs to keep her warm; they have exterminated the red Indians in North America, and built up a great republic, so that their women may live in comfort and luxury. They brought our fore-parents from Africa to work for them as slaves, so that their blue-eyed dames may disport themselves and not be burdened with the care of home and children. When, through force of circumstances, they had to emancipate us, they devised all sorts of machines and utilized electricity for domestic usage. They have invented automobiles, railroad trains and aeroplanes so that their dear ones may travel in comfort; for the upkeep of which they exploit the darker peoples and their lands, so as to get coal, rubber, oil and iron. They ill-treat

Chinese so as to get silks in order to clothe the white bodies of their women. They oppress Indians in India and Malays in Ceylon, so that "me lady" can serve five o'clock tea in her silken boudoir. They lynch and burn black men for daring to look at white women; in short, they will go through hell itself so as to provide luxury for their women.

Mr. Negro, who has no love for his woman, loses the incentive to achieve, and the race is that much poorer because of his slothfulness. Tell him to go out and get diamonds and adorn his woman; he will readily tell you that he isn't going to risk his life for her; yet his dependency on white people makes every minute of his life a risk. He is always out of a job because he is too lazy to go out and make a job for himself; he prefers to hang around the white man's factory doors begging for a job, and oftimes gets what he deserves—a kick.

He makes no effort to provide for his women, nor does he protect her. He will cheerfully sit down to his wife's table and enjoy the good things on it without contributing a nickel to it. When he does find a job he tells her that they must run the home on a fifty-fifty basis; nor does he care if through necessity her morals are fifty-fifty with his. Small matter, as long as he can get a free meal sometimes and not be bothered with the landlord every month. Such are the parasites that most Negro women have for husbands, and we appeal to them at this time to be brave and take hope for the future. Their suffering will not be in vain, although their duties are becoming greater. Nationhood calls for brains and ability. The children must be prepared to shoulder the burdens of the next generation with honor and ability; they must not be allowed to fall into the weaknesses of their fathers, but must be inspired to go out and face the world, and make their separate racial contribution to humanity. Yes, mothers! Yours is a great task, but methinks you will shoulder it bravely. As you bore the rigors of slavery so will you bear the hardships preparatory to nationhood. Let not the apathy of your men discourage you, but seek inspiration from the youth of the race. In them lies our hope.

Parenting/Children and Youths

In "More Attention Given to Our Child Life," Jacques Garvey praises those in the medical profession for their care of children, and she urges Blacks to support their physicians and pharmacists instead of depending upon Whites. Jacques Garvey maintains that the consequences of bad parenting go beyond the individual family and affect the entire race. She fervently believes that the hope of the race lies in the children and thus good parenting is a paramount responsibility. In "The Hand That Rocks the Cradle," "The Duty of Parents to Children," and "Parents Should Learn to Understand Their Children," Jacques Garvey contends that every Black parent has an obligation to the race to raise responsible, self-sufficient, racially aware children, from the time they are babies into young adulthood. To do so, parents need to improve themselves: "You owe it to your children to make good men and women out of them, and you can only accomplish this by fitting yourself for the job." Jacques Garvey believed that both men and women are necessary to raise children properly, but the burden of parenting often falls overwhelmingly on Black women because of the weakness of Black men. She would later have to raise her own two sons often without their father's guidance. In "A Strong Student Unit for the U.N.I.A.," Amy extends the need for adult supervision beyond the immediate family and young children, addressing a group often overlooked by the movement: young adults. Not quite children or adults, this group must be paid more attention, she argues, or else they will fail to participate in the UNIA and become racially conscious adults.

"MORE ATTENTION GIVEN TO OUR CHILD LIFE," MAY 31, 1924

One of the most significant and gratifying signs of the times is the increased attention which is being given by legislators and uplift organizations to child life. The medical profession is carrying the scientific treatment of child life into the home in such a way as to stimulate parents to a higher sense of their obligations in this vital matter. The fact that the activity of our physicians in this respect has been stimulated in a large measure by the organized charities which have built colleges and clinics for the purpose, detracts nothing from the fact that they are active agents in the good work and are doing effective service, often without any compensation, except the spiritual approval, saying, "Well done, thou good and faithful servant." Earning this they may reasonably have the benefit of the finish of the sentence, "enter thou into the Joys of thy Lord."[40]

And right here is a good place in which to make acknowledgment of the splendid service the physicians of the race have rendered, and are rendering, not only in the conservation of child life but in the general health of the race. The fact that in some parts of the country white physicians have not cared to have Negro patients at all, has made an opening for our physicians and enlarged their usefulness in a way that it could not otherwise have been, and which has served as well in the development of our vast drug store interests. The point should be emphasized that our physicians have made a brave effort to measure up to the service required of them, especially in the Southern States,[41] and we are sure that they have done so in a reasonable degree. That is to say, they have done so as far as conditions would allow; and we are all victims of condition, which is another name for environment, upon which so much depends in the life of the child and of the adult.

Our physicians in the more favored States of the North and West have been equally faithful in their service, both in the conservation of child life and of adult life, but they have had more opposition to contend with, in the disposition, unfortunately, of the race to support white physicians and druggists in preference to Negro ones, where they can do it. That is a weakness of the race in all directions of which it needs to heal itself. Each of us can help do so by supporting our physicians and druggists in every situation in preference to the physicians and druggists of other race groups. Selfish? Yes. And who is more selfish than the white man, in matters of sentiment and business?

But let us get back to the conservation of child life. We are all gratified at the awakened sense of responsibility and obligation to their children of the parents of the children of the race. Those of us who watch the army of children attending the public schools, not only of Harlem, but other communities, can easily judge of the sacrifices the parents are compelled to make to enable their children to make the decent appearance they do in the matter of clothing and deportment, because a majority of our parents are very poor and the cost of living is very high, while the average wages they receive is very small, as compared with what others in similar employment get; yet, the appearance of our children and their deportment on the streets will compare favorably with that of the children of more favored groups—more favored in the matter of wage-earning and living conditions. And home influences have much, if not most, to do with the conservation of child life and the healthy development of the mind and body, the disposition and the character, of childhood.

We shall have a stronger man and womanhood in the future, because of the close attention that is being given to the physical and mental oversight and direction of the child life of the race, and the greater preparedness of an educated motherhood to properly mature and develop child life in its home influences. And that we are getting an educated motherhood, not in exceptional cases but as a rule, is a matter of the greatest importance and upon which we are entirely excusable for congratulating ourselves. It is a good and healthy condition, an educated motherhood, one which we can all glory in and do as much as possible to extend and strengthen.

The editor of the Woman's Page of The Negro World is intensely interested in this vital question of the conservation and nurture of child life, and would be gratified to have expressions from the mothers of the race who are readers of this page.

"THE HAND THAT ROCKS THE CRADLE," JULY 5, 1924

Napoleon Bonaparte once said that "the hand that rocks the cradle rules the world." Every man, every woman, who has achieved greatness, who has striven to make the world a safer and better place in which to live, could say as much, if he would. When women take the saying seriously they need not be accused of egotism; they should regard it as a high compliment and strive all the more earnestly to rear children who will be a credit to them and to the race.

The conceit that mere man is the whole thing in the making of good men and women has long been exploded, especially in Christian countries, where proper respect for motherhood and proper care of childhood have become among the most important matters for the attention of legislators and administrators, the medical profession, and the educators, all of whom are working industriously and along the most scientific lines for the safeguarding of child life.

Much needs to be done as yet before motherhood and childhood will be placed upon the scientific basis where the very best results can reasonably be expected in the production of the best and highest type of manhood and womanhood. This will be accelerated by the systematic education which young folks are now receiving in the home and the school; education in how to do things as they should be done, in proper deportment in the home and in public places, and in the development of character, shaping it in the proper way so that "as the twig is bent the tree will incline,"[42] so that when the child reaches the age when it must rely upon its own initiative it will go in the right and not in the wrong way. How important this is we all know. Much of sickness and death, much of running wild and getting into trouble out of which it is difficult to get, of young people is due to bad environment, lack of parental oversight and care, lack of proper education and reproof. "How shall the people know without a teacher?"[43] asks the chief apostle of the Gentiles and which we may reasonably ask ourselves. And none of us ever grows too old to learn and none of us can begin too soon to learn the things necessary and worth while to know.

The obligation is upon the Negro to have progressively more care in the consideration and provision for his womanhood and childhood. Much has been gained in this respect in the past fifty years, but much is required and there can be no let up in the good work. The world expects more of the Negro everywhere today than it did yesterday, and the Negro is expecting more of the world.

We have developed millions of homes in which the parents are educated and thoroughly alive to their obligation and duty to give the children the consideration, reproof and training that make most for strong adultage, for service in home and State and church, and for race, and we shall make greater progress in the same direction in the immediate years. But, however much progress we may make, we shall hardly be able to meet the growing need for a properly trained childhood, in order that we may have a properly trained manhood and womanhood, for many years to come. We need trained men and women everywhere, we need them, as other races need them, to do the larger work that has fallen to the lot of the race in these latter days.

The editor of The Woman's Page is proud of the splendid work our women have done in the home and school and church, and are doing, and are better prepared now to do than in other and more unfortunate days, and she has faith to hope that they will do better work in the coming days, as we tread always on the heels of them in the present, the present and the future being indissolubly lock-stepped, and we should all keep constantly in mind the fact that "the hand that rocks the cradle rules the world."

"THE DUTY OF PARENTS TO CHILDREN," MAY 2, 1925

Much has been said and written about the duty of children to their parents; but so little is heard about the duty of parents to them. The latter duty is by far the more important, because if properly adhered to, would eliminate much ill-behavior on the part of children.

Ill-bred children are a menace to any country. They develop into men and women who take on vices that often wreck their homes and endanger the safety of their communities. Women make the homes, and they rear the children, on them devolves the duty of shaping the young minds and preparing them for contact with the outside world. The fathers provide the means of existence, but the home, like any business establishment, needs the trained, tactful guidance of an expert.

To bring children into the world and through carelessness or neglect allow them to grow up ill-mannered and unkempt, is as much a crime as smothering them in infancy. In fact, the latter course is less harmful to the community and nation; for who can tell what crimes may be committed by one who never knew the gentle guidance or wise councils of a mother? Truly it is said, train up the child in the way it ought to grow, and when it is old, it will not depart from it.

Women who desert their babies do not do it because of innate cruelty, but because of despair, which causes temporary insanity, brought about by the neglect or abuse of the father. A mother's heart is the emblem of self-sacrifice, and who can fathom the depths of her love?

Negro men have contributed in a large way to the backward condition of the race by failing to provide for their children. It is a common expression among selfish men, that what they did not get in their youth they will not worry themselves to give their children. Whether it be an education, a home or a business start, it is the same thing. This belief is as ridiculous as to say that because my great grandfather was a slave, I am willing to let my child be a slave also. Our race is gradually coming into its own, and it is necessary for us to forget all such selfish, ignorant reasoning, and think along new lines, in keeping with the progress of the age in which we live, and for the benefit of our posterity.

"PARENTS SHOULD LEARN TO UNDERSTAND THEIR CHILDREN," OCT. 2, 1926

The great gift of parenthood should not be abused by those upon whom it is bestowed. The care and education of children is a sacred duty, and should not be regarded as a haphazard task that requires no training or skill.

Children are human beings and should not be regarded as domestic pets, never given a chance to express themselves or to develop the creative powers within them. These are the grave mistakes some parents make, yet they blame it on the children, or the age in which we live.

From the time of conception to the time of birth, a mother has every opportunity to make a beautiful child, both physically and mentally. Her thoughts and her mannerisms are all duplicated in the unborn babe, which later environment finds hard to eradicate.

Children are like monkeys, very imitative, in fact, so are all human beings, and for this reason parents and guardians should be very careful what they say and how they behave in children's company. The duty of training the little ones' minds should not be left to school teachers alone, but parents should share this responsibility. Youth is inquisitive, they want to know the whys and wherefores of everything; this is quite natural, in fact, a very healthy sign, it shows that their minds are active. Never tell an inquiring child to shut up, he asks too many questions. If you are unable to answer the question, just say, "Never mind, darling, I am busy now, but will tell you tomorrow." On the morrow be sure to have your answer ready, because Johnny or Mary will remind you of your promise, and it creates a bad impression on a child when you fail to keep your word.

Another mistake that some grown-ups make is to treat all children alike. Each child is a puzzle unto itself, and shows different reactions to pleasure and punishment. The rod curbs some wayward children, while with others a serious talk has the same effect, and being deprived of pleasure does some immense good. The most scientific way to control them is to take them into your confidence and in turn they will place confidence in you. If a child does wrong and confesses to you, don't flare up and make a big noise in the presence of others; take him into your bedchamber and show him the evils attendant on such wrong-doing; he will be more careful next time and respect you all the more. To his companions he will brag, "Oh, I can tell mother anything, she'll help me out of it." He regards you as a trusted friend, and refuge in the time of trouble.

Never let your children get ahead of you mentally. They lose respect for you, and are intolerant of your company. In this world of progress grown-up folks can go to night school, get good books and magazines from free libraries, and pay only a few cents for newspapers. Why, then, should children have to remark, "Mother is so dumb, she doesn't know whether the world is moving or standing still."

Parents and guardians, you owe it to your children to make good men and women out of them, and you can only accomplish this by fitting yourself for the job. Don't abuse them, study them. It is you who are all wrong, not they, adjust yourselves to the task and perfect the great handiwork of God.

"A STRONG STUDENT UNIT FOR THE U.N.I.A.," APRIL 23, 1927

We desire to address ourselves to the members of the Universal Negro Improvement Association particularly regarding the importance of a strong student group within our membership. While divisions and chapters have conducted membership drives time and time again, yet no special appeal has been made to attract this element to our ranks. One might be tempted to say that our program is attractive enough as it is. We concede this, but young people are not ready to rush into serious movements; they must be specially invited and coaxed into it.

Our juveniles have increased marvelously—they are the children whose parents bring them to the U.N.I.A. meetings; they have found a welcome place in this unit, where they are trained to be good Garveyites. They render great service in participating in the musical programs of the various divisions. But the boys and girls over fourteen years of age are the ones we want to see drawn into this organization by the thousands. They consider it infra dig[44] to mix with the juveniles or to be called juveniles, and the old folks are too dull for them. So the organization loses hundreds of thousands of young blood because no special appeal is made to them.

The majority of these youngsters are either being taught in white schools or they are not receiving a racial education, hence they are badly in need of the teachings of Garveyism to let them know from whence they came and whither they ought to go. Garveyism also needs them, as the students of any movement for the oppressed are like the perennial flowers of a garden—lasting and hardy. They have two parts to play—as youths and as grown-ups; therefore they make two contributions to the organization. The juveniles make three, but if there is one student unit, after they reach fourteen or fifteen years they drift into the general membership unrecognized and therefore they lose interest.

Gone are the days when "youngsters should be seen and not heard"; they are very much heard nowadays, and their chatter should be directed in the right channels. The young minds need wholesome topics and clean atmosphere. So we appeal to all the divisions and chapters of this great organization in every nook and corner of the globe to start a campaign for students. Don't be jealous of young brains outshining yours. What we want is results, not competition and rivalry.

One of the many attractions to be instituted for the students should be a monthly discussion, conducted entirely by them, at which the general public of the community should be invited. So as to make the discussions uniform for all divisions, we will publish the subject the first week in every month. Anyone can send us subjects appropriate for discussion. The students taking part in the discussion should read up on the subject for a week after it is announced and before the discussion takes place. Art exhibitions, musicales and plays could be staged, at which the students could be featured. We leave it to the enterprising officers of locals to get busy and gather in the youngsters and when they are in the fold to hold their interest and employ their talent. They will be the men and women of tomorrow, so shape their minds for the great task.

May we also remind you to give publicity to the discussions. Young folks like to be mentioned in print.

An Examination of the Race: Advice and Criticism

In her editorials, Jacques Garvey often provides practical life tips to help people in their daily lives. She maintains that Blacks need to utilize all their resources and unless all members of the race are fully functioning in their personal lives, they will not be able to advance the cause. Therefore, in editorials such as "The Joy of Living," "What Are You Doing with Your Money?" and "He That Endureth to the End," she gives inspiration and advice to UNIA members. She also, however, can be caustic in her criticism of those whom she considers lazy, selfish, and hypocritical as is demonstrated in "Away with Lip Service, "Moral Cowards," and "Play Up, and Play the Game!" Jacques Garvey asserts that the UNIA must expunge such leeches and traitors from the organization in order for its message to succeed.

"THE JOY OF LIVING," JUNE 21, 1924

Every human being that is born into this world is born for a purpose. The Almighty Creator, in the arrangement of this earth, made a place for each and every one of us; therefore, it is the duty of every individual, on attaining the age of wisdom, to ask himself or herself the question, "Am I in my right place, according to the Divine arrangement of things?" The next great duty of man is to find the purpose for which he was created.

A woman may be born into this world for the purpose of mothering and training the President of a nation; another may be born to be the wife of a great statesman, whose single word could decide the destinies of millions of people; yet, these women may be born in very humble stations in life, but, having seized every opportunity that presented itself and done the most trivial and menial jobs conscientiously and well, they fitted themselves for the big purpose of their lives.

Shirking duties and ignoring opportunities shunt us right off the track of the big purpose, and when we come to the end of our life's journey and ask ourselves the question, "Have I fulfilled my purpose in life?" That wee, small voice within us will whisper, "No, pal, you left the track years ago." It is the little particles that form the whole; likewise it is the little things in life, well done, that lead to the goal.

One gets very little happiness out of life in living for oneself; the greatest joy in life being the joy of living for others. The sight of happiness makes one happy, and the knowledge of having contributed to another's happiness makes one profoundly happy. It is said that man's duty is to man—meaning that each individual owes a duty to his fellow man, that each one of us should contribute something towards the well being of humanity.

It is well, therefore, that at the end of each day, just before we retire to rest, we should ask ourselves the question, "Have I made my contribution to humanity? Have I done my duty to my fellow man?" This personal daily reprimand will help to keep us near our purpose and make our lives worth the living.

Christ died that we should live and enjoy life more abundantly. We should so live that mankind can enjoy life more abundantly. In this we would fulfill our purpose in life and partake of the joys of living.

The poet, Bailey,[45] clothed his thoughts in beautiful language when he wrote:

> We live in deeds, not years, in thoughts, not breaths,
> In feelings, not in figures on a dial.
> We should count time by heart throbs. He most lives
> Who thinks most, feels the noblest acts the best.

"WHAT ARE YOU DOING WITH YOUR MONEY?" JAN. 3, 1925

What are you doing with your money? As an individual ask yourself this question. Then get a piece of paper, set down the amount of your weekly salary and other sources of income on one side of the paper. Next, tabulate your expenses. Compare the two totals and see if you can subtract your expenses from your income. If so, what is left?

Are you saving your surplus money? Are you investing a part of it, so that it can work for you while you are working, and even when you are unable to work? Be fair with yourself, dear reader, and admit that you are a bit surprised at your detailed expense column. How many trivial things you could have done without. How many more dollars you would have saved or invested. Wasted money means wasted energy, expended in the earning of it, and so much time subtracted from a life of usefulness.

Every Negro knows how difficult it is for members of the race to get work, as white employers see that their own people are employed first before employing others. Hence it amounts to criminal negligence for us as individuals to spend money foolishly. Such squandering not only hurts us personally, but hurts the race. Money accumulated can be invested in business, which would not only bring profit to the investors, but give employment to members of the race, thereby serving a two-fold purpose.

White people have built up a financial and industrial prestige for their race, that will take us years to equal. Knowing this we cannot afford to imitate a few spendthrifts of the other race. Their recklessness does not materially affect their race, while ours will, because they have reached the goal of their ambition and we are just starting out. Men and women, married and single, should all feel that they owe it to their race to be worth something financially, bearing in mind this truism, "If money go before, all ways do lie open."[46]

"HE THAT ENDURETH TO THE END," JAN. 17, 1925

One of the greatest failings of the Negro is his lack of continuity of purpose and action.

He will start out in some undertaking with so much zeal and enthusiasm that one would be inclined to think that he could achieve his goal in less than given time. Watch his progress and you will observe that when he should be striving hardest his interest wanes, he gives up. Ask him his reason, and he will retort nonchalantly, "I couldn't be bothered any longer," or "Something went wrong." This indifferent attitude is exhibited in the actions of Negroes in all walks of life. They lack stick-to-it-iveness, and do not realize that it is the plodder that rights wrongs, surmounts difficulties and eventually reaches his goal.

Nothing in this world that is worth while is easily obtained. Whether it is a good position, a business, a profession or a life-companion, these prerequisites all require the elements of stamina, perseverance and endurance in one's character to acquire them. Use this thought as an incentive when faced by difficulties and they will disappear before your intrepid onslaught.

The youth who has to work and struggle hard to acquire a profession usually appreciates it, and puts it to better use than one whose parents paid his expenses and furnished him with an office or the necessary appurtenances[47] to practice such profession. The struggles to attain one's ambition brings [*sic*] out either the best or worst in us. If we fail to overcome our difficulties, we exhibit a weakness of character that could not stand the test of endurance because the elements of self-confidence and courage were undermined by fear and doubt. If we overcome our difficulties, we conquer our own weaknesses and thereby gain two victories at once—the attainment of our ambition and the conquest of our weaker self.

As in the lives of individual members of our race, so in the activities of groups, we find the same progressive characteristic lacking. Most Negroes regard every endeavor as a "nine days' wonder" and support it enthusiastically for just that length of time; after that it takes the grit and determination of a few to keep things humming. It is for this reason that men of other races are surprised and even alarmed at the large membership and progress of the Universal Negro Improvement Association. No other organization of Negroes, controlled by Negroes, could have withstood the vicious attacks of governmental agents and treacherous Negroes. The leadership of the U.N.I.A., having a thorough knowledge of the failings of the race, launched an educative program whereby Negroes throughout the world are educated to live up to the highest and best in man. In so doing they see no difficulties nor opposition that cannot be surmounted; fear has no place in their hearts; a redeemed country and an emancipated race is their objective and no earthly impediment will discourage them in their journey toward their goal.

"AWAY WITH LIP SERVICE," FEB. 6, 1926

In this age of materialism and selfishness it is exceedingly difficult to find people who are faithful to anybody or anything for any length of time. Some of us start out with the best of intentions to "stick to the end," but fail when the test is applied. Others never intend to beat any hardships and often those are the ones who make the most noise but mean nothing.

To discover falsity in one's friend is heart-rending; in one's business associate, spells ruin; but to unmask the traitor to a cause is a task that calls for great Christian charity to deal with him, as the welfare of thousands or millions may depend on the fidelity of the one who is proven false.

In a large organization of oppressed people we suffer greatly from men who enter our ranks for selfish ends, for treacherous purposes, and still others with no purpose at all; just for the sake of being in it. The last named class often gives more trouble than imagined because they are stumbling blocks in the way of others, and are sometimes mistaken for sincere by the "sweet nothingness" that they say and the grandiloquent manner in which they say it. They are heavy on the lip service and render no real service at all.

These are the type of barnacles that have gravitated into offices in the Universal Negro Improvement Association and who have sought to impede its progress by sticking like leaches [*sic*], and it is hard to get them out, as some of our members are not keen enough to analyze their frothy mouthings.

Our organization has reached a stage where a big speech cannot advance the cause if there is no real thought and action behind it. A great talker is not the type of man to place at the head of affairs, unless he has the attributes of a deep thinker and knows the art of diplomacy. Again we warn our membership that the U.N.I.A. is getting too large for some of us, and this is more so evidenced since our leader's imprisonment. When the association should be organized to a man to put over its program in the same aggressive manner in which he carried on its affairs, we find some Negroes so spineless and cowardly as to give comfort to the enemy, whose aim is—imprison Garvey—keep him in prison—and you can handle his colleagues who will shrink with fear and hesitate to move forward.

But the Negro women of the U.N.I.A. serve notice on you, who are in charge of locals, diplomatic posts or headquarters in Africa or America, that if you don't get a move on, to use the common parlance, you will have to go. The longer you remain making set speeches and repeating eloquent meaningless phrases the longer you keep Marcus Garvey in prison and stultify the progress of the organization. You are but the agents of the oppressor and consciously or unconsciously doing his bidding.

Away with the lip servers! Let us have eleven million Garveys to push forward the program of Africa for the Africans, and who can imprison that many? Not even the League of Damnation[48] with America thrown in for good measure. Then President Coolidge will get the first pen he can lay his hands on and mark "Pardoned" on Marcus Garvey's release papers, and Atlanta prison gates will swing open and Father Garvey will pass out to thank his eleven million children for holding the fort during his absence.

Go to it members, if you want Marcus Garvey free.

"MORAL COWARDS," FEB. 13, 1926

It is in adversity that one knows one's friends. It needs only a slight shift of the wind of good fortune for one to discover the true character of some folks. In love, in business, in organizations and other groups, we find it evidenced daily that friends and associates, red hot, lukewarm, indifferent and traitorous, exist; and the more material and selfish the world becomes the more we must expect to find men and women who are purchasable and whose sincerity cannot stand the test.

The race that suffers most from insincerity among its members is the Negro race. Why? Because we have not shaken off the old habit of telling all we know to the other fellow. Any Negro would have a life-time job trying to find a white man whom he could bribe to do something harmful to the white race, or that would jeopardize its interest. But on the contrary is it not a daily occurrence to find Negroes who can be paid off by the other fellow to disrupt a movement in the interest of Negroes, or to get rid of a man who stands up for the race?

It is not pleasant to admit this but it is true. And we trust that as time goes on, and we get more strongly organized, we will be able to be rid of men of the type complained of. Unfortunately we cannot deal with our traitors as they deserve, we being domiciled in lands of aliens, who encourage treachery in our ranks so as to exploit and oppress us, but we will mark them well, and hand their names down to generations to come, so that their children may suffer from their misdeeds.

As Marcus Garvey sits in his prison cell in Atlanta and looks back over the nine years of contact with members of his race in America, how his heart must be saddened at [the] thought of men whom he brought from obscurity and placed in high positions in the association; men who could not find work and were penniless, and to whom he gave employment. In what way did they recompense him? By fattening themselves at the cost of his good name, and selling out the secrets of the association to the enemy. Had it not been for those traitors in his cabinet, Garvey would never have been in Atlanta prison, and the organization would not be handicapped in its progress.

Our natural enemy stands ever ready to grease the hands of the Negro traitor, and we must be on the lookout always for the cowards who fall prey to this pernicious system.

"PLAY UP, AND PLAY THE GAME!" SEPT. 25, 1926

In all walks of life we have laggards—persons who are determined to loaf or mark time while the other fellow does the hard work, or bears [the] brunt of the fight. The Universal Negro Improvement Association suffers from this type both within its membership and from the outsiders. There are some Negroes who believe that the program of this organization is the only salvation for the race, but they will not come into its fold and help put it over. Why? They can't afford to mix with the masses; they don't want to be ridiculed and abused like Garvey; Negroes are too ungrateful anyhow; and they have to look after their families, let the others go scratch for themselves. The result is that a race of 400,000,000 suffers from lack of patriots because very few are willing to pay the price.

Besides these we have a standing army of lookers-on. Interested, yet disinterested spectators, who are seeing how "that thing" is going before they join. While the team is short of fit men, and playing against tremendous odds, they are looking on, too mean even to give an encouraging yell; still waiting until victory is indicated; then they will wear our colors, and beat their chests, saying, "see what OUR team has done."

Within our organization we have "chair warmers," who never put a penny in the collection plate, but still they come night after night, filling the best seats, but expecting the other fellow to pay for the lights and general expenses. The "would-be greats" are another problem, whose egos are over-developed; they make ranting speeches of what they could accomplish if only given a chance, yet given that chance they flounder around—helpless incompetents. Another parasite that we used to have in our ranks was the high-salaried official, who would loaf all during the year knowing that he could not be displaced until a convention was in session. After he was voted out, he would sue for salaries he never earned, which of course the white man's court would readily order paid, so as to break up the organization. In three years the organization paid to such parasites through the courts $63,000.00.

At the present time we have with us "When-Garvey-Comes Negroes." They are waiting with folded arms for the release from prison, to do everything.—Put out the traitors; contribute financially; or to go to Africa. Meanwhile the traitors are destroying what Garvey sweat blood to acquire: the organization needs funds, and white people are stealing every square foot of land in Africa.

Friends! it is time for us to wake up, and see ourselves as others see us—enemies to our own progress. Bestir yourselves like men and women, put your colors on, and strengthen your team. The gong has sounded! Man your bases, and put your whole strength in the game, for the result warrants the efforts, however hazardous. Play up, and play the game!

Call for Contributors to the Woman's Page

One of Jacques Garvey's most onerous tasks was the necessity to dun her readers periodically for contributions to the Woman's Page. She made these appeals, sometimes pleading and sometimes chastising, to Black women, regardless of whether they were UNIA members or not, throughout the life of the page as represented in "An Invitation to Our Teachers and Student Women," "Have a Heart," "Do Negro Women Want to Express Themselves?" and "How You Can Help." Even while lamenting the poor quality of the writing that she had received, she would continue to solicit more material. If the women themselves did not have the skills to compose their own letters, she asked them to "get some one who is better equipped to clothe [your] sentiments in proper language and send same in to our office." While celebrating the anniversary of the page ("Our Page Is Three Years Old") Jacques Garvey warns that without help, "then we think it best to discontinue [the page], or pass it over to another lady" who would likely make it a more conventional woman's page. Unfortunately, the demise of the page came shortly after this final appeal. Winston James feels that Jacques Garvey received so few submissions, in part, because her "ideas were far too radical for many black middle-class women" (148). That may well be true, but whatever the reason, Amy clearly grew increasingly "frustrated with women who did not contribute" (Bair "Our Women" 120).

"AN INVITATION TO OUR TEACHERS AND STUDENT WOMEN," JUNE 7, 1924

The Editor of The Woman's Page of The Negro World desires that the women of the race should understand that her sympathies are as comprehensive as the Negro race. They extend to other races, as a matter of course, but the women of the Negro race, by the nature of the case, have the first call upon her interest and sympathies. Ain't that entirely human? I think so. It is true or the women of all race groups; their own come first in their interest and sympathies. Why not? And the Negro women have a more urgent necessity to have an interest in and sympathy for their own than have the women of other race groups. [. . .]

One of the objects of the Editor of this Woman's Page is that it shall so be ordered that it will make for the unification and cooperation of the women of the race for the betterment of the race. To this end, we must desire to enlist the sympathy and support of the women teachers and students of the race in race work unification, uplift, child life, and the conservation of race ideals. We want our women to know that our interest and sympathies are not by any means limited to the membership of the Universal Negro Improvement Association, but include the womanhood of the race, and that we earnestly desire that all should feel free to send us contributions on phases of race conditions in the places where they are as they affect our women, on phases of child and woman uplift work, and original contributions of prose or verse. But we are sure that it will be taken in good part if we suggest that persons who have not a common school education and who have not studied the rules of composition, of prose and verse, should not send us contributions in prose or verse.

The teachers and students of the race, along with other women members of the race, who have a bit of information or an original thought, are invited to send it to the Editor of this page, whether members of the Universal Negro Improvement Association or not, and it will receive sympathetic consideration.

"HAVE A HEART," AUG. 2, 1924

We welcome contributions to this page, whether in the form of news articles, poems or otherwise. It is our aim to encourage Negro women to express their views on subjects of interest to their communities, and particularly affecting our struggling race.

Our appeal is not only made to members of the Universal Negro Improvement Association, but to all Negro women of all climes. You have an opportunity of airing your views in English, French and Spanish. By your expressions and opinions you will be able to help the race materially. Our men will be inspired on reading our lofty ideals and aims; they will respect us the more when they learn of our activities for racial uplift, and our struggles and sufferings for the betterment and advancement of our children.

You women who have had the advantage of higher education, use it, and for God's sake, don't use it selfishly. Help your less-informed sisters. Mix among them a little more; hear their woes and sufferings, and let the world know that our race has noble women, living lives of love and service.

Those of us who, unfortunately, cannot express ourselves on paper, can get some one who is better equipped to clothe our sentiments in proper language and send same in to our office. Don't be discouraged because in your day you did not have the educational facilities your children are having. You can improve yourself now. It is common knowledge also that some of the most beautiful sentiments and lofty ideas can emanate from the brains of women who have had very little education. This is especially true of our race.

Years ago in the days of slavery when we had nothing to inspire us but the lash of the overseer's whip and the snarl from his cruel lips, we tried to have our children in the great house; where they could escape some of the horrors of plantation laborer [*sic*]. That, then, was our highest ambition. Later on when slavery was abolished we washed and ironed from night until morning in order to get enough money to send our children to schools and colleges, so that they might be educated, cultured men and women. Now the time has come for them to demonstrate in a practical manner their education and culture, and certain spheres in politics and business are closed to them by their white brothers; therefore, we are working and striving to establish a strong government in the dear old home-land of Africa, where the ambitions of black men and women will not be confined to menial jobs; but where they will be able to demonstrate to other races of the world the progress they have made since emancipation, and make their independent contribution to civilization as other progressive races.

The modern sciences of the West will be combined with the mysteries of the East, and Ethiopia shall once again boast of her achievement and accomplishment and nations shall welcome her as "Risen Ethiopia," and accord to her citizens the world over the respect and consideration due to persons who are citizens of strong and powerful nations.

We are working toward this glorious goal. Have a heart sister and join us now! The larger the band of workers, the quicker the goal will be reached. Have a heart! Help put it over!

"DO NEGRO WOMEN WANT TO EXPRESS THEMSELVES?" APRIL 11, 1925

Due to the repeated reque[s]ts by our women for a page through which they could express themselves on all matters relating to hu[m]anity at large, and our race in particular, the Managing Editor[49] saw fit to allot us this page for the purpose.

Usually, a Woman's Page in any journal is devoted solely to dress, home hints and love topics, but our Page is unique, in that it seeks to give out the thoughts of our women on all subjects affecting them in particular and others in general. This pleases the modern Negro woman, who believes that God Almighty has not limited her intellect because of her sex, and that the helpful and instructive thoughts expressed by her in her home, with the aid of this page, could be read in thousand [*sic*] of other homes and influence the lives of untold numbers.

But, the question now is, are these modern women helping to keep this page interesting by their weekly contributions? No. They read, but they do not contribute their articles regularly, feeling that some one else will write this week, and putting it off week by week; hence the editor finds it extremely hard, at this time, to make up a page without proper material, and, when it is considered that she has to put in eighteen hours of work daily and sometimes gets only three or four hours of sleep, it is certainly a hardship.

Now, Ladies! We appeal to you, who have the ability to write, to forward your articles to us. Write on one side of the paper in ink, if possible use the typewriter, double space. Write prose, unless you know the rules governing versification.

By your contributions you will be showing to the world the worth and ability of Negro women, and gain the appreciation of our own men, whose lives are guided by our influence, and who get inspiration from us. Trusting we will not have occasion to remind you of your duty.

"HOW YOU CAN HELP," FEB. 13, 1926

Some of our readers who are unable to write an article for this page can certainly write a letter to the editor setting out your views on any given subject in simple language. All contributions are edited before being sent to press.

Others of you who are unable to express themselves in writing can send us clippings of interesting topics that you may read in magazines from time to time. Mark on the article the name of the newspaper in which it appeared and the date of the issue.

With the large membership of the Universal Negro Improvement Association domiciled in many lands, there is every reason why the members should, by their contributions to its columns, make the Negro World the newsiest newspaper in the world. This is one of your duties, members. Do not fail to do your bit.

"OUR PAGE IS THREE YEARS OLD," FEB. 12, 1927

Our page has reached its third year this week, and we take this opportunity of reminding our readers that they have not taken advantage of the space allotted them to express their views, this being the purpose of the page.

The writer has had to produce this page under great strain, especially within the last two years, and if our women readers do not care to contribute to its columns, then we think it best to discontinue same, or pass it over to another lady, who will write on fashions and housewife's topics only. This last resort will be a reflection on the intelligence of our women readers, who should endeavor to use this opportunity to impress their opinions on the rest of us, and also on the men. In this way we will be able to command a respectful hearing before the world, and prove that Negro women are great thinkers as well as doers.

Religion

Although the UNIA did "not advocate any particular form of religion," Jacques Garvey, like most UNIA members, was a Christian. She believed in a Christianity that venerated Christ's teachings; however, at the same time she was often critical of the Christian Church.[50] She saw Christ as a model of brotherhood, but she laments in "Christianity the Best Solution of the World's Ills?" how Whites fail to practice brotherhood toward Blacks. In "Wanted—Missionaries for Africa," she complains of the hypocrisy of White missionaries who pave "the way for the exploiter and land-grabber." She opines in "Christian or Moslem Africa?" that it is up to Blacks to teach Africans about Christianity, or else they may turn to Islam. Despite these criticisms, Jacques Garvey pleads for Christian unity in "Division is the Scandal of Christendom" when she feels the religion might be threatened by Eastern doctrines: "It is necessary for Christians to forget denominational rivalries, and unite to make Christianity a living gospel and not a theory."

Jacques Garvey is ambivalent in her treatment of Jews. On the one hand, in essays such as "Solving the Jewish Problem" and "New York Jews Raise over Six Million Dollars—What of Negroes?" she sees them as models for Blacks because of their unity. On the other hand, "she clearly embraced the negative stereotypes of Jews as shrewd, wealthy, money-grubbers" (Broussard 120). She also tends to overgeneralize by lumping all Jews as Zionists, which is perhaps not surprising given her own nationalistic impulses. Jacques Garvey envies what she feels is Jews' desire to make sacrifices on behalf of a Jewish state in Palestine, and she criticizes Blacks for not having the same zeal that most Jews have in creating their own Black homeland.

While she sympathizes with Jews' quest for a homeland, she criticizes them in "Man's Inhumanity to Man" for their lack of empathy for a Black national homeland in Africa. Although they should be natural allies as oppressed minorities in search of a homeland, Jacques Garvey feels that when it comes to Blacks, the Jew "becomes an one hundred percent. American and adds his share to the misery of the Negro by hampering his nationalistic program."

"SOLVING THE JEWISH PROBLEM," MARCH 1, 1924

Abraham Bragin,[51] organizer of the All-Russia Agricultural Exhibition, has presented a new solution for the Jewish problem in Russia. He proposes that the Soviet Government allocate to the Jews the district of northern Crimea, and the adjoining portion of the Ukraine, including the Black Sea cities, to be designated as the Jewish Autonomous State.

There are about one million Jews residing in this region and with the development of colonization and industries by Jews, it is proposed to make this district self-governing in the next three years. This proposition is reported as being favorably considered by the Soviet leaders, and will not alone help to solve the Jewish question, but is a splendid effort in teaching Jews the art of government.

If the above solution was advanced to alleviate the acuteness of the Negro problem in this country, we wonder what would be the attitude of white public opinion.[52] Yet if Negroes were given a chance to administer the affairs of their own colony here in America, when they will have overpopulated the territory allotted them, the same old question would arise. Hence the sanest solution of the Negro problem is the one advanced by the Universal Negro Improvement Association—that of building a national home in Africa, where Negroes can go when they so desire.

All factions of Jews in America are uniting their efforts to create a corporation to provide $5,000,000 annually for promoting industries in Palestine. This is a part of the big work of building a Jewish nation in Palestine, which Dr. Weizman,[53] the president of the World Zionist Movement, says "would fulfill the prophecy of the Jewish sage that Palestine will unite the Jewish people of the world."

All Negroes, unlike the Jews, cannot see the advisability of a national home and forget their factional differences and work toward that end; but those who interpret the prophecy that "Ethiopia shall stretch forth her hand unto God"[54] to mean the re-establishment of our Motherland, are working with might and main to fulfill that prophecy, and secure to themselves and to posterity the independence and glory that was once their forebears. Generations unborn shall call them blessed.

"CHRISTIANITY THE BEST SOLUTION OF THE WORLD'S ILLS?" AUGUST 16, 1924

It is more than nineteen hundred years ago since Our Father sent [His][55] Only Begotten Son to redeem fallen mankind. Christ came to this world as man. He lived on earth for thirty years, teaching the gospel [of love] and true brotherhood, and living a life of exemplary Man. He [was] rejected by men; crucified, died and was buried. But His teachings [did] not die with Him. On the contrary, His death was a rebirth of His teachings (which is called Christianity). Today millions of men and women all over the world claim the teachings and ideals of the Lonely [Man] of Galilee[56] as their religion.

Quite recently a white clergyman on Long Island delivered a sermon [on] "The Brotherhood of Man." Among other things he said: [. . .] "In His teaching that man is a member of a spiritual family of which God is the Father and all men brothers, we have the noblest and wisest solution for the problems of life and cure for its ills."

We quite agree with our white brother when he asserts that the teaching of Him who died on the cross is the secret of peace and goodwill among men. The white race has had this secret for hundreds of years, but they have not yet started to practice this secret, this Christianity. They have been generous enough to pass on this religion to the other races of the world; they advocate it, but, because of selfishness and greed, they speak with their lips, but their hearts are evil, and they practice evil.

As individuals, in all races we have good Christians, but as a Christian race willing to practice Christianity we believe that the Negro race [is] the one most prepared and willing to practice the true brotherhood of man. But it is more than apparent that the other races are not prepared, and it would be foolhardiness on the part of a weak, struggling race to give love and fellowship in return for hate and prejudice. The other races practice Christianity scientifically, based upon the material things of life, and they will not be willing to lift up weak races and place them on equality platforms until weak races on their own initiative get material power, such as wealth, munitions, ships and airplanes in a homeland of their own. Then the strong white race will be willing to say "Welcome brother!" to the black race, because the former will then have nothing to lose materially and could well afford to practice spiritual love and fellowship.

We of the U.N.I.A. do not advocate any particular form of religion. We are uniting Negroes the world over for their betterment in [all] walks of life, and believe that they should worship God after their [missing words] in spirit and in truth.

[A] fundamental truth of all forms of religion is "Love thy brother [as] thyself [missing word] in other words, "Do unto others as you would that they would do unto you." This ethical truth applies alike to individuals, to nations and to race. When this truth is observed the period of peace, plenty and happiness will be ushered into the world, and the problems of race, pestilence and war will cease.

"CHRISTIAN OR MOSLEM AFRICA?" NOV. 15, 1924

Christianity as taught by our Lord and Saviour Jesus Christ, is the most ethical religion in the world, but Christianity as practised by the majority of Christians is a farce and a mockery. The Divine injunction, "Love the Lord thy God With all [thy] heart... and thy Neighbour as Thyself," is interpreted in terms of race and color. The fatherhood of God and the brotherhood of man is preached but not practised.

If Christ the Redeemer returned to earth today he would not recognize Christianity as the same doctrine he taught and practised in Jerusalem over nineteen hundred years ago. Christian man has fallen short of the glory of God, and has allowed this material, sordid world to rob him of his spiritual ideal and to despoil him of his moral ethics. It is, therefore, difficult for Christians to convert heathens (?) to Christianity, for the latter disregards their own teachings and imposes upon the non-Christians doctrines and religious obligations that they themselves ignore. [. . .]

It is time the Negroes realized the hypocrisy of white missionaries and send black missionaries to Africa to teach their brothers how to live clean, progressive lives on earth and prepare them for the Great Beyond. Africa needs new missionaries. Men of vision, self-sacrificing pioneers, who will take education and progress to satisfy the material needs of the people and a Christianity that will satisfy their spiritual wants. Black men should teach black men.

We of the Western Hemisphere should feel that a duty devolves on us to carry the Gospel of light and leading to Africa. Our brothers in Africa feel the urge of uplift and betterment, but they want their own people to preach to them and elevate them physically and spiritually.

Mohammedanism will triumph in Africa if Negro Christians are so selfish [a]s to allow it[.] Islam knows no color bar, no segregation; hence the teaching of Mohammed finds a quicker response in the hearts of the non-Christian, who, in his awakened consciousness feels that his spirit cannot be uplifted and his physical degraded. There must be co-ordination of the spiritual and physical.

We appeal to the Negro churches of all denominations to unite in this work of helping the African in Africa to know Christ and to know his own possibilities as a man. If we fail to heed the cry of awakened Africa Mohammedanism will conquer and a further breach will be created between Africans at home and Africans abroad.

"WANTED—MISSIONARIES FOR AFRICA," FEB. 21, 1925

Within the last century thousands of men, and even women, have been sent to Africa by white churches and mission societies to Christianize and civilize the so-called heathen. Rum bottles have played as important a part as the Bible in the process of civilizing the poor native. The result is that after he imbibes the white man's firewater he is helpless to protect his property and land, which the good missionary hands over to the traders and teaches the native African to sing, "Oh! Take me as I am," and "Take all the world but give me Jesus."[57]

The white missionary is the forerunner of the trader in Africa. He paves the way for the exploiter and land-grabber. He plays on the innocence of the native until he gets him looking toward the pearly gates of the New Jerusalem; while his brother trader takes the African's gold and diamonds. Far-thinking Negroes in this Western world now realize the chicanery practiced on their brothers in Africa, and are determined that these things shall no longer be.

Africa needs missionaries, 'tis true; but she needs black men and women who have mastered the sciences, literature and the art of modern government in this Western Hemisphere to go over and teach their brethren. Africa needs the plough instead of the rum bottle; she needs medical men with their medicines, instead of a preacher with a long coat. The vast continent of Africa, with untold mineral wealth, cries to black mining experts to come over and show them how to mine the gold, platinum and diamonds, and teach them the value of precious stones. She needs schools and hospitals instead of "gospel houses." Mother Africa stretches out her bleeding hands to her lost sons and daughters and begs them to return home and restore her ancient glory.

Our brothers in Africa are only contaminated by the hypocritical Christianity as preached to them by white missionaries. They need black men and women to teach them the true gospel of salvation as enunciated by our Lord and Savior, who came to earth to save all humanity. When Christ lived on earth as man, He went about doing good. He healed the sick and fed starving multitudes. He did not come preaching a gospel that He himself did not follow. His life was a living example of the truths He taught. Are the men who call themselves missionaries today following after the example of Christ? Are they practicing what they preach? No. They have fallen short of the glory of God, and no one suffers more from their sins and omissions than so-called backward peoples.

Man cannot be successfully taught to look forward to mansions in heaven, when he has not where to lay his head nor proper food to eat. He must be fed, taught to live decently, and then of his own volition he will lift up his thoughts to God in praise and thanks, whether he be a Christian or a Mohammedan.

Shakespeare puts it in the mouth of one of his characters to say, "Sweet are the uses of adversity,"[58] and we believe there is much truth in this reflection. The adversity of slavery could be made to bear sweets if Negroes could realize that after all there might have been some divine intention when so many Negroes were taken from their homes in Africa and brought to this Western world to work as slaves. They learned the "ins and outs" of the white man's civilization, the ways of peace and the methods of warfare. May we not hope that as they have been such good scholars here, they will become good teachers and carry back to Africa all the good they have learned of commerce, industry, science and good government? [. . .]

"NEW YORK JEWS RAISE OVER SIX MILLION DOLLARS—WHAT OF NEGROES?" JUNE 5, 1926

The United Jewish campaign to raise $6,000,000 in Greater New York alone for the relief of Jews in Eastern Europe ended a few days ago. The amount was over-subscribed by $656,000. The national campaign aims to raise twenty-five million dollars, and from all indications this amount will also be over-subscribed.

The Bureau of Jewish Social Research estimates that there are only 3,600,000 Jews in this country, yet their ambition is to raise the enormous sum of twenty-five million dollars; not for their own benefit here, but to send to Europe to help their fellow-Jews who are in need. Such an example of racial love cannot be too highly commended, and as we ponder over the fellowship of these people, our thoughts return to our own race; but ah, how different it is with us. Fifteen million Negroes in America and what genius could get them to subscribe one dollar each for any laudable purpose that would benefit them here? As for sending money abroad to benefit Negroes in other countries, why almost every Negro newspaper would raise a storm of protest, and petty Negro politicians would shed greedy tears at the idea of American dollars going to help "foreign" Negroes. "Let them help themselves," some of us would growl, "and if they can't, that's their hard luck."

This accursed selfishness of the Negro has been his undoing, and until the Universal Negro Improvement Association has reached the heart of each and every one, he will continue to think of national boundaries and ignore racial ties. [. . .]

This organization has a drive on for one million new members and one million dollars, to carry on its work of Negro uplift and African redemption, and we sincerely hope that the Jews will not put us to shame; but that in proportion to our meagre [*sic*] earnings we will oversubscribe the amount, which is a small amount indeed for the great work planned by our leader.

Jewish women have played an important part in making their campaign a success, and it is up to Negro women to rally to the call and round up the recruits and the dollars. One Jewish woman alone collected $161,200. Surely Negro women who have collected moneys to build so many churches, will now turn their attention to nation building, and thereby ensure the future for posterity.

This money must be raised and raised quickly. Extending the campaign over long indefinite periods will not help. A few hundred thousand dollars in the treasury of the organization could accomplish much along all lines, but small amounts coming in spasmodically cannot be used to advantage. Women! This is your opportunity to make your contribution to the race. Let the world know that Negroes can and will support their own cause and protect their brothers anywhere and everywhere.

"MAN'S INHUMANITY TO MAN,"[59] JAN. 8, 1927

A few days ago we were attracted to an advertisement appearing in the New York Times, with headlines as follows: "Mass meeting to protest against anti-Jewish excesses in Rumania," and listed among the speakers was Judge Julian W. Mack,[60] who needs no introduction to our readers, he being the star in the final act of the farce, "Garvey Must Go!"

Fate plays peculiar pranks with us poor mortals, for while the good judge is holding mass meetings and protesting against outrages on his people in Rumania, Negroes the world over are holding mass meetings and protesting against his imprisonment of their leader, Marcus Garvey. He is appealing "to enlightened public opinion of the world to stay the hand of Rumania," while Negroes plead to white America for justice and fairplay [sic] to their persecuted leader.

There are 16,000,000 Jews in the world, and 400,000,000 Negroes. Both groups are persecuted wanderers without the protection of a government of their own, no flag and no aeroplanes. Yet the Jews are better treated than Negroes in all countries, because they control big finances and are large producers, while Negroes are poor consumers, dependent on other races for employment. However, during the last World War the Jews woke up to the fact that they needed a national homeland to give them prestige and protection. So they emerged from the conflict with the plum, "Palestine for the Jews." Since 1920 through the Zionist movement they have invested something like $15,000,000 in Palestine, and are bending every effort to make it truly a home for the oppressed Jews of the world. We may state here that Judge Mack is an ardent Zionist, in other words, he believes that his people should become a national unit.

In 1917 Negroes, too, caught the echo of the cry for self-determination for weaker peoples. Through their inspired leader, Marcus Garvey, they rallied to his slogan of "Africa for the Africans, those at home and those abroad." And for this laudable undertaking he has been ridiculed and persecuted by ignorant Negroes and selfish whites, resulting in his imprisonment. Even the erstwhile persecuted Jew of Eastern Europe becomes an one hundred percent. American and adds his share to the misery of the Negro by hampering his nationalistic program. But opposition of Jews and Gentiles to African redemption will not stop it, because nationalism is what they are also striving for, so why shouldn't the Negro, the second largest race group in the world, also strive to get this permanent cure for all his ills. Isn't he a human being, with feelings, hopes and ambitions like white and yellow people? Why should he remain the servant of all men? Is he not one of God's masterpieces, and therefore arbiter of his own destiny? All honest and fair-minded persons will laud the Negro's efforts to work out his own salvation along national lines, and while they do nothing to help us, yet we thank them for leaving us alone.

Negroes tried to run ships and were put out of business mainly by Jews, but fate again stepped in and when Jews tried to run their Palestine line, they failed.[61] The only difference was that a Jewish district attorney prosecuted the Negro leader, and a Jewish judge sentenced him, but there was no Negro district attorney or judge or any action taken against the Jewish leader. The Palestine line failed—that's all. The rest is a closed book.

While Jews and Negroes work for their respective homelands, pogroms in Europe and lynchings in America continue to take their toll; yet in the face of all this, the Jew is heartless enough to persecute the Negro. How does the honorable Jewish judge feel when he asks Almighty God to save his people from Rumanian outrages, knowing that one word from his own lips would bring joy to the hearts of millions of Negroes, and that word he refuses to utter.

No, says he, let Marcus Garvey remain in prison. So let it be, says the Jewish district attorney.

And so the world moves on,

To each his sufferings: all are men
Condemned alike to groan;

The tender for another's pain,
The unfeeling for his own.[62]

"DIVISION IS THE SCANDAL OF CHRISTENDOM," APRIL 2, 1927

Considerable discussion has been caused by the suggestion of Frederick L. Collins[63] in the Woman's Home Companion, that 100,000 churches in the United States should be abandoned and demolished, so that the remainder could be more efficient. He points out the 200,000 churches in the country belonging to 200 denominations represent an investment of three billion dollars and cost three hundred million dollars yearly to maintain, but, he says, they are only open three times per week for religious services, therefore he offers the following suggestions: "Immediate reduction, by at least one-half of the number of existing places of worship without reducing existing opportunities for worship." [. . .]

Mr. Collins exempts the Catholic church and he gives this reason that this church "performs so many services for its people which the Protestant church does not attempt, that it cannot be judged by the same standards."

The surplus of churches, despite the continued increase in population, has been created by the rivalry of denominations in erecting buildings, without a thought as to the possible shifting of congregations due to economic causes. The all-important work of most church-goers is to build and pay mortgages, the other requirements, such as saving souls, leading exemplary lives, social and welfare work, is secondary because the results cannot be seen by every passerby to evoke their envy. Each little church-group wants to be housed in a magnificent structure so that they may have something to show off on.

Christians are divided into so many denominations that their influence is becoming negligible among the so-called heathen of Asia and Africa. They cannot understand why Roman Catholics commit a sin when they enter a Protestant church to worship God; or the Baptist submerge their candidates, while the Episcopalians believe that laying on of hands by the Bishop is the correct form and condemn the Baptists for their form of submerging; or why the Holy Rollers should roll on the ground as a manifestation of praise to God; and above all, the heathen is at a loss to understand why all Christian preachers should say after Jesus of Nazareth, "Man love thy brother as thyself," when they make no effort to carry out His doctrine in their contact one with another.

With an awakened East, questioning and accusing it, it is necessary for Christians to forget denominational rivalries, and unite to make Christianity a living gospel and not a theory.

Reading and Learning Business and Technical Skills

Jacques Garvey was consistent in her call for Blacks to gain training in jobs that went beyond professions such as doctors and lawyers. In this, she was like Booker T. Washington, who encouraged Blacks to gain industrial skills and the requisite ability in business. These skills would be important for Blacks to survive in a racially segregated United States, but they would be even more important in the anticipated African homeland. In "The Negro Race Needs Trained Men," Jacques Garvey contends that "[t]rained men are like red corpuscles in the body—the sign of good health." In "What the World Needs You Should Produce" and "Africa Needs Masters of Flivvers; Not Masters of Art," she argues that Blacks must use their skills in practical terms. They do not have the luxury to gain an education without putting this knowledge to useful purposes that will help advance the race.

Jacques Garvey asserts that the key to knowledge is twofold: thinking independently and through reading. Like other Black Caribbean leaders of the time such as Arturo Schomburg, Hubert H. Harrison, Richard B. Moore, J. A. Rogers, and Marcus Garvey,[64] she felt that reading was essential to gain true independence. As she says in "Enslave the Mind and You Enslave the Body," "Truly the man or woman who teaches others to think, emancipates them altogether." She reinforces this message in "Reading Is to the Brain What Food Is to the Muscles," urging Blacks to "[q]uench your thirst in the river of knowledge, and be rated among the world's thinkers."

"ENSLAVE THE MIND AND YOU ENSLAVE THE BODY," JUNE 20, 1925

Comparatively speaking the world has few thinkers. Humanity of all climes and races is led by the opinions and conclusions of a few chosen thinkers. Ask the average man on the street why he thinks the earth is round and he will readily tell you because the great Aristotle said the earth is a sphere.[65] Ask the fashionably dressed lady of today when she wears knee-length dresses, and she will answer, "Because Paris decrees it this season." Whether it be in science, politics, or even style, the majority follow the dictates of a few. Man is an imitative animal anyhow, and he depends largely on the leaders of thought in his community, nation and race to think for him, while he executes. Who makes wars? The statesmen, bankers and capitalists of the world. Who fights in the wars? The masses who had no say in the making of them. Many wars of aggression would never have been waged if the people were given an opportunity to think for themselves and to answer the question, "To fight or not to fight."

The educated man is not necessarily a thinker. He reflects the thoughts of real thinkers and, parrot-like, he can quote from the writings and theories of great men. But the really educated man is he who thinks for himself and is able to discover new truths. When the mind is enslaved physical slavery, in one shape or another, soon follows. If a man is taught from childhood that he is inferior, and he believes what he is taught without question, then [h]e is truly inferior, as his mind makes him what he is. The minute he starts to think independently and to believe that he can do what others have done, then the state of his mind frees him from the inferiority ban and enables him to go out and achieve.

Nations hold other people in subjection by enslaving their minds. The oppressed are always made to believe that they are inferiors by their oppressors and that Lord God made them only to be servants. Having acquired this state of mind, they become the willing tools of others[,] their ambition dies in them, they stagnate because of their enslaved minds. Should any one among them discover himself and by thinking independently expose the system that holds his people in thraldom, he is dubbed a radical and an agitator, a dangerous fellow to be gotten rid of, as a columyist [*sic*] in the New York American states: "Socrates was condemned to death for corrupting the youth; that is, he was teaching them to think. To think is always dangerous. The really safe man is the man who does as other people do around him." [. . .]

All men and women who have sought to enlighten the masses of their people have got into trouble, and many have had to suffer even death in their efforts to better conditions which surround them. A reformer must be prepared for sacrifices, even as Jesus, the world's greatest reformer, made them. He is usually misunderstood by his own people, whose minds are in eclipse; his life is eagerly sought after by the oppressors, who see the end of their career if those whom they seek to exploit are taught to think for themselves; hence reformers usually pay the supreme sacrifice, but their efforts are never in vain, even though they are unpopular in their lifetime. Long after they are dead their teaching lives and the oppressed benefit by their contributions.

Two weeks ago a white business man, in a conversation with this writer, said, "Garvey has made the greatest contribution to his race because he has taught Negroes to think for themselves." The white man knows the value of independent racial thought. It is the power that makes or breaks a people. Marcus Garvey knows that and is satisfied to bear his imprisonment cheerfully, because he has given a new thought to black men and women the world over. He has taught them to think in terms of race, to aspire toward nationhood, and the achievement of the highest and best in man, hence it will not be long before they will stand on a platform of equality with other races because of their achievements and contributions to civilization, and demand the respect and appreciation of those who now call them inferior. Truly the man or woman who teaches others to think, emancipates them altogether.

"THE NEGRO RACE NEEDS TRAINED MEN," JULY 3, 1926

To express the belief that the Negro race needs trained men may cause some of our short-sighted critics to view our statement with disapprobation, because many persons of color are prone to consider the race as being limited to America, without taking thought of the teeming millions in Africa and elsewhere; but to us there are 400,000,000 in the world, whose destiny and future are one, whose sufferings are identical, and who are now making common cause to alleviate such sufferings and to lift the entire race to a plane of honor and respect.

Trained men are like red corpuscles in the body—the sign of good health. Our race is anaemic for lack of this material to give it vim and vigor to move it along the road of progress, therefore it is not keeping abreast of the yellow and white races, but lingering and weak, it depends on the support it gets from others.

No one has ever become independent and respected by being a beggar, nor can one become powerful and strong by depending on the charity of others. As of persons, so of nations and races—we achieve greatness and wealth, in proportion to the training we give our minds and bodies, and the manner in which we apply ourselves to the exigencies of the hour.

There are many Negroes, we are sorry to admit, who are content as long as they have something to eat, clothes to wear and somewhere to sleep, caring not how transient these blessings may be. Others are perfectly satisfied to remain in the most menial jobs because they are too lazy to train themselves to become captains of industries. How often one hears a dialogue somewhat like this:

> "Well, I have been working at Mr. Morgan's bank for the last twenty years, and the old man is certainly a nice man to work for."
>
> "What is your position now?"
>
> "I have been portering there since I left high school."
>
> "Why didn't the old man raise you?"
>
> "Raise me? Why the son wanted to put a white man in my job, but the old man said, no, 'I have been such a good boy to him.'"

The doom of the race lies in the lethargy of its men, who are content to be servants, dependents all their lives, and lack the pluck to go out and create positions for themselves.

With them it is better to work for Mr. Whiteman for $15 per week all their lives (supporting wife and children out of it) than to bear a little hardship in their youth and establish some kind of business enterprise that could eventually bring in a substantial revenue, and provide employment for other members of the race. But the eternal selfishness of the Negro cripples him as a man, and keeps the race weak and impotent. He will not suffer for race, many will not consider race at all, and some hardly want to provide for their own children.

The dearth of real men and trained men impoverishes the race. It is a cruel truth, but it is the truth just the same. Four hundred million Negroes in the world, and where are our statesmen? They are the trained men we need to protect our interest in the council chambers of other people, and to direct our destiny in the mother country, where are our commercial magnates and industrial giants to secure outlets for trade and open up plants and factories to manufacture goods, and thereby provide employment for millions of young men and women just out of school? Where are our big laboratories and experimenting stations? Where and oh, where, are our patriots, living for race and country, and ever ready to die for same if the sacrifice is required? Survey the intellectual, political and industrial groups of other races, and ask yourself if black men are measuring up to present day standards. Remember there are 400,000,000 Negroes breathing God's air; where are the trained men commensurate to this great group who will supply their needs, and make them live as God intended they should—Lords of creation?

Black men you are failing on your jobs! Measure height of achievement and breadth of usefulness with others, and be honest enough to admit your laziness. Now shake yourselves, lift your head high, expand your chests, put right foot forward, then left, don't be afraid, now step right off and tackle your jobs. The world expects you to play a man's part, and is fed up on your whinings and "can't-be-done" moans. Be real men, honest, sincere, determined and straightway the race will be lifted up in the estimation of others, who respect those who respect themselves.

"WHAT THE WORLD NEEDS YOU SHOULD PRODUCE," SEPT. 4, 1926

Some Negroes have a peculiar notion that the best future for young men of means is to become lawyers, doctors or preachers. Owing to this short-sightedness, there are more preachers than congregations, more lawyers than briefs, and more doctors crowded into large cities than patients. They lack the courage to spread out into rural districts and small towns; for with them service to others is not the first consideration, and, further, they have no eye for business.

Economics was a poor subject with the Negro student, and, until the advent of Marcus Garvey, industry and commerce were unknown quantities to the race, and strictly "white folks' business." The Black Star Line to some was the hallucination of a weak brain. The idea of black men running ships, building warehouses, handling produce, traveling from America to Africa and the West Indies to negotiate for cargoes and consignments of manufactured products sounded impossible to some Negroes who had never seen a ship, and others who had never even rowed a canoe up a river, nor got any further in an office than sweeping the floors and dusting the desks. Because it was impossible to their narrow minds, they ridiculed it and hampered it in every direction, just to have the satisfaction of saying, "We knew it couldn't be done." Since they knew nothing about it, no other Negro should be given a chance to do it. "We can't, and you shan't[;] jealousy and selfishness are two despicable traits in Negroes that white men have been able to play upon since emancipation to keep the race divided. Every Negro wants to be a leader, and hates to see another being praised for any worthy accomplishment. But black propaganda has made Negroes see themselves as one race 400,000,000 strong. Domicile is no bar to unity, and all are working to one common destiny.

In the effort toward nationhood all Negroes must learn the value of industry and commerce. Professionals are all right in their respective places, but they get their support from the people, who in turn exist by the products of factories and agriculture. Therefore, the basic foundation of a people's existence must be the means whereby they shall eat bread.

Factories must have raw products to turn their machinery, and these products cannot reach the factories unless ships and trains carry them; so in order to meet the world's demands ships are necessary. This is the logical conclusion of trained business men, not the dream of a fanatic.

Today the two products that command ready markets are oil and rubber. Six years ago Marcus Garvey saw that America, with her growing automobile industry, would be sorely in need of these commodities. The Stevenson Restriction Act[66] having hampered the importation of rubber at reasonable prices from English concerns, he negotiated with Liberia for concessions of land to colonize industrious American Negroes, knowing full well that Liberia produced good rubber at little cost, and that with modern machinery the colonists could have built up a splendid trade with American rubber manufacturers, thereby making themselves wealthy. Liberia, through customs duties would have been able to pay off her foreign debts, and America would have benefited by reasonable prices from her former citizens. Marcus Garvey's critics could not see the feasibility of encouraging Negroes to go to Liberia. One old preacher, with the "I-can't-you-shan't" idea uppermost in his mind, boasts of having shown Firestone samples of Liberian rubber, which got him interested in exporting the rubber resources of the country. So Garvey had to go make room for Rubber Barons in Liberia, and the ships of the Black Star Line had to be destroyed so as to dishearten his followers and turn their minds from trade and commerce.

Mons. Roland Dorgeles,[67] writing for Asia magazine, in an article on rubber farming in Indo-China, gives a graphic description of the industry and the great financial returns it brings. He states: "[N]ow those accursed lands that were not worth one piaster[68] bring fortunes. Vessels load millions of tons of rubber at Saigon. On the balance sheet of a corporation that is still young I read, 'Capital, $10,000,000; net profit, $4,500,000.'"

Millionaires are not made from lawyers and doctors, unless they invest money in big business, but from men who have vision, courage and determination to produce what the world needs. Get in that class and you will be respected.

"AFRICA NEEDS MASTERS OF FLIVVERS;[69] NOT MASTERS OF ART," OCT. 23, 1926

Were we to use this column every week only to dilate on commerce and industry, and the Negro's need of them, we feel that it would be space well used, as these are the pivots on which this workaday world turns.

Africa, with its untold mineral resources, fertile soil, large rivers and lakes, and extensive coast line touching two oceans and one sea, naturally requires the hands and brains of industrialists, farmers and scientists, rather than masters of arts, doctors of philosophy, poets and jazz players. This is what we want to rub into the brain of every Negro who intends to answer the call of the Motherland. The Asiatics have begun to appreciate the value of practical knowledge to meet the needs of their people, and surely the Negro's mind is not more dense than his yellow brother.

Ninety-nine Chinese students are now taking post-graduate courses in Ford plants at Detroit, while hundreds of others have been placed in other industrial plants and business offices. Their purpose is not to remain in America after graduation and compete with white men, but to return to China, and bless their country with the knowledge they have acquired. Cannot Negroes in this Western world do the same thing for Liberia, Abyssinia, and other parts of Africa?

Julean Arnold,[70] United States commercial attache in China, writing in The Educational Review, states as follows: "China needs today more masters of flivvers and fewer masters of arts. What the Chinese students in the United States will do for the China of the next decade will depend upon the sort of practical training they receive supplementary to their academic or scholastic education." [. . .]

The first thought of any student, especially one belonging to an oppressed race, should be, what can I do to help my people and my country? Out of all the practical needs of a struggling people, he surely will be able to pick out one line of endeavor which he feels inclined to pursue, and through which he could employ others, or relieve their suffering. In this desperate struggle for the survival of the fittest race, no one should be stupid enough to try to live unto himself and for himself alone; mankind is grouping itself racially, and each race is preparing for the struggle—this every Negro must be made to understand. If he refuses to see, then he should not be allowed to jeopardize the welfare of millions of his own race.

Africa's needs are many, but all her needs could be satisfied if her scattered sons and daughters abroad could wake up overnight with a racial consciousness; then bleeding Africa would not call in vain, for the prodigals and those that were kidnapped would assemble their tools, pack their overalls and return home to make of Africa what the Pilgrim Fathers and their descendants have made of America—the richest and most progressive country in the world.

Yes, Africa needs flivvers, tractors, river boats, ocean-going vessels, and all machinery for refining minerals, and manufacturing—mineral products such as are used in these United States, a few feet of lynch-rope may be handy, too, as a pale-face visitor may forget his western prejudice and attack a queenly daughter of Ethiopia; then we would be obliged to deal with him as he deals with such culprits of our race in these United States. You know what is good for the goose is also good for the gander, and the Associated Press would flash news like this:—

> Athens, Ga.—Burly Negro lynched by mob for attacking frail white girl.
>
> ———
>
> Timbuctoo,[71] Africa—Vicious white man lynched by giant African for attacking beautiful Africa girl.
>
> ———

The Negro woman wants protection and comfort, and to her we make our appeal this week to exert every effort on the men to make them answer the call of Africa and supply her needs, thereby lifting our race to the level of others, and relieving the millions of enslaved and oppressed Negroes.

"READING IS TO THE BRAIN WHAT FOOD IS TO THE MUSCLES," OCT. 30, 1926

If an individual is to amount to anything he or she must think, and to be able to think one must read and make deductions from what one hears. The world would not be as progressive as it is today were it not for the great men and women who have made their individual contribution through deep thought and study. There would have been no aeroplanes, automobiles, steamships, locomotives or electricity if men had accepted theories, without reasoning for themselves, and experimenting with ideas.

The Negro race is backward as it is in this age, because we do not read enough, hence we do not think. It is true there are millions who have never been blessed with an education, but take the millions in America, who are within reach of free schools and libraries, do they take advantage of these benefits? No, the poolrooms, dance halls and dives have more attraction for them. Some would pass a night school and a library every day of their lives, and never once enter either institution, yet being badly in need of education and knowledge. This accounts for the abominable condition of the race, because the men are like rudderless vessels, big hulks drifting along. Their thinking machinery has never been used. Why no, white folks think for them. [. . .]

The disease that is sapping the life out of our race is mental inertia. Instead of our men being energetic and forward looking they slouch around—dull, apathetic, purposeless beings, too lazy even to think for themselves, therefore the tools of a bustling, vigorous, determined race.

Reading good books is like eating good, wholesome food, the former acts on the brain, while the latter acts on the muscles. Think of the millions of Negro brains being fed only on funny sheets, racing hints and scandal. It is just as if you fed your stomach on vinegar and pepper instead of food. Then picture the brains of other people who never read at all, and who never attend serious lectures or indulge in uplifting talks. Their minds are numbed from non-use, and they react to their surroundings like a parrot or a monkey. [. . .]

Go to your nearest library, and let the librarian select a course of reading for you, in keeping with your education. Gradually you will improve, and be able to digest "deep" books. Visit the second-hand book stores, where you can obtain literature at a low cost; when you call on your friends, scan their books over, and when you borrow from them be sure to return it, as this is a terrible fault of booklovers.

Decide within yourself that you will improve your mind. Leave the cabarets for a while, and sit at home with a good book. Your body will be rested, and your mind improved. Remember that reading is also a recreation, especially to those who do manual labor. All varieties of books are printed, just as all varieties of foods are eaten, therefore one should be careful to have a balanced reading course. Ice cream instead of food is bad for the stomach, so are romantic tales alone for the mind. Select your books, as you would select your food, and above all let the reading habit grow on you. Quench your thirst in the river of knowledge, and be rated among the world's thinkers.

Black Nationalism/African Redemption

No task was more important to Garveyites than the redemption of Africa from colonial domination and the establishment of a Black nation in the Motherland. Every other goal revolved around this one central belief. Thus, the quest for establishing a Black homeland is a chief concern of Jacques Garvey and is a theme that recurs in her editorials. She pleads for all Blacks, in "World Renaissance," to dedicate themselves to this sacred "duty and obligation." She expresses hope, in "White Prophecy Concerning Black Africa," that this "dream of a redeemed Africa for Negroes will be realized in less than twenty-five years." She speaks of these natural desires in "Wherefore a National Urge?" "The Urge for Nationhood," and "Our Pledge to Africa." She addresses the painful history of Negroes in America and expresses the empirical urgency for a migration to Africa in "The Strong Must Rule, and the Weak Will Die, Policy of Imperialists" and "Has the Negro Served His Purpose in America?" In "Going to Africa?" she advises those who are planning the trip home to have the requisite skills to advance the development of the Continent. She hopes that the liberation of Africa will be without bloodshed in "Africa Bides Her Time!" but she states "that what is worth living for, is worth dying for." This is a clear reminder that Blacks must be willing to give up their lives if necessary for the cause, and it is a warning to Whites that continued exploitation of Africa will come at a bloody cost.

"WORLD RENAISSANCE," MARCH 8, 1924

(This editorial is written at the request of Mrs. Caroline Gray of Puerto Barrios, Guatemala.)

The world is moving faster today than it did a century ago. All peoples and races are restless. They are shuffling about seeking permanent places for themselves and their posterities. Nations that are already established are not contented with the territory they now occupy, and are foremost in the mighty struggle for a larger share of this earth's surface. They are not thinking only in terms of the present, but are making provisions for their unborn generations. Smaller nations finding themselves pressed on all sides are making desperate effort to, at least, maintain their ground. Oppressed peoples have taken up the cry of liberty and independence, and have declared that they shall no longer be exploited and robbed by powerful nations; but that they shall fight and, if necessary, die in the attempt to throw off the yoke of the oppressor and establish for their children mighty nations and empires.

The great conflict is on. Nation pitted against nation and race against race. Each trying to produce its best in man power and science, to be able to conquer in the struggle for "the survival of the fittest."[72] This is the period of world renaissance. All races are awake to the importance of the hour, realizing that if they do not formulate and carry out some definite plans for themselves respectively, they will be exterminated by the more powerful and aggressive groups. The Negro race, although on the lowest rung of the ladder of present day achievements, is awakened to the consciousness of self, and the responsibilities of the hour.

Five years ago the Universal Negro Improvement Association made a survey of world affairs, and having sensed the danger, pledged itself to organize the scattered and dispersed members of the race and prepare them for the conflict. Today Negro men and women in every quarter of the globe feel the call of race, and have endorsed the primary object of the Universal Negro Improvement Association—that of redeeming Africa, the land of our forefathers. The Negro who does not make every day count for something done toward African Redemption is not spiteing [*sic*] the Universal Negro Improvement Association, but is criminally negligent of his future. An old adage says, "To be forewarned is to be forearmed." The man who is warned of a fight and does not gird on his armor, not alone exposes himself to defeat, but endangers his comrades; because when the onrush comes, and one yields, he creates an opening for the enemy.

Negro men! Beware of your listless attitude towards the progress of your race. You were not created by God to live for your own selfish interests. You may have a good job. You may have wealth, but think of the millions of your own race who are destitute and being brutalized by other races. Have you no love or pity for your own flesh and blood? Can you sit idly by and enjoy your own prosperity while the agonizing cries of your unfortunate brothers and sisters go up to heaven for help and succor? Rich men! Intellectual men! Satisfied men! Bestir yourselves and abandon your selfish mode of living. Help your brothers and sisters, and in helping them you will help yourselves. Build for the race a national home in Africa, that can lend prestige and protection to the poorest Negro in any country where he may find himself. Men! Live, so that the world will always remember that you lived. We pass this way but once, in passing leave the imprints of good deeds, so that posterity will bless your memory because you planned and worked for their security and happiness.

Negro mothers! What are you doing for your boys? Must they suffer and be humiliated as you, or are you training them to become the warriors of the future, who will protect the womanhood of the race at all costs? Mothers, you have a wonderful opportunity to perform service to the race by training your children in terms of race, and preparing their minds and bodies for the march toward nationhood.

Young women! Urge your male relatives and friends to take an active part in this nationalistic program. This is not an age of contented people. All peoples are discontented. They are discontented with their positions, and are reaching out and striving for larger opportunities and higher achievements. The young man who is not ambitious for his race's betterment, is not the man any woman should accept for a husband; because the man who will not help to elevate his race, is not the man who should be the father of children and help populate a down-trodden race.

Women! Wake up and realize your duty and obligation to your race, and get behind your men and see to it that they shoulder the responsibilities of race as white and yellow men are doing. Negro women, it is up to you to win the day for Africa.

"WHITE PROPHECY CONCERNING BLACK AFRICA," JAN. 24, 1925

A few weeks ago Sir Harry Johnston,[73] an Englishman, who spent forty years exploring Africa, made a rather prophetic statement about our Motherland when interviewed by a newspaper correspondent in England. The interview in part states: "I don't expect to see a black Africa in any time," said Sir Harry, who is 66, and living in retirement in his Sussex home after his years of service throughout Africa. "However, it is entirely possible that within half a century all of Africa from the Zambesi to the Sahara may be a great black republic." [. . .]

It is peculiar to note how many Negro newspapers reproduced extracts from the above statements, and topped them with glowing headlines such as, "Vast Black Republic Foreseen for Africa. Africa Will Again Belong to Negroes." These same Negro journals ridiculed Marcus Garvey when he predicted eight years ago that Africa will some day belong to the black man. They continued to call him fanatic, dreamer, even mad man. How could Africa, or any part of it under the control of England, France, Belgium or Spain, become the property of black men, they argued? Until now that a white man makes the same prediction, their argument against the feasibility of it ceases. It is a fact. It will surely come to pass.

This attitude displays the slavish mentality of some Negroes who can never see good in the members of their own race, but will readily believe what men of the white race say. Their erstwhile masters have loosened the shackles from their wrists but their mentality is still enslaved. This is the unseen power that keeps the race where others would have it be. Regardless of ridicule and opposition members of the Universal Negro Improvement Association have rallied to the slogan of "Africa for the Africans, those at home and those abroad," and have not allowed alien races to think for them, but to think about them.

Now black and white are envisioning a vast African commonwealth, controlled by Negroes, and stretching its powerful arms of protection to Negroes throughout the globe. "Glory be to God," the old woman in the Amen Corner[74] in church would say. So let it be, we repeat.

The desire for independence and nationalism for the Negro is the cry of the Universal Negro Improvement Association, for that its members work, and it is gratifying to see how the cry has gone throughout the world and awakened to consciousness sleeping Negroes who never thought in terms of nationhood before.

The dream of a redeemed Africa for Negroes will be realized in less than twenty-five years if all Negroes will forget their petty jealousies and insular prejudices and fall in line with the members of the Universal Negro Improvement Association. The more workers for the cause the sooner will the objective be reached.

The leadership of this great nationalist movement is linking up the scattered members of the race by steamships, teaching them that they are of the same blood, no matter where they may be domiciled; educating and preparing them as future citizens of the African Commonwealth. It is a great task, a noble effort, and should appeal to every man and woman with one drop of Negro blood in their veins.

"THE STRONG MUST RULE, AND THE WEAK WILL DIE, POLICY OF IMPERIALISTS," MARCH 28, 1925

For the last six years Marcus Garvey, through his far-seeing vision and knowledge of world affairs, has been sending warnings to every nook and corner of the globe where Negroes live, pointing out to them the grave dangers facing weak and unorganized groups in an age of world materialism and selfishness.

Some self-satisfied Negroes, who cannot see further than their noses, and are only interested in their immediate surroundings, laughed at him, others called him crazy. But when one follows closely the activities of world powers, and learns the policies motivating their actions, one is bound to admit, "of a truth he is right."

H. H. Powers,[75] a rather outspoken exponent of imperialism, gives us, as a weak race, much food for thought. In an article in the February issue of the Atlantic Monthly he says:

> "Exploitation is the primary and legitimate aim of imperialism. . . . The weak, the ignorant, and the slothful races cannot expect to remain undisturbed in their habitat. It is much that they are allowed to remain at all, a concession rather to the humanity of their betters than to their own right. Interference, guidance and control are the indispensible conditions of this tolerance. . . . We cannot leave them to their indolent siesta if they hold in accidental and unconscious keeping the energies needed for advancing civilization."

This emphatic declaration speaks for itself. The writer goes on to show that weak and oppressed peoples all over the world are clamoring for self-determination, then he asks the question, "What would be the result of this much-invoked race-forbearance, save to give the child of the future a Hottentot[76] for a father instead of a white man?" This is the crux of the whole situation. If white nations were to honestly and sympathetically help and train Negroes along the road to self-government, when they reached the highest possible perfection they would become the masters of the world. Their physical strength, prowess in battle, virility as a race, and adaptability to strange surroundings, would tend in a few years to produce a splendid type of black humanity, whose very self-sufficiency, would cause him to say, "I call no man master." Instead of the child of the future being a Hottentot, the man of the future would be a Negro.

The imperialistic writer closes his article with the arresting thought, "Will the world wait for child-peoples to grow to the measure of these requirements when it can displace them with better stock?" We add, the white race certainly is well protected by its racial thinkers and prophets, who warn their people continuously of the dangers ahead.

This policy of imperialism has been working out for years. Those who have vision see it, but some do not realize it until it is told them in plain blunt, cruel words. The white man is determined to have all the world and its resources, if possible, for himself and his posterity.

The yellow man has sensed this selfish purpose, and is marshalling all the physical, mental and scientific forces at his command and marching abreast of the white man to glory and to power. The yellow man's challenge to the white man is, "What is good for you, is also good for me, and I am going to take mine." The brown man within the last few years has opened his eyes to the fact that he, too, should organize his forces, at least to hold his native habitat and protect it for all times.

Lastly comes the black man, late though he be, and says, "We are also in the fight for the survival of the fittest. God Almighty made us a separate and distinct race, and apportioned to us the great continent of Africa with the command, 'occupy until I come'."

Because of our failure to live up to the high purpose for which we were created, we have been scattered to the furthermost ends of the world, and kept divided through the subtle propaganda of those who fear our united strength. But Marcus Garvey came on the scene six years ago with a message for his race. He showed them a picture of a world that had not enlarged its geographical boundaries, yet, whose population was rapidly multiplying; that this immense mass of humanity was instinctively grouping itself racially, in preparation for the great "pushing off process"; that weak and unorganized groups were being robbed of the territories they occupied and were being gradually exterminated, so as to make room for the more powerful to expand. He pointed us to the vast continent of Africa, the richest in the world, that was being pillaged by bankrupt Europe to resuscitate its treasures, and to bolster up its vaunted superiority. Then he related to us the horrible story of the slave-trade, that had caused us to be brought from our native homes in Africa and distributed as cattle, in North, South and Central America, and the Islands of the Caribbean. He besought us as one race, as one people, although scattered, to link ourselves together in one grand organization, for the ultimate purpose of redeeming Africa from the hands of those who exploit and ravish her. Now the whole world of Negroes has heard the gospel of Garveyism, and is raising the cry everywhere, "We are coming, Mother Africa, 400,000,000 strong." Coming with the latest developments in science, industry and commerce to lead Africa to glory, and to make of her a world power to be reckoned with.

Africa shall be restored to her ancient glory along modern lines by black men, who realize that if we must live, we must be strong. Power is the keynote of this age. When all races shall have acquired that, and reached a common plane of world achievement, each will grasp the hand of the other and say, "BROTHER." Until then, the struggle continues.

"WHEREFORE A NATIONAL URGE?" JUNE 6, 1925

When a race forgets or ignores its history, it loses inspiration and ceases to create history to the glory of itself.

From the time of the destructive fire at Alexandria,[77] Egypt, and the fall of the great seats of learning at Timbuctoo, Africa lost her history; her people started to retrog[r]ade, and today we find ourselves scattered all over the world, laying claim to alien nationalities and even races, many of us not knowing from whence we came and having no complete history to inspire us to perpetuate the ideals for which our fathers fought and died.

It is the policy of the white oppressor to keep us divided, to destroy all traces of our ancient history, and attribute the glory of our ancestors to his race. We are taught that in schools, every conceivable kind of propaganda to that effect is disseminated among us, hence we unconsciously assume an inferior attitude, and the white man stalks through the world labeled "Superior."

The Englishman, when he remembers the slavery of his ancestors, in the Roman period, sings, "Britons never, never shall be slaves."[78] Some Negroes sing that anthem just as lustily as the English. But does it mean anything to the Negro? No! They are merely parrots, imitating, without thinking. While they are singing the pledge or vow of the Britons, their blood-brothers are being murdered and brutalized by the same English in Africa in order that "Britons never, never shall be slaves," even if they have to retain their freedom at the price of all Africa and by the bombing of millions of natives there.

At the time when Rome had her English slaves,[79] Africans were cultured, refined people, teaching the world art and sciences. How can any Negro call himself a Briton, and succeed in tracing his ancestry back to the Angles? He may essay to, if he is a half-breed, but under the white man's law he is a Negro if he has one drop of Negro blood in his veins.

Under the French rule we sing, "Aux Armes, Citoyens! Formez vos Battalions! Marchons, marchons."[80] For whom are we shouldering our arms? For France, or for Africa? Black men! Use your BRAINS as well as your ARMS. THINK, then ACT.

In America we sing, "My country, 'tis of thee, sweet land of liberty." But can our hearts really swell with pride when we sing these words? Is it "my country" that jim-crows, lynches and burns me? Is it my "sweet land of liberty" that denies me equal opportunity with others, and a fair trial in its courts of law? The naturalized German can truthfully sing this anthem, because he enjoys all the blessings of citizenship in this country, but not the Negro who saw the light of day here, and fought "the brutal Hun" in 1914–18, for the sake of democracy.

We of the Universal Negro Improvement Association respect the national anthem and flag of all peoples. We think it is right and proper when one is in another's country that he, in common with others, should rise and sing the national anthem of that country in public places, and that he should pay due respect to that flag, as it is the symbol of the nation, and the national anthem is the patriotic expression of the people. We have such a high regard for such expressions and symbols that we too have composed our own anthem, and made our own flag. And we are working and praying for the day when the scattered members of our race shall be reunited in Mother Africa, with the flag of the red, black and green[81] unfurled to the breeze; and sing from the fullness of our hearts:

O, Jehovah, thou God of the ages,
Grant unto our sons that lead
The wisdom Thou gav'st to Thy sages
When Israel was sore in need.

Thy voice thro' the dim past has spoken,
Ethiopia shall stretch forth her hand,
By Thee shall all fetters be broken
And Heaven bless our dear Motherland.

This is a verse of the new African national anthem,[82] and the Universal Negro Improvement Association, under the leadership of Marcus Garvey, its founder, strives to establish a homeland for Negroes on the great continent of Africa, from which we were taken hundreds of years ago, there to build up a mighty nation along modern scientific lines, based on an ancient African culture and racial refinement.

"HAS THE NEGRO SERVED HIS PURPOSE IN AMERICA?" NOV. 7, 1925

That the Negro was brought to America against his will is common knowledge; that he intends to remain in America is the determination of many; but under what conditions and to serve what purpose are questions that do not seem to be considered in the desire to stay.

Negroes were enslaved and transported to America years ago for the purpose of doing the laborious work in building up the country. The country has been built up, the slaves have been freed, and for sixty years the presence of these ex-slaves here have created a problem, commonly called the race problem. Divers have been the solutions offered for the problem; but up to now no organized, legalized method has met the popular approval of both races.

Some whites say, "Let the Negro remain here and gradually work out his salvation," yet secretly knowing that by economic pressure he may be exterminated in another century. Others say, "Let him go," yet they offer no recompense for his contribution in America, and no help to re-establish him in Africa. In brief, white America is heartless and cruel and is not concerned about the fate of the Negro because he has already served the purpose for which he was brought here. Therefore the Negro's future rests in his own hands, and should be a matter of deep concern to him at this time, seeing he is no longer the ward of the nation.

Some Negroes believe that by miscegenation he will be absorbed into the white race, and enjoy social equality with his erstwhile master.[83] Others believe that it is a crime to mongrelize the race; and by active campaign and propaganda, are endeavoring to get white America to realize its moral obligation to the Negro, and secure its aid in helping ambitious, industrious Negroes to return to their ancestral home and there establish a government of their own along modern lines based on their own racial culture.

The advocate of this latter group is Marcus Garvey, who has made a thorough study of the industrial, political and economic life of the Negro in America and is convinced that the Negro can rise no higher than his present status—that of the underdog in the nation. His development is circumscribed by an overwhelming white majority, whose prejudices and intolerance increase daily. He cannot employ himself and is entirely dependent on the white man for work (which brings him bread and butter) and that work is of the most menial and for which he is underpaid. Even these jobs are being jeopardized with the introduction of labor-saving devices. Where twelve Negroes were formerly employed to dig a ditch, now two white men can operate a machine that not only digs the ditch, but shovels up the earth and puts sane into a motor truck, in less than half the time. [. . .]

Electricity and motor power are now doing the work of the Negro, and it is imperative that he create his own jobs, or face unemployment and consequent starvation. The life of the black consumer is short unless he starts out immediately to produce those essentials of every day life, which will take him out of the servant class and at the same time ensure his livelihood; but the question of protection lies in the establishment of a government of his own in Africa, strong enough to protect him in any part of the world he may reside.

Truly the Negro has served well the white man's purpose for bringing him to America; and the enlightened wide-awake Negro is now determined to serve his own purpose, that of living and enjoying life as any other man, without limitations and without barriers against his development and progress.

Who can stop the onward march of ten million Sons of Ham, to nation[h]ood and to power!

"THE URGE FOR NATIONHOOD," MAY 1, 1926

The test of a real man is the difficulties he overcomes, the situations he masters, and the test of a genuine movement for good is similar, in that it will weather all storms, because it is basically sincere; and misfortunes will but serve as stepping stones to success.

Unfair though this world may be, sceptical to a marked degree, yet it is compelled to credit the scattered sons and daughters of Ethiopia with the urge for nationhood, and the determination to bring to a fruition this ideal.

The idea of African nationalism has been scoffed at and ridiculed: its exponent has been dubbed crazy, framed up by his enemies and imprisoned; the organization or vehicle used to promulgate the idea has been exploited by traitors, and oppressed from every angle, but still, notwithstanding ridicule, the idea has thrived, the leader is stronger in prison because of his martyrdom bravely suffered, the organization has gained many millions of converts and sympathizers from its admirers because of the buffeting it has withstood. In short the cause has triumphed, and no adversity can shake its foundation.

The hope of millions of Negroes cannot be crushed, the future of a race is at stake, and those who, for paltry gold, try to jeopardize it, will never succeed, but, on the contrary, go the way of traitors, or will their offspring not escape the curse. Who can overthrow a bulwark of righteousness? Who could be successful in frustrating the plans for redemption of an oppressed people? 'Tis said that God hears prayers, and surely the daily prayers of oppressed black humanity are not offered in vain, and the great All-Seeing and All-Wise Providence will crown their efforts with success. Of this the members of the Universal

Negro Improvement Association feel assured, and with confidence in themselves and their Creator, faith in the cause, the battle is half won.

The urge for nationhood is born of the travail of oppression, and will continue to develop until its destiny is fulfilled. Obstacles will arise, reverses will come, but these things must needs be, in the life of any individual, movement or nation. We are not dismayed because of treachery within our ranks. We shall not be moved because of the machinations of the oppressor. The spirit of our dead slave ancestors urge us on and on toward the goal. The glorious history of ancient Ethiopia inspires us to duplicate what has been, and for these and other present day occurrences, African nationalism is deeply implanted in the breasts of millions of Negroes, and from the fullness of our hearts we say:

> Light of the world, arise! arise!
>   On Africa thy glory shed.
> Fettered, in darkness now she lies,
>   With weeping eye, and drooping head.
> Light of the world, arise! arise!
>   Millions in tears await the day.
> Shine cloudless forth, O cheer our eyes,
>   And banish grief and wrong away.[84]

"OUR PLEDGE TO AFRICA," MAY 22, 1926

The love of home and the love of country are the two loves that can outlast others more demonstrative and more impetuous. These are loves that call for sacrifice, daring and the most exacting service; yet withal man has no regrets in making his contribution when the opportunity offers itself.

Women have worked themselves sick trying to make home comfortable; men have weathered all storms to provide for home, and until recently were known as the bread-winners. Now the honors are divided almost equally between both sexes in countries where the motto is equal opportunity, equal responsibility. The love for country has caused men to sink to the depths of perfidy in order to expand, or protect their homeland; but such acts are committed in the name of patriotism, and as such the world applauds them. Frenchmen invading Riff[85] territory in North Africa, in order to expand the French Empire. A D'Annunzio[86] proclaiming, "Awake Italy! March and drive Moslems out of Asia Minor." Englishmen dropping bombs on Africans in Africa, because they refuse to pay these white invaders exorbitant taxes. All these offenders are called patriots, yet the man who kills another even under provocation is called a murderer and punished as such. The difference is that the former is actuated by altruistic motives, and his acts are considered only a means toward an end.

The Negroes scattered over the western world under the banner of the Universal Negro Improvement Association, have pledged their lives and fortune to free Africa from thraldom and to lift their brothers at home to the heights of progress and achievement commensurate with present-day standards. We offer no apology to any one in our endeavor to pursue this course; nature makes us feel we are right; when we commune with our God in prayer he inspires us to go on; the atrocities heaped on members of our race daily impel us to action; the memory of our slave dead urges us on in the cause of African redemption, and who dare stop our course?

Men of other countries have dared death and hell for love of country; Negroes are no less patriotic than they. Negroes who have served all nations in their quest for power and conquest, can now serve Africa, their ancestral home, and insure for black posterity a place in world affairs.

Negroes under the leadership of Marcus Garvey are serious, and consider the redemption of the homeland a sacred mission from which nothing can swerve them. In the few choice words of poesy we vow:

"Oppression! I have met thee face to face,
And met thy cruel eye and cloudy brow:
I swear . . .
Still to oppose and thwart with heart and hand
Thy brutalizing sway: til Afric's chains

Are burst, and Freedom rules the rescued land
Tramping Oppression and his iron rod.
Such is the vow I take—So help me God!"[87]

"AFRICA BIDES HER TIME!" FEB. 5, 1927

It takes some big physical demonstration to make some Negroes appreciate the necessity for and worthiness of the program of Garveyism. The Chinese war now being waged[88] has done it. Ten years ago when Marcus Garvey started his crusade and informed a warring world that peace could only be brought about when each race group and nation learned to respect the rights of the other, and that as Europeans claimed Europe as their exclusive possession, so should Asia be for the Asiatics, and Africa for the Africans. He was laughed at by some Negroes and dubbed a "dangerous man" by European landgrabbers. Today the slogan "Asia for the Asiatics," created by a black man, is the war-cry of millions of oppressed Chinese, who are letting Europeans know and feel that their home is in Europe, unless they are willing to be governed by Chinese. Today thousands of white people are packing up bag and baggage and leaving China for the Chinese. Hundreds of years of prayers, petitions and appeals made no impression on the powerful nations of Europe, who were busy exploiting China, but less than one year of fighting made them decide to leave China alone to work out her own destiny. Under the caption, "Want It? Fight for It," Mr. [Arthur] Brisbane[89] of Hearst's publications, writes: "If you want anything, in selfish civilization, fight for it. China starts fighting, and Europe suddenly becomes polite. Russia wishes China well, thinks she should rule herself." [. . .]

Asia has learned what Africa is now learning, that what is worth living for, is worth dying for. But Africa is not asleep, she is in the organization period, uniting her tribes, linking hands with her scattered children in all parts of the world, educating them for the great task of self-government, and instilling in their minds the love of race and the love of country. It is a great task, but once this task is done, the battle will be comparatively easy, for what human forces could be successful in defeating 400,000,000 determined, well-trained Negroes. They have better sense than to try such unequal conflict, they will yield as gracefully as they have yielded to the Chinese. Africa will be redeemed, perhaps, without the shedding of blood. In the meantime:

Africa bides her time! And from the ocean strand
O'er jungle, mountains, vale and mead
The sweet word "unity" will speed on wings of winds
And woo her fretful folk into one dream, one voice, one heart, one hope.
And yet again she'll claim her sacred right
To rule herself apart from alien right.

But if once more the pale face men shall say,
Not yet, thou backward race, still thine to pay;
I quake to think how swarthy arms shall hurl
Thundering terrors at a grasping world
When Africa awakes.[90]

"GOING TO AFRICA?" APRIL 16, 1927

All members of the Universal Negro Improvement Association hope to go to Africa. Their greatest handicap, however, is the necessary cash to get there. But, remembering that cents make dollars, it is only a question of time when the thrifty ones will have their wish. Some will go to stay; others will go to visit friends and relatives. And still others, who may not go in the flesh, yet their bodies will be sent over to rest in peace in the Motherland.

To those who intend to live in Africa, we want to remind them of a few things essential to their well-being and the progress of Africa. First, get a map of Africa, decide within yourself in what direction you are going, and where will be your location. Then find out the fare, and the cost of packing and shipping your household goods. That done you now have a workable figure as to how much money you will need to go, plus extras to maintain you for a few months after you have landed.

The next point to consider is, what are you going to do when you get there. If you cannot read or write, then it is time for you to kick yourself for having missed the opportunity afforded you through free education. Africa does not want illiterate people now. One of the first requests a native will make is, "We want learn book." How would you feel if you had to admit that you can't read yourself[?] What have you been doing in America and other parts of the Western World to improve yourself? Gambling and jazzing? That won't help you in Africa; you will have to leave your bad habits here and only take to Africa that which is helpful.

It is not the numbers that Africa needs, it is the well-equipped, sober, honest few who will act as a leaven for the mass of untrained people there. Where are the farmers who can till the soil with modern machinery, and produce food all the year round? Take your farm implements with you, and let your brothers in Africa see that you have not wasted your time here.

The forests of Africa invite the lumberman with their saw mills. The minerals are under the earth awaiting the shafts of the mineralogists; chemists are required to make experiments; physicians and surgeons are necessary to heal the sick; engineers to bridge the rivers, and shipbuilders to build ships to carry the freight to the markets of the world. Yes, Africa needs skilled men, hard-working men, jobmakers, not job-hunters. The fellow who is looking for a job had better stay right here and keep looking.

It is far better for those who are not fitted for pioneering work to remain here and help those who are equipped to go. Furthermore, those who remain can establish agencies for African products, and conduct an import and export trade, which is a paying concern, if properly handled. Such products as sugar, hides, coffee, rubber, gold, oil, diamonds, platinum and lumber can be sent from Africa by the pioneers in exchange for machinery, cloth and other manufactured goods.

Africa must be redeemed—first through industry and commerce, conducted by Negroes, and political redemption will follow. So, if you are going, know what you are going to do before you start, and if you are staying, know what you are going to do while here. Above all, do something for Africa and stop talking. Let us see action and hear less gab.

Garvey as a Leader While Imprisoned

Marcus Garvey was either under indictment or imprisoned during the entire run of the Woman's Page. Therefore, it is not surprising that Garvey, the man, would be a central topic for many of Jacques Garvey's editorials as the UNIA tried to keep their absent leader alive in the mind of the members. This was especially the case in 1925 (all of the writings here are from this year) when Garvey was sentenced to a five-year term to be served in Atlanta Federal Prison. "Go Ye Into All the World and Preach the Gospel of Garveyism!" was published shortly after Garvey was imprisoned on February 8. As was the case in many references to Garvey, his message is compared to the message of Christ. "Garvey in Prison but Garveyism at Large," "If Garvey Dies in Prison, What Then?" and "Imprison a Leader and You Boost His Cause" are upbeat messages emphasizing that despite Garvey's imprisonment, the movement continues. The leader himself is seen as being patient, cheerful, and brave in his suffering; his spirit cannot be crushed. In "Lest We Forget," Jacques Garvey makes perhaps the most explicit connection between Christ and Garvey (the article itself was published on December 26, almost perfectly coinciding with Christ's birth). She reminds the reader of the noble suffering of Garvey in prison during this joyous season and urges them to remember him, stating that they should go into their church (Liberty Hall) "and join in the well-known hymn: 'God Bless Our President.'"

"GO YE INTO ALL THE WORLD AND PREACH THE GOSPEL OF GARVEYISM!" FEB. 14, 1925

All movements for national and racial expression have met with opposition; even by those to be benefited by the progress of such movements. Through a system of intimidation and bribery the powers in control of weak and unorganized groups make every effort to crush the rising spirit of self-consciousness among those whom they desire to subjugate and exploit; hence he who initiates such movements for freedom and liberty must be prepared to encounter opposition, persecution and treachery, in his own ranks.

The struggle for emancipation politically, religiously or racially is always a long drawn out fight, carried on sometimes for centuries; while its advocates pay the price in money, property and blood. Marcus Garvey knew all this when he started his great organization and made up his mind to bear the sacrifices necessary in the struggle upward. Therefore, his enemies find in him a brave soldier, who knows no defeat until the cold hand of death beckons him to follow. Even in death there will be no defeat, for the ground that he has gained will be held by his fellow comrades, who will lift high the flag of the red, black and green and sing, "Advance, Advance to Victory, Let Africa be Free!"[91]

The determination of the millions of members throughout the world to carry on the work of the organization is Marcus Garvey's tower of strength during his imprisonment, and though he cannot be with them in the physical, yet his spirit will lead them to greater achievement and success. He is President-General of the Universal Negro Improvement Association in prison and out of prison, and his strong personality has permeated the hearts of his followers who are obeying his command, "GO YE INTO ALL THE WORLD AND PREACH THE GOSPEL OF GARVEYISM."[92]

"GARVEY IN PRISON BUT GARVEYISM AT LARGE," FEB. 28, 1925

Garvey is in prison—the tiger is bagged[93]; the lion is caged, according to his enemies. They have wired the Warden of the Federal Penitentiary, Atlanta, Ga., to ascertain if he is really behind the high stone walls of the prison; if he is treated like any other Negro in a Southern prison, and the answer comes back, Yes. Some Negroes (who sell their newspapers, not on their merits, but on the mere mention of Garvey's name) had five-inch deep headlines in red on their front page. "Garvey Safely Behind Bars," and "Garvey, in Prison, Loses Identity." The carefully laid scheme "to get Garvey" is successfully accomplished. Rewards are already distributed, and toasts are drunk in honor of the greatest capture of the age. Now that the hysteria is all over, one asks, "Are Garvey's enemies satisfied?" No. They have found out that in their effort to brand Garvey as a criminal, they have made him a martyr. Instead of destroying the Universal Negro Improvement Association by publishing malicious news about it, they have advertised it throughout the length and breadth of the world. In their attempt to disrupt the membership of the organization they have cemented the members together in a closer bond of fellowship and created new friends for the organization among both races. They conjured up in their minds a picture of Marcus Garvey shackled with head bowed down and tears streaming from his eyes, cursing fate for his predicament, or cursing himself for being a fool to have tried "the impossible," and they gloated over the thought of such a picture realized; but how different was the reality. Garvey was shackled, 'tis true, but his head was erect, his eyes bright and sparkling; he smiled to his followers and said, "I expected all this and more; it is the price that one pays for leadership of reform. Carry on until I return."

Garveyites all over the world, instead of being ashamed of the picture of their leader shackled to a white marshal, have framed same and point with pride to it and say to their children, "That's the price he paid because he dared to teach us to say 'Africa for the Africans, those at home and those abroad.'"

Garvey's enemies staged a big play, but it was crudely acted. The plot was too evident from the beginning of the play. The characters put too much personal feeling in acting their parts. Each character acted, not in keeping with the play, but changed the play in an effort to vent their spleen on the "villain." Hence, the "villain" received the applause and sympathy of an admiring multitude. Something was rotten in Denmark,[94] and the world knows it now.

Marcus Garvey, during the last seven years, made every effort to spread his doctrine far and wide, knowing not the day nor the hour when he would be taken from his followers. He caught the ears of Negroes in every nook and corner of the globe, and now, that they have imprisoned Garvey in the physical, the spirit of Garvey or Garveyism goes steadily marching on.

"IF GARVEY DIES IN PRISON, WHAT THEN?" MAY 23, 1925

The persecution of Marcus Garvey which culminated in his imprisonment has won for him and the Universal Negro Improvement Association more sympathizers and followers than thousands of dollars of propaganda and months of canvassing could have done.

In their efforts to "down Garvey," his enemies have outdone themselves. All the adjectives that qualified a villain were employed by them in the hope of destroying the confidence of his followers in him, and to make the public suspicious of him and his movement, but his persecutors were neither diplomats nor psychologists, they hammered him too hard, and in their feverish anxiety to destroy him they showed plainly their malicious, envious motives. The trick is now turned, and Marcus Garvey in prison is heralded as a martyr for the cause he espouses; while his persecutors are sneered at for the selfish, jealous men they are who feared his power and resorted to the meanest methods to get rid of him.

He has been called a fool. Granted that he is a fool, then he is the only fool that the world has ever given so much publicity to and in fairness the adjective should be applied to those who advertise him.

Some say he is a lunatic. If that be so, then he is the only lunatic, in or out of confinement, that causes the statesmen of Europe to fear him.

He is dubbed a dreamer. True, but his dream for his race is the best dream any Negro has had so far, and his efforts to realize it the most creditable, because he has met and overcome so much opposition. Some refer to him as a fanatic, yet those who listen to him and read his reasonable, logical contentions for his oppressed and much abused race, are convinced that such a charge emanated from fanatics, and not from the brains of sound thinkers.

Others say he is ambitious. If it were so, he is ambitious, not for himself alone, but for an entire race. Else he would not have suffered the many privations he has, in order to carry on the work of the association, when with his ability he could have continued his studies and become a prominent lawyer, living in ease with only his family to think for.

Some who do not know him, write of him as an opportunist. If this is true of him as an individual, he would have feathered his own nest, sold out his race when the opportunity presented itself, because he has "the goods" that the powers that control Africa want. He would have compromised when untold wealth was offered him, "to ease up on certain folks," or to retire, but Marcus Garvey elected to remain penniless, and even go to prison, dependent upon the charity of his followers, than to accept the opportunity offered him of wealth and affluence. He is an opportunist for his race, because he has sworn by the memory of his slave-grandparents, that he will seize every opportunity that presents itself in order to better the conditions of his people in communities where they live, and to establish for them a national home, powerful enough to protect them wherever they are domiciled.

Few men would have had the courage to live under the hailstorm of abuse showered on him by his jealous rivals, and fewer still, of like aggressive temperament, could endure the humiliations and cruelties of a Southern prison, without hastening their end. Yet in spite of it all Marcus Garvey smiles, and says to his followers: "Don't fret for me, but carry on, until Africa is redeemed."

All reformers have been misunderstood and persecuted in their day. It is only those who come after them that are able to place a fair estimate on the work of those who suffer, and often die for their ideals. Marcus Garvey smiles, because he realizes this, and knowing his cause is a just one, his objects are pure and righteous, his soul can lift itself from an atmosphere of malice and hate, and as a real Christian he says, "I forgive my persecutors, for they know not what they do."

Hundreds of his followers in this country have signified their willingness to serve the prison term in his stead. Thousands contributed of their moneys to pay the best lawyers to take his case to the highest tribunal in the land. The very Negroes that he is supposed to have defrauded have signed a petition to President Coolidge asking him to pardon their leader. Yet Garvey lingers in prison.

The Negro voters, who regard the mistreatment of Garvey as an insult to the race, are silently watching the outcome of his plea for justice. The millions of Negroes in other parts of the world, who outnumber whites ten to one in some sections, are also silently waiting to see what white America will do with Garvey. His well-being concerns the members of his race everywhere, and they are seeing after it. How long will he be kept in a cold damp prison? Has he been given work in prison that will aggravate his asthmatic condition and cause him to die "a natural death?" they ask. Those who seek to keep him in prison would do well to consider carefully their actions, and ascertain if they are not playing a fool's game after all. Because the Negroes who love Garvey are not confined to any one country, nor even to one hemisphere, but are scattered in every nook and corner of the globe, and long after his maligners have passed away and are forgotten, the name of Marcus Garvey will be revered, and black posterity will pay homage to him as the father of African redemption.

"IMPRISON A LEADER AND YOU BOOST HIS CAUSE," AUG. 15, 1925

It is pleasing to note the awakened consciousness of Negroes everywhere. Traveling as we are from State to State, and visiting the large cities of these United States, receiving letters and dispatches from the remotest parts of the world, we rejoice at the fact that the ideals of economic independence and nationalism expounded by Marcus Garvey have permeated the minds of men and women of African descent everywhere, and no human agency can stop them in their onward march to progress and to power.

The imprisonment of Marcus Garvey has not served the enemies' purposes. On the contrary it has intensified the determination and zeal of his followers, and roused to a sense of sympathetic understanding the apathetic members of his race. White men who did not realize that a new type of Negro made up the membership of the Universal Negro Improvement Association are now alarmed at the growing proportions of the organization, and the large-hearted of them declare that such a splendid group of ambitious people ought to be helped and not persecuted. Yellow and brown men of Asia are reaching out the hand of fellowship to us, and saying, "Let us join forces and throw off the yoke of white oppression."

When a man can serve his people cheerfully and without material gain, in spite of unjust and vicious attacks by his own people, and opposition and persecution by others, then he is truly a leader, and when he can go to prison and although suffering physically send out from week to week the most inspiring messages, surely his enemies are defeated in their plans, and the thoughtful are bound to admit the greatness of such a man and the righteousness of his cause. It is the suffering of martyrs that bring speedy success to any movement, and we are glad that the race at this time can produce one unselfish enough and courageous enough to bear imprisonment and even death for a free and redeemed Africa. His sacrifices are not being made in vain, and although his contemporaries are non-appreciative of him, yet posterity of his own race will bless him, because of his determined and unyielding stand for race and homeland.

The longer Marcus Garvey stays in prison, the bigger strides will the organization take. It may seem paradoxical to say this but it is true. His imprisonment is a blow aimed at independent Negro leadership, and knowing this Negroes are falling in line with the organization, as they never did before, and have pledged their lives to support their own leader, whether he be in New York, Atlanta, Timbuctoo or Liberia. Had Marcus Garvey been "picked" by the white people to lead Negroes, he would have had smooth sailing in his career, because he would have been the mouthpiece and tool of white oppression, hence only hearty co-operation would have come from the system in control, and Negroes would not have dared to oppose the white man's candidate who had financial and political backing. But when Marcus Garvey sounded the tocsin "Africa for the Africans, those at home and those abroad," he trod on the toes of greedy, exploiting European countries, who are tapping the economic resources of Africa, in order to feed their half-starved population[;] when he stated that "Negroes should be governed by Negroes everywhere," he sounded the doom of the Colonial systems of exploitation and aggression by whites, and a strong independent Negro race loomed up on the horizon, which was termed "a black peril." When he declared that "Negroes should evolve a leadership of their own," the white man's candidates for leadership got busy and sought to destroy him, knowing that their salaries and "hands out" would cease, and they would have to lead on their own merits and racial achievements. So these combined forces succeeded in putting him in prison which, apart from affecting his health, has not worried him in the least, because Marcus Garvey has already spent eight years of ceaseless toil teaching his people, and the millions of converts he has gained and the territory that they have covered spreading the gospel of a redeemed Africa is bound to bring about the realization of his dreams in a shorter period of time than he anticipated.

No one can imprison the soul of a man. The mind will soar far beyond prison walls and iron rails. A brave man lives, even in confinement, when his beautiful thoughts are his boon companions, and any movement for the liberation of God's people will prosper if only because of the righteousness of his cause.

"LEST WE FORGET," DEC. 26, 1925

We feel it our duty at this season of the year to remind those of our readers who are members of the Universal Negro Improvement Association that they should not lose themselves in rounds of pleasure and forget the serious side of life as expressed in the aims of objects of this great organization, but that they should assemble themselves in their respective Liberty Halls all over the world and give thanks to God for what has been achieved so far, and pray for added strength and wisdom to carry on to its fruition the grand noble task of Negro uplift and the redemption of Africa.

God, the Father, sent His only begotten Son to redeem fallen man. He was rejected, crucified and buried, yet we commemorate His birth with rejoicing and festivities although nineteen hundred years have rolled by. Many of us profess the Christian religion, yet few practise it, the lack of which causes the world to be in turmoil, and despite the millions of so-called converts to the doctrine of Christ, man is no nearer perfection than when God looked down on a world of sin and sent His Son to direct sinners into the path of righteousness.

If Christian man would adhere to this Divine Command "*Man love thy brother*" there would be no need of machine-guns, poison gases and submarines; there would be no need for Negroes to organize and redeem Africa from exploitation; there would be no need for Negroes to mass themselves to protect their very existence against extermination by selfish, cruel races; but man has fallen short of the glory of God and maybe it needs the second coming of a Messiah to set this old world right and to have peace and good-will on earth as it is in heaven.

We feel sure that every member of the Universal Negro Improvement Association will be saddened in the midst of his rejoicings when one thinks of the founder and leader of this organization in the cold, damp prison in Atlanta, Georgia, suffering for his ideals—a free and redeemed Africa. This is the common lot of reformers—persecution and suffering. No cause for the betterment of any people survives unless it has its martyrs, and none is worth while unless it is opposed. The oppressor has never yielded willingly to the demands of the oppressed; the weak must always gather strength by organization and force the strong to treat him fairly and honorably, and in the course of this process, leaders we must have—men of character and moral courage, who are not afraid to face any danger and to undergo any suffering in the furtherance of a cause. They will be ridiculed and misunderstood by some who don't want to understand them; framed-up and imprisoned, perhaps assassinated; but all these persecutions only tend to strengthen the movement and to gather more converts to the cause, for after all who does not admire a brave man? Who does not sympathize with the persecuted? Leaders do not think of themselves, it is the welfare of others that gives them great concern. Real leadership is a labor of love; it is spontaneous and knows no regrets, no "ifs" and "buts," no hesitancy and no repining; a goal must be reached, a struggling people must be made happy, and the sighs and tears of the oppressed masses are the living urge that presses one forward despite the forces of even Satan and all his hosts. Do you wonder that leaders have been led smiling to the scaffold? Is it strange that a Negro man should be committed to a prison cell for five years, his only comment to his followers being: "Carry on until I return?"

Ah, men and women, when we find such Spartan leaders we should honor them, and try to lighten their burdens incurred in advocating our cause; if we fail, we are ingrates and unworthy of help. Think of home and comforts denied your leader. Picture him, asthmatic and suffering behind four gray walls, and know that leadership is not applause and hurrahs alone, but the test of a strong man. Lest you forget him at this season, enter into your Liberty Hall and join in the well-known hymn:

"God Bless Our President."[95]

Race Pride/ Racial Propaganda

One of the core messages of Garveyism was an emphasis on Black pride in order for Blacks to counter negative images of themselves that predominated White media. Jacques Garvey criticizes the desire of some Blacks to adopt White standards of beauty, and reminds them to honor their own bodies in "Are We Proud of Our Black Skins and Curly Hair?" and "Each Race Sees Beauty in Itself." She counters the notion that there are gradations of race in "The Myth of Superior and Inferior Races." Jacques Garvey was a fervent adherent to the notion that race is a biological designation determined by god. To defy this is to question the wisdom of the creator. She makes her case for the differences between races in "Black Skin Is not an Accident, But Purpose of Creation." One of Jacques Garvey's most intriguing editorials is "I Am a Negro—and Beautiful." In her editorial, she praises Langston Hughes for his "splendid article," commending him for his criticism of those of the race who look askance at those who are "too Negro." She supports his statement that Black writers should not care what Whites think of them but should "express our individual dark-skinned selves without shame or fear." She does not know whether he is a Garveyite or not, but she holds him up as a leader other Black artists should follow.

Propaganda is closely tied to racial pride. In "The High Cost of Propaganda," Jacques Garvey defines propaganda as "a system of educating others to one's viewpoint." She is proud that her own writing and that of others included in the *Negro World* is openly propagandistic. Whites have long used propaganda against Blacks in newspapers, schools, and textbooks.

To combat such pernicious images, she argues, Blacks need their own propaganda: "Money must be spent [on propaganda] and plenty of it." She reinforces the power of propaganda in "White Idolatry in Movies," stating that "Negroes' minds are being vitiated every day with the poison of movie propaganda." Until Blacks demand positive images of themselves in film, the race will continue to revere White actors and actresses. Jacques Garvey stresses that it is possible to reverse negative stereotypes of a group in "Five Mission Dollars for German Propaganda in 1927." As part of the Allied effort in World War I, Germans were portrayed as "Teutonic barbarians." In the ensuing years, Germany invested millions to counter these images. Jacques Garvey wished that the UNIA had the resources to do the same for Blacks.[96]

"WHITE IDOLATRY IN MOVIES," SEPT. 20, 1924

The moving picture industry is one of the most lucrative industries of this age, and has on the other hand been used, particularly by the white race, for propaganda purposes. It is really the most effective method of propaganda at little or no cost to the propagandists. For the reason that people pay to see moving pictures for recreation, and during those hours of relaxation unconsciously swallow more propaganda than months of reading could accomplish. The masses who can't or won't read books go to the movies; hence this method of propaganda is being overworked by those who desire to disseminate certain ideas among certain people.

Negroes' minds are being vitiated every day with the poison of movie propaganda. It is quite time we woke up to the danger of it. Our children, our young men and women become white hero worshippers; they see white; they imitate white. Is it any wonder that they mar their beautiful dark skins and stiffen their curly locks to "look white"? Their scrapbooks abound with faces of white actors and actresses, whom they consider the most beautiful and charming on earth. When their young minds are so trained is it any wonder that they try to "get out of the race"? Is it any wonder they associate clandestinely with members of the other race?

Negro men and women, the evils resultant from a continuance of this form of propaganda are legion, and it is your duty to demand of the theatre managers in your community colored actors and actresses on the silver sheet. Let your children see the beauty of the race in the movies. Let them applaud handsome black men and beautiful black women.

The demand for actors and actresses of our race will not only stimulate race love and respect, but will be a means of providing employment for our intelligent, artistic girls and boys. Therefore from the economical and racial point of view we will be benefited considerably. If we were to take a census of the number of colored movie-goers in the world and compute the amount expended for tickets yearly, it would run into millions of dollars. And all this money goes to support white players and producers. There are only two colored children employed by a white company in Hollywood,[97] and about six colored men and women financed by a Jew, who produced five colored movie dramas. This record is certainly a shame on the race, and if all local theatre managers in colored districts are asked to show colored pictures, they will certainly please their patrons, or be compelled to close their doors. The slogan from now on should be: "Negro plays and Negro players."[98]

"ARE WE PROUD OF OUR BLACK SKINS AND CURLY HAIR?" AUG. 1, 1925

To study the Negro race carefully and to note the lack of initiative, the slothfulness in seizing opportunities, and their warped racial perspective, one is bound to exclaim, "What fools these mortals be!"

Negroes have as much ability as any other peoples, they are more physically fit than any other race; yet because of the iniquitous institution of slavery imposed on them for 300 years in this western world, the sixty odd years of freedom and limited opportunities, have not made them individual racial thinkers, and given them that pride of race and country, the motivating forces of all ambitious peoples.

The average Negro is willing to marry into any other race, some only too glad so that their children may be able "to pass" as white, as Japanese, or as Chinese, as the case may be. It is a common occurrence to hear conversations like this in many West Indian and American Negro homes:

> "My brother is passing for a Spaniard downtown. He got a good job."
> "Suppose he is found out?"
> "Oh, no! He has gone to live on Broadway with white people, and is engaged to a white girl."
> "Do you visit him?"
> "No, I am too dark. If I saw him on the street with his white friends I would pretend not to know him."

The above conversation intimates that a Negro has crossed the racial border. He has forsaken sister, because she is "too dark." He despises the mother that brought him into the world, because she is "too black." Too black for what, you may ask. Is she not made in the image of God? Surely, the Almighty did not make a mistake when he created millions of black men and women. No. He did not, but Negroes have fallen short of the glory of God, and instead of being proud of their black skins and curly hair, they despise them rather than build up a great nation, with a proper economic basis, as other races have done and are doing. Negroes use the laboratories, not to discover serums to prevent disease and experiment in chemicals to protect themselves in case of war, but to place on the market grease that stiffens curly hair, irons that press the hair to look like a horse's mane, and face cream that bleaches the skin over night.[99] Look at God's black masterpiece, after several years of this straightening and bleaching process, and you will see a being that God Himself in anger and disappointment would not recognize, and white men ridicule, because in trying to look like some one else, you admit the superiority of that person. Hence the white man rides to power on the black man's self-inflicted inferiority and proclaims his "white superiority."

Before white women bobbed their hair, black women in this Hemisphere thought it a crime to have short hair, and they spent as much money trying to make their hair grow and buying false braids and switches as they do to buy shoes and stockings. Now that white women have declared that it is unsanitary to have long hair, black women, like monkeys who are incapable of thinking for themselves, echo the chorus, "Long hair is unsanitary," and they, too, shave the nape of their necks, and treasure the boyish bob. It is wonderful! It is so stylish, because white women say it is.

What is the real reason why Negroes want to escape their race? To be perfectly blunt and brief, we say, LAZINESS IS THE ROOT OF THE WHOLE EVIL. The white man has built up great nations, even when he has done so by using the enslaved blacks, and he does not intend to share and share alike with them in the benefits to be derived by citizens of a great nation, caring not how you pray to him, and petition him. He has built up trade, commerce and large industries all over the world, even in the black man's land, and he does not intend to give Negroes an equal opportunity in his economic and industrial life. If the Negro is not satisfied to be used as a peon or a cheap laborer, he can go out and conquer and build like the white man. The yellow and brown races realize the selfish attitude of the white race and they are emulating him in every particular. Now, Mr. Black Man, how long do you expect to close your eyes to the realities, and solve the degraded condition of your race by "jumping the racial fence?"

The Negro masses are to be pitied, but the false leaders are worse than murderers who tell you that miscegenation will cure your ills[.] That by gradual wholesale absorption of the blacks by the whites, the former will come into their glory, and enjoy all the benefits of white civilization. Lazy, good-for-nothing, as we are looked upon by the whites, is this, the highest ideal to which you can aspire? Must the salvation of the race lie in the extinction of the race? No, God forbid that we should lose sight of the Divine purpose of our creation. We of the Universal Negro Improvement Association, under the leadership of Marcus Garvey, are laying the foundation of nationhood, and all that goes to make a prosperous race, so that if we do not live to enjoy the protection and blessings of a powerful black government, our children will, and when we return to our Father in Heaven, we will go to him in the image and likeness in which he created us—fine, ebony skins and curly hair, masters of the earth and all that dwell therein,[100] and fit subjects for the Heavenly blessings in an Eternal Kingdom.

"EACH RACE SEES BEAUTY IN ITSELF," MAY 8, 1926

The Bible teaches that God made men in His own image and likeness,[101] and through scientific deductions we learn that the differences in man's pigmentation and hair are caused largely through the influence of climactic variations. In other words God or nature is kind to the black man when in apportioning him to the torrid regions of Africa he makes him with black skin and frizzled hair, which enables him to withstand the heat of even Equatorial Africa, that defies the white man.

The white man's pale pigmentation is essential for him to live in the frigid zone of the earth, and his straight long hair keeps his head warm. The yellow and brown peoples are made for the temperate zone. Thus, the different distinct racial physiognomy is not an error on the Creator's part, but was intended for the good of all.

The white man in his arrogance believes that all beauty begins and ends within his race, and by every conceivable means of propaganda he endeavors to make others believe likewise. His religious preachments wreak [*sic*] of this propaganda, when he paints a Christ as a white man, surrounded by little white angels with white wings, and takes these pictures into foreign lands, and tells black, yellow and brown heathen (?) about a white God sitting on a white throne.

It is no wonder that Christianity as taught by white men has failed to impress Africans and Asiatics as it should, because they argue that if God is a big white man, he could not be a good spiritual father to them, as he would naturally have the same double-dealing traits of the white missionaries who teach them to sing, "Take All the World, But Give Me Jesus," while these same messengers of God rob them of their lands and minerals.

Yellow men also see beauty in their own race, and glorify their own type on the canvas and by the printed word. The following are the impressions of a cultured Chinese woman who saw white people for the first time:

> The door was suddenly opened, and a tall male 'foreign devil' stood there, smiling all across his face. I knew that he was a man because he wore clothes like my husband's. But he was much taller than my husband and, to my horror, his head, instead of being covered with human hair, black and straight like that of other people, had on it a fuzzy red wool. His eyes were blue, and his nose rose up like a mountain from the middle of his face. Oh, a frightful creature to behold, more hideous than the God of the North in the temple! [. . .][102]

The brown man moulds his gods in his own likeness and thinks his women the most beautiful on earth; insomuch that he tries to keep her from the gaze of the world, and often imposes the death penalty for intermarriage.

The black man in his native habitat is also proud of his type. Africans in Africa believe that black denotes something genuine. They see in "black" the symbol of strength, and their slogan is "The blacker the better."

Unfortunately, Negroes who are descendants of the African slaves who were brought to the Western Hemisphere hundreds of years ago, being overshadowed in the white man's environment, have swallowed his propaganda of white superiority, and in their blindness many became so dissatisfied with themselves that they straightened their hair and bleached their skins in a mad effort to look white, and thereby reach perfection as they thought; but through the efforts of the Universal Negro Improvement Association under the leadership of Marcus Garvey, Negroes have learned to see black and glorify their true type.

God is a spirit, but when He is [v]isualized by Negroes he takes on the form of a black man, for in the worship of God who looks like us, we worship and respect a black ideal; we become satisfied with ourselves as black people; being satisfied with out type, we become proud of our race, grateful to our Creator, and the impetus grows in us to carry out the Divine injunction, "Ye are the Lords of Creation."

"I AM A NEGRO—AND BEAUTIFUL," JULY 10, 1926

Too much cannot be said in denouncing the class of "want-to-be-white" Negroes one finds everywhere. This race destroying group are dissatisfied with their mothers and with their creator—mother is too dark "to pass" and God made a mistake when he made black people. With this fallacy uppermost in their minds, they peal [*sic*] their skins off and straighten their hair, in mad effort to look like their ideal type. To what end, one asks? To the end that they may be admitted to better jobs, moneyed circles, and, in short, share the blessings of the prosperous white race. They are too lazy to help build a prosperous Negro race, but choose the easier route—crossing the racial border. It is the way of the weakling, and in their ignorance and stupidity they advise others to do likewise. As if 400,000,000 Negroes could change their skins over night. And if they could, would they? Seeing that the bulk of Negroes are to be found on the great continent of Africa, and they, thank Heaven, are proud of their black skins and curly hair. The "would-be-white" few are fast disappearing in the Western world, as the entire race, through the preachments of Marcus Garvey, has found its soul, and is out to acquire for itself and its posterity all that makes other races honored and respected.

This urge for whiteness is not just a mental gesture. It is a slavish complex, the remnant of slavery, to look like "Massa," to speak like him, even to cuss and drink like him. In last week's issue of the Nation Magazine, Langston Hughes, a poet, wrote a splendid article[103] on the difficulties facing the Negro artist, in which he described the racial state of mind of a Philadelphia club woman, which is typical of the group under discussion. He states:

> "The old subconscious 'white is best' runs through her mind. Years of study under white teachers, a lifetime of white books, pictures, and papers, and white manners, morals, and Puritan standards made her dislike the spirituals. And now she turns up her nose at jazz and all its manifestations—likewise almost everything else distinctly racial. She doesn't care for the Winold Reiss[104] portraits of Negroes because they are "too Negro." She does not want a true picture of herself from anybody. She wants the artist to flatter her, to make the white world believe that all Negroes are as smug and as near white in soul as she wants to be."

We are delighted with the frank statement of Mr. Hughes in a white magazine; we do not know if he is a registered member of the Universal Negro Improvement Association; in any event his closing paragraph marks him as a keen student of Garveyism, and with stamina enough to express its ideals:

> "To my mind, it is the duty of the younger Negro artist, if he accepts any duties at all from outsiders, to change through the force of his art that old whispering "I want to be white," hidden in the aspirations of his people, to 'why should I want to be white? I am a Negro—and beautiful'! . . . We younger Negro artists who create now intend to express our individual dark-skinned selves without fear or shame. If white people are pleased we are glad. If they are not, it doesn't matter."

Bravo, Mr. Hughes! From now on under your leadership we expect our artists to express their real souls, and give us art, that is colorful, full of ecstacy, dulcent [*sic*] and even tragic; for has it not been admitted by those who would undervalue us that the Negro is a born artist. Then let the canvas come to life with dark faces; let poetry charm the muses with the hopes and aspirations of our race; let the musicians drown our sorrows with the merry jazz, while a race is in the making, and steadily moving on to nationhood and to power.

Play up, boys, and let the world know "we are Negroes and beautiful."

"THE MYTH OF SUPERIOR AND INFERIOR RACES," JULY 31, 1926

Tut-ank-amen, the Boy King of Egypt, is again in the limelight of modern times. The first photograph of his features has been published in the New York Times in the rotogravure section of the 25th inst. It is a profile view, and anyone who has seen both white and Negro people, would be compelled to admit that the features of this youth are Negroid. The golden mask that covered the mummy shows clearly the thick lips and wide nostrils. As the exponents of white superiority cannot claim him as their own, they make no comment as to his racial stock. Of the 140 articles found in the tomb, each tells the history of the first great civilization on the Nile, the most historical river in Africa, and for the matter of that, in the world. One of the most important, is a dagger with a crystal knob, and a blade of iron, which is the earliest known instance of its use, antedating bronze.

The handle of the dagger is of gold, inlaid with precious stones; the sheath is of gold, beautifully embossed, depicting a hunting scene. Crossed over the breast of the royal mummy are his crozier and flail,[105] symbols of his kingly authority and between the hands lay a huge black scarab.[106] The head was covered with a fine linen skull cap held in place by a gold band; among the treasures found are his crown, oil boxes of gold and silver, and his golden collar, and so the king that was carefully and tenderly laid to rest 3,000 years ago has come to light again, as a mute testimony of the glory of the great African Empire, that gave to the world its arts and sciences.

The peoples of African descent should rejoice that the burning of the library at Alexandria only destroyed their written history, but the tombs of the rulers of Egyptian Africa reveal their culture and progress, in an age when they who now boast of being superior peoples were then barbarians. There are no superior and inferior races. Each race group can boast of a distinct and progressive civilization at some period in its history; while one race may be backward at a given period that does not indicate inferiority of the race. Africa, India, China have all had their periods of advanced civilization, so wherefore this boasted superior white race, the foundation of whose history is based on their enslavement?

Mr. V. F. Calverton[107] in a debate in the August issue of Current History Magazine very clearly explains the shifting of civilization to different centers of the world, and proves that the rise and fall of nations is not due to inherent superiority and inferiority but to changes in their environment. He argues: "[. . . I]t was not a matter of race but of change of social and commercial centers that brought the so-called Anglo-Saxon nations to the forefront of civilization. It was a matter of geographical and economic environments and not racial superiorities that were the determining factors in the change."

The cycle of civilization will again shift to Africa—the east will once more be the center of civilization, and knowing this, the Negroes of the world prepare themselves to hasten the day. The untouched wealth of Africa will attract civilization, the geographical situation of this vast continent, and its ability to accommodate surplus populations will cause her again to radiate culture and material progress to the world; but let not that period be dominated by any but her sons and daughters.

"THE HIGH COST OF PROPAGANDA," AUG. 14, 1926

Propaganda is the most effective weapon used in the world today; whether in peace or war man relies on it to gain support for his cause and make friends of hostile forces.

It is a system of educating others to one's viewpoint, and divers are the methods used to bring this about. It is said the allies won the war through propaganda; to a great extent this is so. They depicted the Germans as war-mad, thirsty for blood, ruthlessly destroying Europe, the centre of white civilization, and asked white America if he would withhold men and money in such a crisis. Uncle Sam was forced to succor the allies, because every citizen was made to sympathize with them through allied propaganda.

Today world attention is being focused on Mexico in her effort to keep the church out of politics by enforcing her religious laws. The Roman Catholic Church, which owns millions of dollars of property there, is putting up a stiff fight to thwart government control, and it is interesting to read the garbled reports emanating from Papal agencies, in an attempt to enlist world sympathy and aid. The Knights of Columbus, the strongest Roman Catholic organization in the world, met in convention and appealed to President Coolidge to intervene, which he could not do, since the property of the church was not American property, but belonging to the Pope at Rome, and the lives of Americans were not threatened. [. . .]

One of the most efficiently organized and highly financed is anti-Negro propaganda. Some Negroes are too dull to sease [*sic*] it, and often are the tools used to disseminate it. White newspapers are the organs used to express it. Their method is to portray the Negro as a rapist, thief and gambler, for these deeds he gets a front page location and glaring headlines. His deeds of valor and achievement are ignored by the white press. White movies also play up the Negro in this role, or as a servant, bowing and bending to the white master. Even the white man's religion when interpreted by him to Negroes reek of this racial antipathy. His schools and his textbooks are all in keeping with this vicious scheme. Hence white men the world over have been propagandized to believe that every Negro was low and good-for-nothing. Negroes themselves were taught that they were only fit for servants and that white men were their natural masters. It rested with some one bold and courageous enough to launch and maintain a counter propaganda to educate white and black to the fact that black men first gave civilization to the world, and it is because of the sinister acts of suppression and oppression why Negroes are unable to achieve much in this age as a people.

Nine years ago Marcus Garvey came; single handed he stepped forth, friendless and lacking means, laughed at by his own and persecuted by whites, yet today the world writes Negro with a capital "N," quotes his expressions, and takes him seriously, while the race devotes its energy to building a nation in Africa, and takes pride in its wonderful physique and beautiful black skin.

It took Marcus Garvey nine years of toil and suffering, even his liberty, to bring about this change. It cost the faithful members of the Universal Negro Improvement Association, thousands of dollars to change world opinion about them: yet a few thousand dollars is nothing compared to millions spent by white peoples to keep Negroes in subjection. The veriest tyro is obliged to admit the great feat accomplished by this organization, and knowing the great value of propaganda, Marcus Garvey will continue to invest more money for this purpose. It is money well spent and brings good returns. Nation building is our program, not building apartment houses or churches; that's too small a job for us; and in laying the foundation of a government, we must, of necessity, educate our people up to the standard of knowing what they want, getting what they want, and keeping what they get. These are invaluable assets, yet cannot be seen in brick and mortar. The Anti-Saloon League[108] and the drys spent about thirty million dollars for propaganda purposes in America in order to bring about the prohibition law. They said it was cheaply done at that figure, and so in any attempt to influence a number of people and enlist their sympathy, and educate them to your views, money must be spent, and plenty of it.

"BLACK SKIN IS NOT AN ACCIDENT, BUT PURPOSE OF CREATION," JAN. 22, 1927

We were distressingly surprised to read the following comment in the Kansas City Call of a recent date: "In failure and in success, men are men. Color is an accident, not a limitation put on anyone as punishment." We have weighed the words carefully and cannot understand how a man in the position of a newspaper editor could make such a silly assertion and expect his readers to digest same. Does he really mean to inform us that the Almighty Architect made 400,000,000 "accidents" or mishaps? Has any one heard of white men saying that their pale skins are accidental, or have yellow men made such a complaint? Yet a Negro in America (where his race is the most religious) essays the opinion that his God made a mistake in assigning different "colors" to mankind. Is it any wonder that before the advent of the Universal Negro Improvement Association in this country Negro women thought they were reaching the height of their ambition by pealing [*sic*] their skins and straightening their hair. But Marcus Garvey launched a campaign against such ignorance, and made his race to understand that the differences in the texture of hair and pigmentation of mankind, was the purpose of the Divine Creator in fitting us to inhabit the four corners of the earth.

Negroes have been particularly blest, in that our race is the hardiest of all races, and fitted to live and inhabit the richest continent in the world—Africa. Had it not been for these physical differences our pale-faced brothers would have overrun Africa, and made it a "white man's country." In other words the natives would have been exterminated (as were the Red Indians of North America, if they could not be enslaved), but the good Lord has so planned it that paleskins cannot endure the heat of tropical Africa, and their straight silken hair keeps their heads too hot, which causes them to fall from the heat of the direct rays of the sun, while Negroes are immune, thanks to their kinky hair, which admits air to their brains, and the extra thickness of their skulls protect them.

If, by some miracle, black men in equatorial Africa were to suddenly become white, with straight hair, they would soon die out, as their resistance to the heat lies in their black skins and kinky hair. So the editor above referenced to is misleading his readers when he says "Color is an accident." Since he is so little informed, we would like him to know that "color," as it relates to pigmentation, is to protect man from the fury of the elements.

A New York physician recently opined that Negro babies here were more easily subject to rickets than were the white ones, for the reason that the rays of the winter sun were too weak to have any helpful effect upon the former's black skins, which nature had so constructed as to withstand strong sun rays. It is also generally known that the large nostrils of the Negro caused him to inhale cold air, and incidentally germs, faster than other races, and but for his robust body he would be more easily a victim of disease. So one could readily see that our Heavenly Father never intended that cold countries should be the natural habitat of Negroes, nor equatorial regions the home of whites. It is a plan of creation, for our own good, not an accident. All that is necessary is for Negro men to go out and build up their section of the globe, as white men have done their own.

Laziness and selfishness are their main handicaps, and the color of their skin nature's blessing.

"FIVE MILLION DOLLARS FOR GERMAN PROPAGANDA IN 1927," MARCH 5, 1927

The Associated Press reports from Berlin state that $5,000,000 will be spent for propaganda this year by the German government. This is a wise move, actuated perhaps by the bitter experiences of the war of 1914–18 when Germany was defeated, mainly by allied propaganda. The horrible tales of atrocities in Belgium stirred the white world to united effort to "save civilization from Teutonic barbarians," as nothing else could have done. No one stopped to ascertain the truthfulness or source of the stories; everyone was too high-strung then to reason why, "their's [*sic*] was but to do or die,"[109] with the feeling of saving the world for democracy.

Today the Nationalists of China[110] are defeating their adversaries by the same effective weapon—propaganda. Foreign governments cannot depend on their hireling generals, they in turn are distrustful of their armies. Why? Because the propaganda of the Nationalists teaches their hearts and they fall, not by the sword, but converts to the program of "China for the Chinese."

If we could tell exactly how much England spends yearly for propaganda many of our readers would be surprised, as it is a very large figure, but it should be remembered that England controls her possessions and bluffs the world by reason of her studied and systematic propaganda, disseminated in such a subtle manner that it is digested without the victim being aware of its poison.

Propaganda is advertisement on a large scale. Germany wants the world to get her views, she wants trade, and to be kept in the limelight, therefore, she apportions $5,000,000 for this purpose for the year, a nominal amount, when it is considered that she has to redeem herself in world opinion, and court new friends and allies. It is the same way with a merchant who has been bankrupt and wants to stage a comeback, he has to spend a good deal of money in advertisement, before he can regain his credit and patronage.

Germany wants back her lost colonies in Africa, so that she can have a steady supply of raw materials, without paying for them, so a large portion of the $5,000,000 will be used for propaganda toward this end. Just as Italy propagandizes the world with the idea that "Italy must expand or die," so is Germany saying "We must have raw material for our industries or our machines will stop humming." In other words they are first educating the world to their viewpoint and desires, when they think they have enough converts, they will go and grab the lands they desire.

Marcus Garvey has been called one of the greatest propagandists of this age, because he is one of the few men that saw the great worth of propaganda in the year 1917, and started to use it, in his effort to educate black men to see the necessity for African Nationalism, and to get white men to appreciate the righteousness of his cause.

One of his hardest tasks is to get "wise" Negroes to realize the value of propaganda. To them it is money wasted, because the benefits derived are not seen in dollars and cents, or brick and mortar. The Knights of Columbus, a Roman Catholic organization in America, voted $1,000,000 at its last convention for propaganda work for the year. If the Universal Negro Improvement Association had done this, a howl of protest would have gone up from "big Negroes" for "wasting the people's money." They would contend that the money could be invested in real estate in America, an investment that he has no means of protecting against white Christian mobs that may covet it, and an investment that would not benefit Negroes outside of America who finance the organization.

To get the Negroes of the world to know that there are 400,000,000 of them breathing God's air; to get this number to realize that they are men and women, not dogs or monkeys; to get them to know that the Creator made them lords of the earth, not to be slaves or peons for other races; to remind those in alien lands that Africa is their ancestral home and it is their duty, in common with those at home, to make of it an earthly paradise, this is the task Marcus Garvey, with God's help, has set out to do. Agents of white governments may persecute him, ignorant, jealous Negroes may scoff at him, but the work goes on just the same. Handicapped by lack of funds, harassed and thrown in prison, yet his spirit soars high above the mean tactics of those who seek his destruction, and in a clear, determined voice he continues to cry "Africa for the Africans," while the tom-toms relay the glad tidings to the remotest corners of the motherland, and languages and dialects re-echo the sound to a startled world. Truly propaganda is a wise investment.

PART 3
POST-WOMAN'S PAGE EDITORIALS

Although the Woman's Page ceased on April 30, 1927, Jacques Garvey continued to write editorials for the *Negro World*. They tended to be similar in subject matter to many of her earlier editorials, but often were slightly longer, which allowed her to elaborate a bit on some of her topics. She discusses problems women face in "A Dearth of Husbands" and "Mothers and Vacation." In the former essay, Jacques Garvey laments the bleak marital prospects of women of the race: "Where can she find a responsible husband who can in truth be called the head of the house; and who would shoulder the financial burdens, and leave her free to manage her house and expand her intellectual gifts?" In the latter essay, she bemoans the devaluing by husbands and children of the ongoing work that mothers engage in on a daily basis. She expresses the belief that mothers need at least a few days of vacation time to re-energize.

She engages political subjects in "Experiments in Government," a pithy examination of "Monarchism, Republicanism, Sovietism and Fascism." "Color-Baiting America" speaks of Whites condemning the atrocities committed by Asians while ignoring those committed by Whites against Blacks in America. Jacques Garvey awaits the day when "a grouping of yellow and brown, and perhaps black" will rise up against their oppressors. "Frenzied Attempts to Make Temperate Africa White" contemplates efforts by Whites to populate the more hospitable areas of Africa. "The Future Control of Africa" is Jacques Garvey's fullest discussion of an eventual battle between Whites and Blacks for control of Africa." "What Makes A First-Class Nation?" is one of her most militant writings, advising Blacks to defend themselves from other races by force if necessary. They

> "must serve others in their own coin, and speak to them in a language they will understand."

"WHAT MAKES A FIRST-CLASS NATION?" MAY 28, 1927

All ambitious youths hope some day to have a home of their own and to become prosperous.The feeling of independence and the desire to direct one's own life is natural, and exerts itself as maturity approaches. Even so all self-respecting groups of humanity long for the day when they will be able to direct their own affairs in their own homeland, and rise to the pinnacle of greatness and achievement. It matters not whether their selfish guardians think them competent or not, independence is a natural growth that cannot be permanently suppressed. It is bound to find an outlet somehow, and gathers greater force when impeded.

Love of home and love of county are two great urges that cause men to give up their lives gladly in defense and protection. It is the right to possession, occupation and use that makes him love it and want to hold it inviolate against all intruders. The glorious privilege of saying, "This is mine" urges them to hurl themselves on cannons and suffer untold hardships. [. . .]

A first-class nation, in this age, must be able to protect itself at a moment's notice, and keep abreast with all other nations in the acquirement of all devices for such protection, as civilized man only fears force. Such nations in the making must be made up of men and women who are not afraid to die, and whose brains must be ever busy devising methods and means for protection, and the striking of the blow for recognition. He must serve others in their own coin, and speak to them in a language they will understand. No other effort will be effective.

"A DEARTH OF HUSBANDS," JULY 9, 1927

There is usually a hesitancy among most people in discussing sex problems, yet such matters are vital to our very existence. Laws governing marriage, divorce and illegitimacy are largely made by men without consulting the feminine sex in the matter, therefore both Eastern and Western standards weigh heavily on women.

The East has just begun to emerge from polygamous practices, which permits a multiple of wives according to a man's ability to support them, while its proponents contend that the system eliminates prostitution and social diseases, yet the ignorance and subserviency of the women retards the progress of those countries.

Monogamy, while supposedly a Western system, is just a theory, the practice of which amounts to indiscriminate polygamy (only one union at a time being legal), which brings in its wake social and mental diseases, poverty and bastardy. Western customs create a double standard of morality. Men have a free license for self-indulgence, while women who indulge likewise become social outcasts.

The spread of the knowledge of birth control has tended to increase sexual indulgence, and this in turn is causing young men to refrain from marriage. Why? Because their physical desires can be satisfied without the responsibility of caring for a wife and without the danger of supporting illegitimate children. The young girl of marriageable age waits in vain for marriage proposals; she must lower herself by resorting to furtive pleasures or employ repressive control, which finally lands some in insane asylums or causes them to be nervous wrecks. The normal physical function of women is to bear children, and when healthy women are prevented from so doing a nervous reaction sets in.

Negro men—who, by the way, detest any sort of responsibility—contend that the reason they do not care to become husbands is because they are not fit for the task economically. But we feel that since they make very little effort to lift themselves to the standard of economic independence, they really have not the proper appreciation or love for their women, and this is the basic reason for the low status of the race and the insults heaped on Negro women by white men.

American Negro women are their own breadwinners, whether they are married or not, and practically their only source of employment is in white men's factories or homes. They are therefore subject to the wiles of such men, who abuse them for pleasure. What can the poor women do? They must either work or starve; quite often they have children dependent on their labor, and the thought of those little ones in need impels them to put up with insults and hardships so as to be able to provide for them.

How often one sees groups of men during the day standing outside pool parlors, leaning against speakeasies as if to give them physical support, and their conversation is in this strain: "My old lady is a good chef, she makes $20 a week"; next voice: "Oh man, mine can't be beat, she makes $40 a week in the factory during the rush and can clean up some good overtime." Third voice: "Say, don't you know my wife does [a] day's work—four,ten a day and carfare—and when I get home the house is all cleaned up and my dinner just sitting on the stove waiting for me." In order to keep up appearances many women tolerate lazy husbands, but their bragging to bachelors about their hard-working wives puts the latter in the frame of mind of doing likewise. They argue: "If George can get a Jane to work for him, I can get one too." The result is lazy husbands or no husbands at all. The ambitious intelligent young woman who is not disposed to support her husband is therefore made to suffer. Where can she find a responsible husband who could in truth be called the head of the house; one who would shoulder the financial burdens, and leave her free to manage her house and expand her intellectual gifts?

We have frankly outlined the situation and hope that our male readers, especially the younger ones, will see the far-reaching effects of their attitude toward marriage and wives, and so act as to prevent a continuation of the existing conditions, and exhibit those sterling qualities of real manhood that go to make up a progressive race and a powerful nation.

"MOTHERS AND VACATION," AUGUST 20, 1927

Only two weeks more left for vacationists! Some persons delight in going off the last two weeks in order to escape the mid-season rush, since a real vacation to some is not the idea of meeting people, but avoiding people, and a chance to enjoy nature at its fullest, with the least possible human contact.

Many of us have not had a vacation in years, like this writer; yet we are appreciative of the great benefits derived from a vacation—change of air, change of scenery, rest from work, a chance to meditate and formulate new plans and resolves for the coming fall. Two weeks of real rest and change is worth a year's doctor's bills.

If we would care for our bodies as diligently as we care for a delicate piece of machinery there would be less sickness and death and humanity made happier because of less grief. But most of us forget that our bodies need rest at times. We keep on working until there is a complete collapse, then there are the usual regrets—"If I had known." Much money has now to be spent for doctors, nurses, medicines and nourishment, and finally the doctor orders you away for a change—the same thing that you needed months ago, and which could have saved you so much expense and worry.

Persons who are so employed that they cannot get a week or two off for vacation, can certainly use their weekends for outings to nearby country resorts or sea beaches. This arrangement is helpful to large families who cannot afford to rent a cottage or pay big hotel bills. And while we are thinking of large families, let us remind our readers of the worn-out mothers of such families. It is generally believed that if all the children are away mother can have a fine rest. But rest is not all she wants, and furthermore she is just likely to busy herself with getting the children's clothes ready for the reopening of school, preserving fruits and changing the rooms around, and at the end she will be prostrated with backaches. Mother needs, not only rest, but an entire change of surroundings. Men have a grand way of saying to housewives: "Oh, you are home all day; I don't see why you should be tired." Yet these same men would not have the patience to stand one-fifth of the annoyances incumbent on a housewife. Hers is a nerve-wracking job—she must make a dollar do the work of two; try to please every crank in the family; nurse them when they are sick and soothe their griefs; yet her work is not really appreciated, and she is the last to be thought of when vacation period comes around. Let this be a reminder to father and children to see to it that mother gets a few days' vacation before the hot days are gone.

"THE FUTURE CONTROL OF AFRICA," SEPT. 17, 1927

Not until the advent of Marcus Garvey with his slogan of "Africa for the Africans" has there been any serious questioning as to the future control of Africa. That this immense continent was parceled out among the strong European nations[1] was a fact, and the idea of Africans at home and abroad ever trying to regain control of all of it was not even thought of it, [*sic*] much less seriously considered. But ten years of intensive campaigning under the magic slogan, "Africa For the Africans At Home and Abroad," has awakened Ethiopia's children to such an extent that, white thinkers are asking the world this question, "to whom will Africa eventually belong?" Before we enter into a discussion of this question, we would like to review the reasons why Africa is such a prize to European Powers. First, Africa has twelve million square miles of land and the products of this great continent are numerous and varied. According to W. D. Hubbard, a white resident of South Africa writing for The Nation Magazine:

> "[. . .] No one who studies the climate and geology of Africa can fail to appreciate her enormous economic resources. [. . .] Will the whites surrender their large concessions in response to demands for land by the natives? Or will they try to segregate the blacks and hold them in reservations? [. . .] I feel that there are three possibilities—first, that Africa will eventually be a black country; second, that the whites will wipe out the blacks; third, that whites and blacks will interbreed and produce a new brown race which will control the wealth of Africa. I believe in the inevitable eventuality of a black Africa. [. . .]"

Now, let us test out Mr. Hubbard's statements. He asks: "Will the whites surrender their large concessions in response to demands for land by the natives?" We would like to know if there is a single European nation that honestly negotiated with Africans for concessions in Africa and kept the terms of their agreement. Every fair-minded person of intelligence knows that from the Sahara desert to the cape[2] there is not a square mile of land under the control of white nations that was not secured by chicanery or taken at the point of the gun from peaceful Africans, and is it not then logical to assume that if a man robs something from you when you are unarmed and unprepared, when you arm yourself and realize the value of the article stolen from you, that you will endeavor to get back your property?

As to the question of segregation and holding the blacks on reservations, we ask in all seriousness: "Can a handful of whites do this to nearly three million[3] blacks? Even, although the handful of whites have the modern implements of destruction of the combined European Powers that exploit Africa, yet God in his infinite mercy and goodness has so created us physically that white men cannot live and thrive, much less fight, in numbers in tropical Africa.[4]

It is true that the whites have developed plantations and mines, but at whose expense? By the sweat and blood of the African, who cannot enjoy the benefits of his labor and sacrifice until he ousts his oppressor. The improvements in Africa rightfully belong to the African who toiled to make them, and so far the whites who supervised the work, repaid through their exploitation of the country's wealth for these many years.

As to Mr. Hubbard's second surmise that the whites may wipe out the blacks. The only way that could be done is by spreading disease germs among them; and pray in what manner would the whites be benefited, when they themselves could not labor to take from the bowels of Africa its wealth, as the climate is deadly to them. Even in South Africa where the climate is temperate, the whites would not be procreative if they had to do laborious work.

As to Mr. Hubbard's third surmise that the whites and blacks may interbreed and produce a new brown race. This is a joke, as a handful of whites interbreeding with nearly three hundred million blacks, is like putting a teaspoonful of milk in a gallon of coffee; Negro blood is so strong that it can be traced unto the third and fourth generation.

Yes, Mr. Hubbard's first surmise is correct. Africa will be a black country, only the tint will be slightly brown in the extreme north and south because of alien mixture and a more temperate climate.

Mr. Ormsby Gare,[5] Under-Secretary of State for the British Colonies after touring West Africa stated in a speech to his colleagues: "Nobody can pretend that any part of British West Africa is ever going to be a white settlers' country. [. . .] The white man can only be a supervisor, and only a supervisor with very frequent spells of leave after comparatively short tours in the country."

This is a very frank confession for the guidance of white men in their future dealings with Africa—They would love to hog all Africa for themselves, but they just can't; their white skins and straight hair make them unable to live and thrive in sunny Africa. No sense of fairness or altruism causes Mr. Ormsby Gare to warn white men that West Africa can never be their home, as he admits, there is no political consideration, but the climate forbids them. This grasping conscienceless, and unfair disposition of the white man is what prevents him from being really happy. When he learns to practise the maximum [*sic*] "live and let live," he will know what true happiness is, because his conscience will be clear before God and man.

"EXPERIMENTS IN GOVERNMENT," SEPT. 24, 1927

GOVERNMENT—FOUR KINDS

There are many different forms of government, but the outstanding ones which are battling to exist are Monarchism, Republicanism, Sovietism and Fascism.[6] Monarchism has had its day, and the Divine right of kings to rule has passed into antiquity, leaving the few crowned heads of Europe as mere symbols under the control of dictators and prime ministers. Republicanism has flourished best in the United States of America, but still a large number of citizens complain that the working man is merely a wage-slave and Communism would give all an equal share in this world's goods. Citizens of color also complain that the democratic principles on which the republic is based, and "the holier than thou" attitude it assumes, is a farce and a lie, as millions of them while being taxed to the limit are denied the rights of citizens, and their lives and property are not protected by the States.

Sovietism and Fascism are new experiments in government, and as such they are being modified and changed daily in an effort to meet the exigencies of the times. Sovietism as represented in Russia is particularly interesting in that it gives equal representation in its council to worker, peasant and soldier, but on account of its social system of communal interest of goods the condition arises where, because of lack of competition in trade, the country stagnates. Fascism as Mussolini of Italy exemplifies it, is absolute dictatorship, the mind, body and soul of Italy being in the hands of one man. While Mussolini in pursuing this policy has pulled Italy out of the financial mire and given her new life politically, yet many Italians say, "Our mouths are muzzled, we dare not act as free men, or express our opinions in the press or on the public platforms; our country is being run by a despot against the wishes of the masses."

Since we find flaws in all forms of governments, then the same question suggests itself to us that Mr. H. G. Wells[7] asked in his article in the New York Times dated 18th inst.: "Whether the political system we live in is to be regarded as an end in itself, a divine unquestionable thing, or whether it is to be considered merely a transitory means to a greater end, to be judged on its merits, to be used, altered and in the end gradually or completely replaced by something better."

Mr. Wells applies this question to the British Empire, and in order that his readers may arrive at a fair verdict, he makes the following indictment against those who control its destinies. The indictment, by the way, is very mild in comparison with the cruelty and oppression practiced by those who are obsessed with the idea of expanding the empire. He states:

> "A British Empire which does not seem to me to be realizing the wide and generous dreams of the liberal imperialism with which the century began

> is of no use to me and I do not believe the universe will suffer it to continue. For ten years I have seen the empire going heavily and dully about its business. I have seen it made an excuse for much meanness and clumsy violence. It suffers in credit and direction by the hard 'loyalty' of stupid adherents and stupid representatives who do not understand how gracious and mighty a civilizing organization it could be. They control it and they cripple it. It carries a vast crowd of parasites who snatch, monopolize and profit in its name. It has lost moral prestige in Ireland, in India, in China and before all the world. Enormously. Perhaps even fatally." [. . .]

It does one's soul good to hear an Englishman of Mr. Wells's standing take his rulers to task about the beneficial function of his government. But he excels in his pen pictures of the "loyal" subjects and the universal system that makes them commit crimes "for king and country." He states:

> "Behind this personal abjection lurks moral corruption, a sort of collective scoundrelism. You must not trade fair and square, you must favor 'empire' goods. You must not publish the scientific truth, but make whatever you discover an 'empire' secret. You may spy, you may lie, for the 'empire's' sake. Such 'loyalty' I repudiate as an insult to humanity. I refuse my pinch of incense on that altar."

Mr. Wells is a free thinker,[8] and is inclining toward the larger brotherhood, but it is my belief that the white race will have to suffer defeat through its big nations at the hands of one or two of the darker races before white men will reconcile themselves to the fact that we are all God's children and should share and share alike in this world's goods.

We watch with interest the experiments in government of the white race, and when we realize our dream of government on a larger scale it will be a democracy in the truest sense of the word, for the benefit of all classes, where money and color will not be the standard by which one will be measured, but by his service to humanity. Happiness for all is our aim, and for that we strive.

"COLOR-BAITING AMERICA," OCT. 29, 1927

Early this year William Randolph Hearst,[9] who owns a string of newspapers in this country, announced to the world his plans for an English-speaking union. This announcement was the climax to a series of subtle maneuvering to influence politicians to get closer to England. Now the American public is asked to believe that such a union will "save the world for democracy," and in order to make them believe in the expediency of Mr. Hearst's plans, his newspapers, from time to time, publish articles and pictures showing the danger of Asian invasion of Europe or America. To him the danger is always imminent, and England and America are asked to embrace each other as blood brothers and form a white vanguard against yellow and brown Asia.

This proposition suits England, as America is the world's banker, and Uncle Sam's marines in the Pacific could be requisitioned to help hold up the standard of white supremacy in India, and keep Australia white. As to the benefits America will derive from such a union, it seems as if John Bull will wink at Uncle Sam's distributing his Marines in Central America, and perhaps hand him over one or two West Indian Islands, in appreciation of any service rendered in Asia.

In keeping with propaganda in favor of the proposed English speaking union, this week the Hearst Syndicate published three hideous pictures, one a Mongolian woman sentenced to death by starvation in a wooden box with an aperture only large enough to hold her head and one hand; the other a Lama with a heavy chain around his neck; and the third that of an image with drawn sword and vicious expression. [. . .]

It does seem peculiar that an American artist should, in his imagination, picture such horrid pictures of Asia, yet he has overlooked much more hideous and real pictures of the beautiful Southland where Negroes are subject to the most fiendish deaths for being suspected of insulting white women. Why see Asia in imagination, and overlook Georgia, Texas and Mississippi in reality? Surely hate-loving white America does not need this continuous dose of propaganda for her to decide whom she should help in case of a European and Asiatic war.

But all this is a camouflage, as Mr. Hearst and his editors well know that an Asiatic invasion of Europe is a long way off. Asia does not want European lands, nor is she in a position to start wars of aggression, all that Asia wants at present is to be left alone to work out her own destiny, and that her nationals should be respected by white nations.

This equitable treatment neither Europe nor America is prepared to accord Asia, hence the color-baiting propaganda to further enrage these nationals against Asia, and to becloud the issues with hate and suspicion.

Any combination of white nations to form a race unit, will perforce cause a grouping of yellow and brown, and perhaps black, in retaliation, and it will certainly not be a pleasant time if they clash. We hope that the far-seeing statesmen of the world will work toward a peaceful adjustment of all differences and prevent such a clash.

"FRENZIED ATTEMPTS TO MAKE TEMPERATE AFRICA WHITE," NOV. 26, 1927

Within the last few years there has been a frenzied attempt to get emigrants to the temperate zones of Africa in such numbers as would even approximate half of the black population, but this has not been accomplished, even although the English Government has in every way helped the immigration scheme. The whites are still a very long way off from reaching the half-mark of the blacks, and so the campaign goes on with greater force and better inducements are offered to Europeans to fill up the open spaces of temperate Africa, as the present settler will not be able to hold the natives in check very much longer, notwithstanding their plentiful supply of aeroplanes and machine guns.

Fortunately, nature has been kind to Africans living in the tropical belt, which includes all West Africa, as well as the central portion: the climate is so warm that Europeans cannot live there and thrive, so they hope to hang on to Africa by controlling the Eastern and Southern portions to the exclusion of the natives.

The following excerpt from the speech of a white settler in Southern Rhodesia gives one an idea of the comparative populations, and how they hope to cope with the situation: [. . .] "We must, in the face of the facts, grow at a totally different rate [i]f we are ever to attain a position of strength in this part of the globe. The pace we must make is not that which we prefer, but that dictated by the grim giant Necessity. It is the same as in other races in life, namely, the pace which our competitors call."

Why all this anxiety to live in Africa one may ask? And we supply the answer in the words of one Major Percy Inskip,[10] one of the campaigners for "more whites in Africa." Of course, he only refers to Rhodesia, a colony founded by a consumptive Englishman named Cecil Rhodes, but the inducement holds good for all Africa. Major Inskip states: "The new settler is secured of a hearty welcome from a progressive and hospitable community, and when it is remembered that Southern Rhodesia is an exporter of gold, coal, asbestos, chrome ore, mica, maize, tobacco, cotton, and cattle [. . .] you will understand why I say that I shall be surprised and disappointed if the population of Southern Rhodesia is not at least doubled within the next ten years."

The white man is in Africa for all he can get out of Africa. He knows the value of minerals and the possibilities of fertile lands, and he further knows that Europe is over-populated and bankrupt, and in order to make a future for his children, he is trying to establish a firm foothold in temperate Africa. We contend that the white man should remain in his own native habitat, but he retorts with the argument of Prof. [William J.] Sollas[11] in his "Prehistoric Man"—"It is not priority of occupation, but the power to utilize, which established a claim to the land." We, of African descent, in the Western Hemisphere, know the value of minerals and fertile lands, and those of us who are true Garveyites mean to go back and possess the land that is ours by Divine right and every law of Nature. The white man's argument is, in everyday language, if a Kaffir[12] is sitting on a heap of diamonds playing with them as if they were stones, and refusing to give them to him, the only logical thing to do is put a bullet through the Kaffir's head and take the diamonds. The argument of shot and shell has been used on the African for a long time, and now that we Western World Africans know all that the white men know, we are going to Africa to teach our brothers how to utilize all the wealth that God so benevolently bestowed on the country. We are going despite the obstacles placed in our way by white governments, who would like to hog the whole world for their race.

The British Government that works secretly to keep Western World Negroes out of Africa, does everything to help and encourage English emigres to go there. [. . .]

Mr. Black Man of the Western World, it is up to you to help your brothers in Africa hold their own against white intruders. Africa has the numbers, we must supply the brains, the skilled labor, and leaven the black population. After that Nature will take its course, and no influx of whites will prevent Africa from being the home of black men. Study the map of Africa and see where your destiny lies. Righteousness must triumph over tyranny, and Ethiopia will rise in her majesty.

PART 4
SPEECHES

Jacques Garvey was a popular figure at UNIA meetings. She was frequently asked to address audiences and was considered to be an effective speaker. Marcus Garvey took advantage of his wife's popularity, but he also had concerns about her as a possible rival, so her speeches were usually brief and were not often recorded in the *Negro World*. As he once half-jokingly remarked, "Now I have a rival, but I am glad she is my wife" (qtd. in James 145). Presented here are three written accounts of her remarkable speechmaking skills. "Mrs. Amy Jacques Garvey in Telling Speech Points out Need for Sacrifice on Part of Each and Every Member," "Mrs. Garvey Delivers Ringing Message to White Women of London at Great Meeting; Tells of Insults and Suffering," and "Mrs. Amy Jacques-Garvey at Bermuda" provide a rare glimpse into Jacques Garvey's abilities as a stump speaker. In the first speech, she touches on many common subjects including the need for total dedication to the race. In the next she appeals, sometimes subtly and sometimes emphatically, through the commonality of their gender and Christian faith. What is most astounding is that she is able to chastise the false claims of British Christianity while in the heart of the Empire. In the final speech, she forcefully defends herself against charges from government officials that she is in opposition to the colonial Bermudan government. She reminds her audience that she is not calling for all Black Bermudans to go to Africa, but she feels it would be wonderful if they could send a representative to the Pan-African nation that Garveyism preaches. Thus, she is cleverly advancing exactly the message that the British officials fear: an independent Black Bermudan government.

"MRS. AMY JACQUES GARVEY IN TELLING SPEECH POINTS OUT NEED FOR SACRIFICE ON PART OF EACH AND EVERY MEMBER," JULY 4, 1925

Tonight was Women's night at Liberty Hall, and an excellent program, with women as the only participants, was enjoyed to the full by the thousands who throng the hall Sunday night after Sunday night to receive inspiration to new endeavor.

Mrs. Amy Jacques-Garvey, wife of the president-general, was the principal speaker, and received enthusiastic applause as she spurred the women of the race to greater efforts, scored the men who had failed the cause and broken their vows, and told of her distinguished husband's unmeasurable devotion to the cause of African Redemption. [. . .]

Mrs. Garvey's Address

"The call of service to humanity, and particularly to one's race, means sacrifice," said Mrs. Amy Jacques-Garvey, as she explained her presence in Liberty Hall that evening even though she was ill, "and the men and women who are not prepared for sacrifice had better not shoulder the thing called service to race.

"We, at this time," she continued, "must be prepared to give our all to this organization. If we are not prepared for such service and such sacrifices we cannot hope to get anywhere. It is not merely a matter of attending meetings, or paying dues to the organization, but it is a question of giving one's whole life to the cause. We have only to look back at the organizations of white men, organizations with great objects in view, that have started from small beginnings, and note the sacrifices that have willingly been made. In the case of the Egyptian movement, the Gandhi movement and the back-to-Palestine movement, we see great sacrifices being made.

We have not started to make big sacrifices. Garvey is the only one who has made an appreciable sacrifice for his race, and many others are to follow. I wish I could say tonight that as many as have stood here and sworn to serve you had truly served you and not betrayed you. If those who had served from the beginning were faithful, we would have accomplished even greater things than we have accomplished today. Garvey would not now be serving five years in Atlanta penitentiary, for he would have had associates and co-workers around him instead of Judases and time-servers. You can't expect one man to shoulder the burden of a race and accomplish wonders. All those associated in leadership must be of like minds, prepared to serve and to sacrifice. Men must understand that when they essay to lead and serve us they must give all or we will take all from them, and if the men do not realize their responsibilities we women must make up our minds to assume the responsibility, if it takes our lives.

White men are serving their race, yes, to the very limit. They are giving their all. They can see none other than a great white race, superior in strength, in finance and in all the things that go to make for worth and material achievement and greatness. Yellow men are doing the same. Only today we read in the New York American where a white American related, how in his visit to Japan he had seen the wonderful preparations being made by that country for the great war that will face the world. And who can blame them? If nations do not prepare, if disorganized peoples and groups do not prepare, their future will be all misery and they will be face to face with extermination. And if after seven years of teaching you do not understand and realize for yourselves all that Garvey has been trying to show you, then you are not worth the salt you eat and you are not deserving of the life you live.

This is a serious age. I wish I had the gift of oratory and the strength to speak to you as I would like at this time. I wish you could see the danger which confronts you at this time. But, unfortunately, there are some of us who will agitate trifles and discuss and lambast our neighbor, and cannot see the evil that impends. And the nearer it approaches, the more you seem to ignore the peril which comes thundering on you. It is not a matter of individuals, for individuals are not worth much, but it is a matter of the combined whole. And if you continue to waste your time and energy fighting among yourselves, being jealous of each other, being envious of each other, airing foolish talk about place of birth and what not, you will not get anywhere, and the other fellow will swallow us up.

Each and every one of us has our part to play. There are many who have not the education or the ability for leadership, but you must remember that those that follow are as valuable as those that lead, because it is the following that makes up leadership. And if you are not good followers, how can you be leaders? And when you select leaders take care to select the proper ones. The only question to consider is whether the Negro will serve you and serve you well, and if you elect a man this year and next year when the organization doubles its membership and has twice as much work to do he can't measure up, you have no other recourse but to put him out.

This organization is going along and we must keep pace with it, and when you have men who don't measure up to the exigencies of the moment, who will not interpret world events and speak to you as Marcus Garvey would, it is no use bothering with them; let them get down and give place to worthier men.

There are some people who believe in marking time. This is not the age of marking time. The world is moving forward at a rapid pace; events that took ten years in the accomplishment are now being accomplished in one and two years and if the Negro sits down and thinks like his great grandfather, he will soon find the chains around his wrists. Don't you realize how much harder it is to get jobs now than two years after the war ceased? Don't you see how much more difficult it is for women to find employment? Can't you see the terrible economic depression as far as my race is concerned? And if you will fathom it out and make the proper inquiry you will find it is the outcome of the other fellow's system to keep you under his heel. He has found that, as the world and civilization are today, it is difficult to enslave you by actual legislation, but by the economic weapon he can reduce you to complete dependence, to actual physical slavery, whether you realize it or not, and if you Negroes do not get busy and cooperate and think, you will revert to a condition of peonage and slavery, a condition where you will be glad to work for a dish of coarse food and something to wear.

Mr. Garvey had these things in mind when he started the steamship line—that the products from Africa and the West Indies could be brought to this country and could be manufactured here, giving employment to you Negroes in your own factories, and the manufactured goods taken back to those countries, thereby building up trade and commerce for the whole Negro race. And when you build up that commerce you will be able to employ your own people, you will be able to live like men and women, and you will be able to link up yourselves with your brothers and sisters across the seas. But there are some foolish Negroes who will not see Garvey's plan. They talk about apartment houses. Apartment houses are all right, but what have you got to protect them? And so Garvey was far-seeing enough to know that anything you built here would not be lasting until you made efforts along national lines to protect what you have.

The world today respects power. You can't fight a man with your fists when he has a gun. And what it took to make other races great and keep them strong and powerful we must acquire. We cannot be contented to be the wards of any particular nation. America has freed us. We are no longer slaves. We are a free people and it is for us to look out for ourselves. White America feels that she is under no obligation to protect us.

We must cease betraying each other. Indeed, had we kept our language we would not have had so many traitors today.

The case of the Jew is a case in point. His case is analogous to ours. He strives and builds, progressively and aggressively, and his unity and cooperation is amply rewarded. But thank God we see every sign that the African is awake and is redeeming himself, and it is for us to play the important part we can in making that redemption speedier and surer.

I hope that when the time comes for a call for women to serve this race, there will be no hesitancy. Fine furs will not redeem Africa, and the time will surely come when the women will be called upon to make a special sacrifice in answer to Africa's call. Take a leaf from Garvey, who could be free today, living in luxury, if for one moment he would have agreed to surrender his principles, to retract and go back upon his word, to cease active service to his race. But Marcus Garvey is not a man that can be bought, and I have made up my mind to go the whole day with Marcus Garvey. (Applause)

And what Marcus Garvey can do for his race, you also can do. If you die serving your race, you have died well, but if you die serving another race, you have died pretty low.

We are on the highroad to success and nothing can stop us. I went to Boston last Sunday where a splendid meeting was staged, and I came away feeling more cheerful and enthusiastic than I have been for a long time. Men, women and children were working together in a noble way for the good of the cause. With that spirit in evidence the world over among Negroes there is nothing that can halt us short of our objective.

When I saw Mr. Garvey recently he begged me to say a special hello to Liberty Hall. He remembers and asks for many of you by name. Some that he can't remember he tries to describe. He wants to know if Mr. So-and-So is still sitting in the same seat; if Mrs. So-and-So has ever missed a meeting. I try to show him the bright side of things and he fairly beams with joy as I assure him that the work he has done these last seven years is bearing fruit.

Men and women, let us dedicate ourselves anew to our task and go on unwavering and unfaltering to our goal. Surely we will live up to the high calling of the Almighty architect who placed us here. And when the call comes and the white man answers, "Lord, here am I; I am the master of this earth"; and the yellow man can answer, "I am here, too; I am master of this earth"; when the Lord looks around and sees the stalwart Mr. Black Man, let us make sure that he will be able to answer, "Lord, here am I, too; you gave me Africa, and, by God, I am holding it." (Loud applause) [. . .]

"MRS. GARVEY DELIVERS RINGING MESSAGE TO WHITE WOMEN OF LONDON AT GREAT MEETING; TELLS OF INSULTS AND SUFFERING," SEPT. 22, 1928

Mrs. Garvey Speaks

Mrs. Amy Jacques-Garvey (who was received with applause) said:—Mr. Chairman, ladies and gentlemen. I have been given 15 minutes to deliver a message from the Negro women of the world to the white women of England. I may say here that it is obviously difficult to deliver such a message within such a short space of time, but if I were to sum up in a very brief form the message from the Negro women of the world to the white women of England I should say this: We greet you in the name of a larger humanity and the hope that as the years go on we will develop to the standard that you have developed to today. (Hear, hear.) You have trod the rough paths until in this generation you, the white women of the world, are nearly on an equal platform with your men in politics, in literature, in art, in music, in trades; in fact, in every standard and walk of life you rub shoulder to shoulder with your men. (Hear, hear.) We ask, ladies, that you will look not unkindly but with a heart full of good will at us, the black women of the world, who are struggling with our men in our upward climb towards recognition as a nation. (Hear, hear.)

We have really just come out of slavery, and we are in the stage where we need all the encouragement, where we need all the help—not that we are asking you to look down on us—no; because we deplore anything like that, but we ask you to think kindly of us, to learn more of our activities, to know this that we suffer even as you do, because the color of our skins does not make us different in our physical bodies, does not make us different in our ambitions and in our aspirations and in our hopes. No. We hope for as much as you have hoped and longed for. We are ambitious to the extent that any path you have trod and any standard that you have set we are climbing up there to. We hope to travel along those paths, and we hope some day to be able to sit as representatives of our nation, the Black Nation, around your conference tables as you sit today with your men. (Hear, hear.)

You, perhaps, know little about our race as a whole; you know still less about the hopes and ambitions of black women; but we ask you this afternoon to know and learn day by day more about the struggling black women the world over. We have struggled with our men in slavery; we have stood the insults and abuses of white slave-masters. We have emerged from slavery, and we have nourished and helped our children to put them through schools and colleges, until today black boys and girls, young men and young women, are trained in all walks of life. We are a coming people, if you please, and we hope for more things. In this climb towards nationhood, day by day, we want the world to know just what we stand for; we want the world to realize that we are not coming with bowed heads or with tears streaming down our cheeks. No; we are a courageous people; we have nothing to be ashamed of because we have just emerged from slavery; because, friends, all groups of people, all races of peoples, have gone though slavery just as we have. (Hear, hear!) It is no condition that has been imposed only upon one group, the black group. Big nations and groups of peoples other than us look down on us; but we want you to know that we are coming, and others who are at the apex of their civilization today should not regard us as inferior, should not regard us with impunity, but should encourage us; and, if they cannot encourage us, at least they should give us a chance to go along and step forward.

Yes, the black women of the world have suffered; the black women of the world are suffering today. You hardly know what struggles we have to make day by day—the insults heaped upon our race because we are black. Is it pleasant for me, as a black woman, when I come into your beautiful city of London, the heart of the Empire, and if I am hungry and I go into a decent restaurant, feeling I want clean food and a nice clean table and cheerful and pleasant surrounds in which to eat my meal—that is why I go there—I am told, "Madam, we cannot serve you"? "Why! I am hungry. I have the money to pay for it. I am cleanly clothed, I am well behaved." "Madam, I am sorry, we do not serve black people in here."

You say you are Christians, and you say this is the heart of the Empire; you say this is a Christian country, a Christian capital; that you are all Christian people. Then why cannot you serve me because my skin is black? Friends, those are the things that make us feel badly, which make us feel hurt; not so much because of the insult, but to think you are the ones who have brought Christianity to us. You come to us in the name of Jesus, and you say, "Love ye one another." Yet this is the way you treat us when we come to your city.

I go to a hotel. I want a clean bed. I want a decent room and nice, quiet surroundings, and I should like such-and-such a room. I have the money to pay for it. I am not begging. I am clean. I am tidy. I am well behaved. But I am told, "Madam, we are sorry, but we do not put up black people here." How do I feel again? After going day after day and hearing the insults from the white Christians—not heathens, you know, but Christians in London—how do I feel when I go back to my people and say I was treated this way and the other way in the heart of the Empire, in the Christian city of London?

Ah, friends, I bring it to you because I want you to realize and to see. I make this appeal to you because, perhaps, no black person has ever brought it forcibly to your attention, and you are at this meeting because you are interested in black people, otherwise you would not have come; and since you are interested in black people, I want you to know the insults which are heaped upon black people by your brethren merely because we are black; and I want you to talk amongst your white friends in your cities and your towns and in your country as a whole that they should remember that the insults they heap upon individual black people create such bitter feeling in their hearts that one never knows what may happen in the future. The black people of the world are down to-day, but they may be up to-morrow. There is such a thing as evolution. One cannot turn the wheels of evolution backward. No; it must go forward; that is the law of nature. To-day we are backward. Yes, we are backward in our civilization because we have no navy. We have no airplanes. But we may acquire all those lovely things which civilization sets up as a standard, and to-morrow may find us going upward and onward. As a people who love all humanity, we want to greet you, the white people, here and to tell you that we have nothing but love in our hearts toward all peoples, and we want you to exhibit that same fellowship and feeling of love toward all children of God because whether you are white or yellow or brown or black one Creator made us all, and when we die we return to another earth; whatever certain religions believe, we are clay and all return to the earth; after all, we are of the earth earthy [*sic*].

Our appeal, as black people, is learn more about us as a race; be kindly disposed toward us. We are not asking charity of you, because we believe in self help; we believe that as a race of people struggling onward and upward we must of ourselves lift ourselves up; and all we ask you is that you treat us kindly and decently. I know that white women, like all women of the world, have more of a heart than the men. I may explain that in this way. We say—at least, it is a general expression—that a woman thinks more with her heart than with her head. After all, that is lovely because women have a finer conscience, or, perhaps, more conscience, in them than men have. A man will go and rush out and do something and not give a hang about it; but a woman will feel a little pang of pain in her heart if she tries to do the same thing. There is more of love in women's hearts. Perhaps it is because they are the mothers of the world; and it is to that little something in the hearts of women that we appeal as black women and ask you to think twice and to remind your men that after all we are all human beings and, as the children of God, we deserve equal treatment, equal fairness, equal justice, in common with all humanity. (Applause). [. . .]

"MRS. AMY JACQUES-GARVEY AT BERMUDA," DEC. 1, 1928

Mrs. Garvey Speaks

Rising amidst great applause, Mrs. Garvey said:

"Friends, I am glad to be with you today, and do hope to instill new hope and courage in you by speaking to you. Before I begin, however, I must relate a very nauseous incident. It was necessary for me to visit the Canadian steamship office on Friday to obtain my ticket for Jamaica, and queerly enough, I at once became the object of attention. 'Where is she?' 'Oh, that is Mrs. Garvey,' were some of the remarks made, with fingers indicating. I completed my business and returned home."

"It seemed, however, in the meanwhile, that some highly imaginative person or persons had fabricated a story and passed it on to the police commissioner. It ran something like this: 'Mrs. Garvey said she thought Bermuda was a self-governed place, but it seems it is better governed by Russia.' Now, I look upon Bermuda's government as a respectable one, but I confess great disappointment when the heads of departments can receive such absolute piffle—unfounded, at that—and magnify it into an offense. Why, I would have driven the person from my office." (Laughter).

"We, of the U.N.I.A. believe in constituted authority, and advocate respect for and a proper observance of the laws of any country in which we find ourselves. Who is Red? We are not Reds! Nor are we Socialists! We are a people banded together whose principles are self-love, self-help and amity with all peoples. (Cheers.) Unfortunately, many misunderstand or underestimate the aims of the Universal Negro Improvement Association. It is not a small, benevolent institution; it is not one with a limited perspective. It is broad in its principles and far-reaching in its effect. Its purpose is too great to be trifled with.

"A great and solemn duty devolves upon us. We must so clearly enunciate these principles that no confusion will remain in the minds of those whom we teach and no mistake is made in its application. The time has come when we must press on, as never before, for the solution of our problem. Already our claims, set forth in a petition, are before the League of Nations.[1] I reiterate, we must press on—and look to ourselves! England has her burdens to bear, notably the caring for of approximately two million unemployed. That entails constant attention and great expenditure. A gentleman in London said to me, 'Do you think we can attend to your matters when our difficulties are ever present and remain unsolved?' That is a natural state of mind and a natural stand to take. It is the Law of Life.

"No, my friends, let us all realize that the new Negro is awake, is looking around and is demanding what he wants (cheers). Nevertheless, remember that you serve the purposes of the association best when you are dignified and honorable, when in treating with others you bring to bear all the fine characteristics of the race (cheers). You can be polite without any evidence of obsequiousness; you can be assertive without rudeness.

"We hope soon to accomplish many things. But let me clear up one point. You must not think we intend to dump the entire Negro population of Bermuda in Africa. Decidedly not. It is not desirable, indeed, the weeding-out process will prevent that. How wonderful it would be, though, for Bermuda to send a representative to the League of Nations or to any other place where one is needed. Our people must work side by side with the exponents of western civilization, absorb the best of it and return with it to our brothers and sisters on the Continent. So do your best, work steadily, and be ready for the day when your call comes. [. . .]

Notes

INTRODUCTION

1. Studies of Garvey and the Garveyite movement that have generally neglected Jacques Garvey, even though they often contain other important information, include Judith Stein's *The World of Marcus Garvey: Race and Class in Modern Society* (Baton Rouge: Louisiana State Univ. Press, 1986); Rupert Lewis, *Marcus Garvey: Anti-Colonial Champion* (Trenton, NJ: Africa World Press, 1988); Elton C. Fax, *Garvey: The Story of a Pioneer Black Nationalist* (New York: Dodd, Mead & Company, 1972); Tony Martin, *Race First: The Ideological and Organizational Struggles of Marcus Garvey and the Universal Negro Improvement Association* (Dover, MA: The Majority Press, 1976); E. David Cronon, *Black Moses: The Story of Marcus Garvey and the Negro Improvement Association* (Madison: Univ. of Wisconsin Press, 1969); C. Boyd James, *Garvey, Garveyism and the Antinomies in Black Redemption* (Trenton, NJ: Africa World Press, 2009); and Adam Ewing, *The Age of Garvey: How a Jamaican Activist Created a Mass Movement & Changed Global Black Politics* (Princeton: Princeton Univ. Press, 2014).

2. The bulk of Jacques Garvey's writings, including her scrapbook containing clippings of most of her *Negro World* editorials, are housed in the Amy Jacques Garvey papers at the John Hope and Aurelia E. Franklin Memorial Library Special Collections at Fisk University in Nashville, Tennessee. Other material is located at the National Library of Jamaica in Kingston, Jamaica. Incomplete holdings of the *Negro World* are available on microfilm in several institutions, including the Schomburg Library (a division of New York Public Library) in New York City. Thanks to these institutions for their support.

Significant work on Jacques Garvey is included in my Works Cited, particularly the writings by Adler, Bair, Broussard, James, and Taylor. See also the multivolume *The Marcus Garvey and Universal Negro Improvement Association Papers* (Berkeley: Univ. of California Press), edited by Robert A. Hill, et al.; Theodore G. Vincent's *Black Power and the Garvey Movement* (San Francisco: Ramparts, 1972); Henrik Clarke's *Marcus Garvey and the Vision of Africa* (New York: Vintage, 1974), assembled with Amy's assistance; and Colin Grant's *Negro with a Hat: The Rise and Fall of Marcus Garvey* (Oxford: Oxford Univ. Press, 2008). See also Rupert Lewis, "Amy Jacques Garvey: A Political Portrait," *Jamaica Daily News*, July, 29, 1973, and Rupert Lewis and Maureen Warner-Lewis, "Amy Jacques Garvey," *Jamaica Journal* 20 (Aug. Oct. 1987): 39–43. Several younger scholars who are working on manuscripts that deal with aspects of the role of Black women intellectuals in the Garvey movement include Keisha Blain [Benjamin], TaKeia Anthony, Natanya Duncan, Asia Leeds, and Ashley Farmer. Thanks to Ula Taylor for pointing out several of these scholars to me.

3. Some sources list 1896 as the year of birth. However, Ula Taylor cites the Registrar in Jamaica as indicating 1895 (Taylor, *Veiled Garvey*, 240, note 2).

4. In *Garvey & Garveyism* Jacques Garvey indicates her year of arrival in the United States as 1918 (113). However, all other sources indicate the correct year is 1917.

5. I describe her as Amy Jacques Garvey after her marriage. The complicated relationship between Amy Ashwood, Amy Jacques, and Marcus Garvey goes beyond the scope of this work. For various perspectives of it, see Taylor, *Veiled Garvey*, 23–38; Grant, 212, 236–7, 305–6; Tony Martin, *Amy Ashwood Garvey: Pan-Africanist, Feminist and Mrs. Marcus Garvey No. 1 Or A Tale of Two Amies* (Dover, MA: The Majority Press, 2007), 61–6, 343–4, and Lionel M. Yard, *Biography of Amy Ashwood Garvey, 1897–1989: Co-Founder of the Universal Negro Improvement Association* (Associated Press, 198?), 58–63.

6. In this work Black nationalism is used as an umbrella term for any organization that promotes a self-governing, independent Black homeland, whether in Africa, the United States or elsewhere. Garveyism entails an entire program of Black self-sufficiency and advocates a black homeland specifically in Africa. African Redemption means the freeing of African nations from any foreign, colonial control.

Garvey was certainly not the first to promote an African homeland for Blacks. Others who preceded him include Martin Delany, Henry Highland Garnet, Alexander Crummell, Edward Wilmot Blyden, and Henry McNeal Turner. However, he was the first to galvanize such a large following to its cause. For more on this subject see Wilson Jeremiah Moses, ed., *Classical Black Nationalism: From the American Revolution to Marcus Garvey* (1996) and Wilson Jeremiah Moses, *The Golden Age of Black Nationalism* (1978).

7. In addition to Amy Jacques and Amy Ashwood, these women included Henrietta Vinton Davis, a stalwart Garvey advisor for several years, and

Maymie Leona Turpeau De Mena, a Nicaraguan-born Garveyite for over twenty years. For more on these women, see Lionel M. Yard, *Biography of Amy Ashwood Garvey, 1897–1989: Co-Founder of The Universal Negro Improvement Association* (Associated Press, 198?); Tony Martin, *Amy Ashwood Garvey* (The Majority Press, 2007); Tony Martin, "Women in the Garvey Movement," *Garvey: His Work and Impact*, ed. Rupert Lewis and Patrick Bryan (Africa World Press, 1991); and William Seraile, "Henrietta Vinton Davis and the Garvey Movement," *Afro-Americans in New York Life and History* 7 (July 1983): 7–24.

8. Jacques Garvey began the *Philosophy and Opinions* "as a personal record" of Garvey's speeches and sayings, but she came to believe that disseminating his ideas through the book would be a means to help exonerate him from criminal charges. As she says in the Preface to the collection: "By his own words he may be judged, and Negroes the world over may be informed and inspired, for truth, brought to light, forces conviction, and a state of conviction inspires action."

9. For a discussion of the literary contributions of Garveyism to the Harlem Renaissance, see Tony Martin, *Literary Garveyism: Garvey, Black Arts and the Harlem Renaissance* (Dover, MA: The Majority Press, 1983); Tony Martin, ed., *African Fundamentalism: A Literary and Cultural Anthology of Garvey's Harlem Renaissance* (Dover, MA: The Majority Press, 1991); and David Krasner, *A Beautiful Pageant: Theatre, Drama, and Performance in the Harlem Renaissance, 1910–1927* (New York: Palgrave Macmillan, 2002), 167–87.

10. For a description of more typical Black woman's pages, see Ula Taylor *Veiled Garvey*, 68–9.

11. See note 6 for some of the Black nationalists that preceded Garvey.

12. For a detailed discussion on race, see Michael Omi and Howard Winant, *Racial Formation in the United States*, 3rd. ed. (2014).

PART 1: EARLY WRITINGS

1. The couple lived at 133 West 129th Street in Harlem.

2. A one-act opera by Pietro Mascagni with a libretto by Giovanni Targioni-Tozzetti and Guido Menasci. The book was adopted from a short story by Giovanni Verga. The opera premiered in 1890.

3. Tutankhamun lived ca. 1341–1323 BCE. Howard Carter and George Herbert, 5th Earl of Carnarvon, discovered his tomb in 1922. Amy takes the

controversial position that the ancient Egyptians were Black. The racial heritage of the Egyptians has been much debated since the 19th century. See Martin Bernal's three-volume *Black Athena: The Afroasiatic Roots of Classical Civilization* (1987) and the collection of essays entitled *Black Athena Revisited* (1996), edited by Mary Lefkowitz and Guy MacLean Rogers for very different views on the subject.

4. In Amy's preface, dated Feb. 23, 1923, she states:

> My purpose for compiling [Marcus Garvey's speeches and articles] was not for publication, but rather to keep as a personal record of the opinions and sayings of my husband during his career as the Leader of that portion of the human family known as the Negro Race. However, on second thought, I decided to publish this volume in order to give to the public an opportunity of studying and forming an opinion of him; not from inflated and misleading newspaper and magazine articles but from expressions of thoughts enunciated by him in defence of his oppressed and struggling race; so that by his own words he may be judged, and Negroes the world over may be informed and inspired, for truth, brought to light, forces conviction, and a state of conviction inspires action.

5. The article (*Negro World* July 14, 1923) is purportedly a defense of Jacques Garvey from charges that she was attempting to take over the UNIA. However, the defense was done in such a condescending manner that Amy was more disturbed by it than by the original charge.

6. A news agency organized by Cyril Briggs (1888–1966), a member of the militant communist-leaning African Blood Brotherhood. Briggs, a light-complexioned native of Nevis, frequently pilloried Garvey in his newspaper columns, particularly in the *Crusader*. For more on him, see Robert A. Hill, intro. and ed., *The Crusader*, 3 vols. (New York: Kraus, 1987).

7. William Sherrill was president of the Black Cross Navigation and Trading Co. and became acting president of the UNIA when Garvey was imprisoned in 1925. Garvey denounced him in 1926 on grounds of maladministration and disloyalty, leading to a major rift in the organization. Robert Lincoln Poston was the Secretary General of the UNIA. As a representative of the UNIA he met the King of Liberia in 1924 in an unsuccessful attempt to gain land for settlement by UNIA members. He contracted a fever and died on the return trip home. Jacques Garvey had a favorable relationship with him, as seen in her essay written upon his death (*Negro World* April 6, 1924). Barbadian

Clifford S. Bourne was appointed High Chancellor of the UNIA by Garvey in 1923. He had organized a UNIA post in Guatemala in 1921.

8. Shakespeare, *Romeo and Juliet*, Act 5, Scene 1. Shakespeare uses "hangs" not "hangeth." Many texts indicate "starvest," not "stareth."

9. The name here is used ironically. Originally, El Dorado was the name given by Europeans to a legendary, wealthy Indian chief in what is now Colombia, South America. The name has been extended to describe any wealthy place, a city of gold.

10. This is an example of a "sunset town" (also called "sundown town" or "gray town") in which all people of color had to leave the town by sunset or face violence. See James W. Loemen, *Sundown Towns: A Hidden Dimension of American Racism* (2005).

11. A stereotypical Jewish villain in Shakespeare's *The Merchant of Venice.*

12. Hearns' was one of the largest department stores in New York City. The company ceased operating in the 1970s, but its flagship Manhattan store closed in 1955.

13. For more on Garvey's relationship with Washington, see Martin, *Race First*, 280–3 and Grant, *Negro with a Hat*, 66–70.

14. Robert Russa Moton (1867–1940) was the principal of Tuskegee Institute from 1915–1935. He advised several presidents on Black issues and wrote such works as *Finding a Way Out: An Autobiography* (1920), and *What the Negro Thinks* (1929). For more on him, see Ronald L. Heinemann, "Robert Russa Moton (1867–1940)," *Encyclopedia Virginia* March 1, 2014, Web. Accessed Nov. 19, 2014.

15. A paraphrase of English Romantic poet John Keats' line, "A thing of beauty is a joy forever," from *Endymion* (1818).

16. "Atlanta Compromise Speech," 1895.

17. From *Up From Slavery* (1901).

18. Undoubtedly, Jacques Garvey is referring to W. E. B. Du Bois, a graduate of Harvard University, and other Blacks who attended elite White-run academic institutions.

19. Ernest (Ernie) Morrison (1912–1989) was an original *Our Gang* member. In 1919, he was the first African American actor to sign a long-term contract. Morrison left the Our Gang series in 1924, continued acting into the 1940s, and had a final appearance in the television series *Good Times* in 1974.

20. *Our Gang* comedies were short comic films about a poor neighborhood gang. They were produced by Harold Eugene "Hal" Roach Sr. (1892–1992) from

1922– 1944. The films were unique for their inclusion of boys and girls and Blacks and Whites. Beginning in 1955, eighty sound films were syndicated for television under the title *The Little Rascals*. For more, see Richard Lewis Ward, *A History of the Hal Roach Studios* (2005).

21. Robert F. McGowan (1882–1955) was the senior director of the *Our Gang* comedies from 1922–1933.

22. Born in 1879 and died in 1935. He was a film and vaudeville star whose homespun humor was enormously popular in the 1920s and 1930s.

23. Allen Hoskins (1920–1980) played the character Farina in over 100 *Our Gang* comedies in the 1920s. During his years in the films (1922–1931), he was one of the most popular and highest-paid members of the cast. For more on Hoskins and Morrison and *The Little Rascals*, see Donald Bogle, *Toms, Coons, Mulattoes, Mammies, and Bucks: An Interpretive History of Blacks in American Films* (1973) and Leonard Maltin and Richard W. Bann, *The Little Rascals: The Life and Times of Our Gang* (1992).

24. An elaborate dance developed on slave plantations. A cake was often awarded to the winning couple. The origins of the dance are debated, but many historians maintain that the dance began as a satire by Blacks on dances held by their White masters.

25. Canadian-born actor and film director (1880–1933) who acted in or directed over 120 silent films between 1912–1931.

26. Marie Osborne Yeats (1911–2010) was the first major American child star of the silent film era. Her best-known film is *Little Mary Sunshine* (1916).

27. Richard A. Rowland (1880–1947) was an American film producer and executive. He headed Metro Pictures Corporation from 1915– 1920. Rowland sold Metro in 1920 to Marcus Lowe; subsequently, it became part of Metro-Goldwyn-Mayer studio.

28. Born in 1894 and died in 1957, she was a silent film actor and film producer who starred in such films as *Smilin' Through* (1922).

29. Swanson (1899–1983) was an early silent-film star, but was later featured in *Sunset Boulevard* (1950), ironically portraying a character, Norma Desmond, that some critics believe was based on Norma Talmadge.

30. A reference to silent-film star Rudolph Valentino (1895–1926). The Italian-born heartthrob was featured in *The Sheik* (1921).

31. Born in Baltimore, Maryland in 1880 and died in 1956. He was a journalist, essayist, and magazine editor of works including *The American Mercury*

(1924–1933). He is also well known for the multivolume *The American Language* (1919). Although he maintained cordial relationships with many Black writers and published them in his magazines, he often had shockingly racist views. Mencken ridiculed many aspects of the South, particularly in his essay "The Sahara of the Bozart," first published in 1917 and then expanded in 1920. See Charles Scruggs, *The Sage in Harlem: H.L. Mencken and the Black Writers of the 1920s* (1984) and Fred Hobson, *Serpent in Eden: H.L. Mencken and the South* (1974). Mencken wrote a column "Mencken and the Negro" in the *Negro World* published July 23, 1927, praising the progress of the race.

32. Born in 1882 and died in 1958. In addition to his editorial work with Mencken, Nathan was a leading drama critic.

33. A literary magazine that ran from 1900 to 1930. During the years H. L. Mencken and George Jean Nathan edited the magazine (1914–1924), it featured such authors as Sinclair Lewis, Eugene O'Neill, Aldous Huxley, Edna St. Vincent Millay, and Dashiell Hammett. The magazine published two stories from James Joyce's *Dubliners* in 1915, marking the author's first United States publication.

34. Although the term dates back to the 1890s, it gained popularity during the Harlem Renaissance years, particularly with the publication of Alain Locke's *The New Negro* (1925). The New Negro is generally marked as more assertive and proud of his race than his predecessors. For more, see David Levering Lewis' *When Harlem Was in Vogue* (1981).

35. Those blacks who blindly obey the master.

36. Patricia Wiegmann writes insightfully about the trip in "Amy Jacques Garvey 'On A Trip from Coast to Coast': Roots, Routes, and Emancipation," *Comparativ* 21.5 (2011): 88–105.

37. Pullman porters were Black men hired by owner George Pullman to operate on his sleeping car trains after the Civil War. The porters, under the leadership of A. Philip Randolph, formed a union, The Brotherhood of Sleeping Car Porters, in 1925.

38. Philip Jenkins points out that "[b]y 1925 the Klan may have had 250,000 members in Pennsylvania." "The Ku Klux Klan in Pennsylvania," *The Western Pennsylvania Historical Magazine* 69 (April 1986): 120–37.

39. After being sentenced to five years in prison on charges of mail fraud on June 21, 1923, Garvey was soon taken to the Tombs Prison in New York City. He was released on bail of twenty-five thousand dollars on September 3, 1923. He was, however, incarcerated in Atlanta Federal Penitentiary on February 8, 1925.

40. W. S. Vaughn, from Youngstown, was a delegate at the UNIA Convention in 1924.

41. Republican William C. Reese was mayor of Youngstown in 1922–1923.

42. The story of Daniel's imprisonment and rescue is from the Old Testament Book of Daniel.

43. The god of dreams. He is mentioned in the Roman poet Ovid's *Metamorphoses* Book 11 (8 AD).

44. The Klan, led by D. C. Stephenson, was particularly active in the state between 1920 and 1927. By 1925, the governor and over half of the elected members of the state assembly were members of the organization. See Leonard J. Moore's *Citizen Klansman: The Ku Klux Klan in Indiana 1921–1928* (1997).

45. The *Sun*, under Bagby's editorship, was one of the most important sources for Black news in Indiana.

46. Old Testament (Gen. 9:20–27). In the story, Ham shames his father, Noah. He is cursed as a result. The specious linking of Ham's descendants to Black people has long been used as a justification for their enslavement.

47. Samuel R. Wheat, a coal merchant. He and his partner, William M. Green, sent a petition in July 1923 protesting Garvey's imprisonment. See Robert Hill, ed., *The Marcus Garvey Papers* V (Sept. 1922–Aug. 1924) 47, note 2).

48. Leonidas C. Dyer, a Republican Representative for St. Louis, Missouri, introduced an anti-lynching bill in 1918. By classifying lynching as a federal offense, the federal government would be allowed to prosecute rather than the government of the state in which the act was committed. The bill was filibustered by Democratic representatives from Southern states beginning in 1922 and never came up for a vote.

49. To be deep in serious thought.

50. One of the bloodiest riots in American history occurred in East St. Louis on July 2, 1917. After simmering tensions between White unions and Black migrants hired to work in the city, White mobs began burning homes of Blacks and shooting or lynching those found in the streets. Well over one hundred Blacks and nine Whites were killed. W. E. B. Du Bois and Martha Gruening, sent by the NAACP to investigate, compiled a report entitled "The Massacre of East St. Louis." The riot led to the infamous silent protest parade by 10,000 blacks in New York City. See Elliot M. Rudwick, *Race Riot at East St. Louis: July 2, 1917* (1964).

51. William W. Gordon was mayor of Kansas City, Kansas, from 1923 to 1926. His brief term was marred by scandal, and he was found guilty of willful

official misconduct (charges included permitting bootlegging and using city funds for personal business) and removed from office.

52. A medium-security prison established in 1903. It is located in Leavenworth, Kansas, twenty-five miles north of Kansas City, Kansas.

53. These lines echo Marcus Garvey's words in "The Negro's Greatest Enemy," *Current History* (September 1923): "I asked: 'Where is the black man's Government?' 'Where is his King and his kingdom?' 'Where is his President, his country, and his ambassador, his army, his navy, his men of big affairs?' I could not find them, and then I declared, 'I will help to make them.'"

54. A reference to Exodus 33:3: "Go up to the land flowing with milk and honey."

55. Although slavery was banned in the Oregon territory in 1844, several laws were passed between that year and 1857 attempting to exclude Blacks. It took until 1927 for an amendment to be passed voiding Oregon's constitutional exclusion clause.

56. The Fourteenth Amendment, designed to protect the rights of citizenship for former slaves, was passed over the fierce resistance of Southern states in 1868. The Fifteenth Amendment prohibited the federal government or individual states from denying a person's right to vote based on that person's "race, color or previous condition of servitude." It was ratified in 1870.

57. During the 1920s, the Ku Klux Klan had marches in various cities in Washington that drew crowds of 20,000 to 70,000 followers ("The Ku Klux Klan in Washington State, 1920s," *Seattle Civil Rights and Labor History Project*, Web, Accessed Nov. 19, 2014). The Oregon Klan had some 35,000 members at its peak in the 1920s (Eckard Toy, "Ku Klux Klan," *The Oregon Encyclopedia*, Web, Accessed Nov. 19, 2014.

58. Marcus Garvey believed that the Ku Klux Klan represented the view of the majority of White Americans. In 1922, he held a controversial meeting with Klan leaders in Atlanta to discuss race issues. The Klan agreed with Garvey's belief in returning blacks to Africa, but for entirely different reasons. For more on this meeting, see Tony Martin, *Race First*, 344–7.

59. Again, likely a reference to Du Bois and his supporters.

60. The Great Kanto Earthquake that struck Yokohama and Tokyo on September 1, 1923. The death toll was about 140,000.

61. William Wrigley (1861–1932) co-founded the chewing gum company that bears his name in 1891.

62. August Anheuser Busch (1865–1934), CEO of the Anheuser-Busch Brewing Company from 1913–1934. His father, Adolphus Busch, co-founded the company.

63. The Eighteenth Amendment declared the production, transport, and sale of alcohol illegal. The law was in effect from 1920 to 1933, when it was repealed by the Twenty-first Amendment.

64. A play on Shakespeare's "Lord, what fools these mortals be," from *A Midsummer Night's Dream* (Act 3, Scene 2).

65. Born in Baltimore in 1878, Thompson, a journalist on the staff of the *Evening Express* and *Morning Tribune*, became an influential Black leader in Los Angeles, California. He was the husband of writer Eloise Bibb-Thompson. Thompson was openly critical of the UNIA's handling of the Black Star Line's finances, which caused a schism in the Los Angeles UNIA division. Garvey's visit to Los Angeles and his praise of Thompson was an attempt to heal this rift. For more on Thompson, see Emory Tolbert's *The UNIA and Black Los Angeles: Ideology and Community in the American Garvey Movement* (Los Angeles: Univ. of California, 1980).

66. Probably the influential *California Eagle*, which operated from 1879–1964. It was owned and managed by the progressive Charlotta Bass from 1912–1951.

67. Amy is alluding to three different references here. The first, to "the mills of the gods," is taken from popular American poet Henry Wadsworth Longfellow (1807–1882). The poet writes in "Retribution," "Though the mills of God grind slowly/Yet they grind exceeding small." The reference to sowing what one reaps is from the Bible (Galatians 6:7–9): "For whatsoever a man soweth, that shall he also reap." According to the Gospel of Matthew (26–27), Judas Iscariot betrayed Jesus in exchange for thirty silver coins. After feeling remorse for his actions, Judas hanged himself.

68. Jacques Garvey probably means silent-film star Rudolph Valentino. See note 30 for more on him.

69. Normally used as a derogatory reference to a White person, usually from the rural South.

70. Such a scenario can be seen in Amy's sketch "Whither Goeth Thou?"

71. A legendary figure who was said to have tormented Christ on the way to his crucifixion and as punishment is doomed to walk the earth until the Second Coming. Jacques Garvey is also alluding here to the Great Migration,

beginning in 1915. By the end of the 1920s, well over one million Blacks had migrated from the South to the North. See Isabel Wilkerson's *The Warmth of Other Suns: The Epic Story of the Great Migration* (2010).

72. A dedicated Garveyite from Norfolk, Virginia, Ward worked unsuccessfully to overturn the ruling on Garvey's deportation.

PART 2: EDITORIALS FOR THE WOMAN'S PAGE

1. Saad Zaghloul (1859–1927) was Prime Minister of Egypt in 1924. He was a long-standing advocate for Egyptian independence, but British opposition to him and widespread rioting in the country soon forced him to leave office.

2. David Lloyd George (1863–1945). He was Prime Minister of the United Kingdom from 1916–1922.

3. The French believed it was their moral obligation to assimilate their colonial subjects, hoping to make them "little Frenchmen." Unfortunately, the system was inherently studded with racial prejudice and paternalism. See Martin D. Lewis, "One Hundred Million Frenchmen: The Assimilation Theory in French Colonial Policy," *Historical Problems of Imperial Africa*, ed. Robert O. Collins, (Princeton, NJ: Markus Wiener Publishers, 2000).

4. Édouard Herriot (1872–1957) was a Radical French politician who served as Prime Minister for brief periods in 1924–25, 1926, and 1932.

5. An American geologist, explorer, and author who lived from 1870–1950.

6. Woodrow Wilson, in the Fourteen Points address on January 8, 1918, gave several moral reasons attempting to justify United States involvement in World War I. One of these was the right of European nations such as Poland, which was occupied by Germany, to self-determination. He gave a speech on February 11, 1918, reiterating that "[n]ational aspirations must be respected." Garveyites interpreted this to include those peoples living in Asia and Africa as well as Europe.

7. There are several Biblical passages implying that we should do unto others as we would want them to do unto us. One is from Matthew 7:12: "Therefore all things whatsoever ye would that men should do to you, do ye even so to them."

8. The first self-created being. For many Christians this means God.

9. One of the fundamental beliefs of many Gnostics: "As ye dissolve the world and are not dissolved yourselves, ye are the Lords of creation and

destruction." It is intriguing that Amy would choose to quote this passage since it would be considered blasphemous by orthodox Christians because it made man, not god, master of the world.

10. Colonel E. Alexander Powell was a war correspondent during World War I. *Asia at the Crossroads* was published in 1922.

11. A Eurocentric term referring to Western Europe and the Americas.

12. The country was the chief focus of the UNIA's attempt to establish a Black homeland in Africa. The Liberian government, "after providing Garvey with initial encouragement, repudiated the agreements." See Tony Martin, *Race First*, 122–37. Amy thought enough of this essay that she marked it as "important" in her scrapbook, the only editorial indicated this way by her. For more on Garvey and Liberia, see C. Boyd James, *Garvey, Garveyism and the Antinomies in Black Redemption*, 177–291.

13. Large tires filled with air at a low pressure.

14. After World War I ended, the British were left with a glut of rubber. The British Rubber Growers Association, led by its chair Sir James Stevenson, attempted to stabilize prices by limiting the amount of rubber exported. They did this through pressuring Ceylon and British Malaysia (chief growers of rubber) to pass the Export of Rubber (Restriction) Enactment in 1922.

15. A national personification of England. He is usually depicted as being well meaning if not always authoritative.

16. Two densely populated islands that are part of what is now Indonesia. At the time Amy was writing, the islands were part of the Dutch East Indies.

17. Harvey Samuel Firestone (1868–1938) was head of the tire and rubber company that bears his name. In 1926, Firestone signed a 99-year rubber-rights agreement with the Liberian government.

18. Barclay (1882–1955) was President of Liberia from 1930–1944.

19. Fought between the Spanish (and later French) and natives of the Rif region of northern Morocco between 1920–1926. The Europeans with overwhelming force won.

20. Luke 23:34.

21. The British fought several wars between 1823 and 1901 with the Ashanti Empire in what is present-day Ghana. As a consequence of the British victory, the Ashanti territories became part of the Gold Coast colony. The British fought the Zulu in Southern Africa in 1879. As a result of the British victory, the Zulu Kingdom was annexed by the British.

22. The Ethiopian or Abyssinian Empire dates back to the 12th century. In the modern era, Ethiopia and Liberia remained the only two countries not to be colonized by European nations in the late 19th century. Emperor Haile Selassie ruled the country from 1916 to 1974 with the exception of the Italian occupation from 1935–1936. He and Garvey had a contentious relationship. The Italians and British had long discussed the status of Ethiopia, and when the two nations made a series of agreements in 1938, England gave tacit permission for Italy to take control of Ethiopia.

23. Women in the United States were given the right to vote through the Nineteenth Amendment in 1920. Women over thirty who owned property were given the right to vote in Great Britain after the Representation of the People Act in 1918. All women over twenty-one could vote as of the passage of the Equal Franchise Act in 1928.

24. A political movement that advocated a constitutional monarchy rather than an absolute monarchy in late 19th-century Turkey. The term now generally refers to a progressive political movement.

25. Mustafa Kemal Pasha (Ataturk) (1881–1938) was the founder of the modern state of Turkey. Madam Kemal, Latife Hanim, was a Western-educated woman who married Mustafa Kemal Ataturk in 1923. She fought for women's rights in Turkey. The marriage lasted only two years.

26. Amy probably intends 350,000,000 people.

27. There were attempts at prohibition in Great Britain and the Scandinavian countries from the 19th century up until the 1930s. The Bolsheviks, with limited success, banned the production and sale of alcohol in the Soviet Union from 1917–1925. Women's groups and religious organizations often abetted this temperance movement.

28. The quotation is generally attributed to American William Ross Wallace (1819–1881), from his poem, "What Rules the World" (1865). Napoleon had stated that the future destiny of a child is determined by the mother.

29. Perhaps Jacques Garvey is thinking of the Dutch Jewish philosopher Baruch Spinoza (1632–1677), who said, "Peace is not the absence of war, it is a virtue, a state of mind, a disposition for benevolence, confidence, and justice."

30. "Love your neighbor as yourself" (Mark 12:31).

31. Florence E. S. Knapp, Republican, 1925–1927.

32. Nellie Tayloe Ross, Democrat, Wyoming, 1925–1927; Miriam A. Ferguson, Democrat, Texas, 1925–1933.

33. From "A Comparison: Addressed to a Young Lady," by English poet William Cowper (1731–1800).

34. Rhodes (1853–1902) was a British businessman and politician in South Africa. He was president of the De Beers Company, which at one time controlled 90% of the diamond industry. A champion of colonialism, Rhodes founded the British colony of Rhodesia (present-day Zambia and Zimbabwe) in 1895.

35. Amy published a similar article with a similar title ("Scanty Clothes—Healthy Bodies," *Negro World* July 16, 1927).

36. Bustles are frames worn under skirts that extend the back of the dress; hoops were worn to hold skirts out from a woman's legs; stays are flat strips of metal, plastic, or bone to stiffen corsets.

37. Hill (1866–1952) did research on blood pressure. He was a fellow of the Royal Society and was knighted in 1930.

38. As Winston James points out in *Holding Aloft the Banner of Ethiopia*, at least two men did muster up enough strength to send letters in defense of Black men (154–5).

39. Jacques Garvey was very suspicious of the American Birth Control League, headed by Margaret Sanger (1879–1966) and other pro-abortion rights organizations, which she saw as an attempt to curtail the growth of non-White peoples.

40. Matthew 25:23.

41. Although a relatively small percentage of Black doctors graduated from White medical schools, by 1923, there were only two Black medical schools: Howard University Medical School in Washington, D.C. and Meharry Medical College in Nashville, Tennessee. Duke Univ. Medical Center Library Online, accessed Nov. 19, 2014.

42. "As the twig is bent, the tree's inclined." British poet Alexander Pope (1688–1744), "Epistles to Several Persons" (1732).

43. "How shall they hear without a preacher?" (Romans 10:14).

44. Short for Latin, *infra dignitatem*, meaning "beneath one's dignity."

45. British poet Philip James Bailey (1816–1902), best known for the volume *Festus* (1839), from which the quoted lines are taken.

46. Shakespeare, *The Merry Wives of Windsor* (Act 2, Scene 2).

47. Accessories.

48. Garveyites often were critical of the League of Nations (which the United States never joined) due in large part to their denial of African land for repatriation after World War I.

49. Marcus Garvey was the managing editor from 1918–1932.

50. The Christianity of both Marcus Garvey and Amy was rooted in Black nationalism, a religion that would support both the earthly and spiritual needs of Black people. In his essay "African Fundamentalism" (*Negro World* June 6, 1925), Garvey states, "God and Nature first made us what we are, and then out of our own creative genius we make ourselves what we want to be." Despite their beliefs in Christ's teachings (Marcus was born a Roman Catholic; Amy was an Anglican), both Garvey and Jacques Garvey were skeptical about organized Christianity. Garvey established the African Orthodox Church in 1921, headed by George Alexander McGuire, which espoused the doctrine of a Black god. See Randall Burkett, *Garveyism as a Religious Movement* (1978) and *Black Redemption: Churchmen Speak for the Garvey Movement* (1978). See also Tony Martin, *Race First*, 67–80.

51. A Russian-born Jew who was an early advocate of the creation of a Jewish state in the 1920s "on the shores of the Black Sea." Benjamin Pinkus, *The Jews of the Soviet Union The History of a National Minority* (1988): 71.

52. The creation of a Black nation within the United States was advocated by the Communist Party at the Sixth World Congress held in Moscow in 1928. The Comintern declared that the so-called Black belt in the American South had the right of self-determination as "a subject nation." The controversial idea did gain some support from Black radicals such as Cyril Briggs ("For Self-Determination in the Black Belt," *The Liberator*, August 1, 1932), but it was not seen as credible by most Americans, either White or Black.

53. Chaim Weismann (1874–1952) was a biochemist and Zionist leader who eventually became the first president of Israel (1949–1952).

54. The passage, a favorite of Garveyites, is from Psalms 68:31.

55. Unfortunately, parts of this important essay are missing or illegible. I have supplied what seem to be the missing words in brackets.

56. A reference to Christ.

57. Two well-known hymns. Elizabeth H. Hamilton and Ira D. Sankey composed the former in the late nineteenth century. Fanny Crosby and John R. Sweeney composed the latter in 1879.

58. Spoken by Duke Senior in Shakespeare's *As You Like It* (Act 2, Scene 1).

59. The quotation is attributed to Scottish poet Robert Burns: "Man's inhumanity to man/Makes countless thousands mourn!" It is from his poem *Man was made to mourn: A Dirge* (1785).

60. Mack (1866–1943) was a United States Federal Judge. He presided over Marcus Garvey's trial on embezzlement charges in 1923. "Mack sentenced

Garvey to five years in prison, fined him one thousand dollars, billed him for court costs, and denied him bail" (Judith Stein, *The World of Marcus Garvey: Race and Class in Modern Society* (1986): 200). He was also one of the leaders of the Zionist movement.

61. The American Palestine Line was opening in 1924 to take transport passengers between New York and the Holy Land. The general manager, Hyman Epstein, was charged with embezzling funds but was exonerated in 1925. The business closed shortly therefafter.

62. From Thomas Gray's "Ode on a Distant Prospect of Eton College" (1747).

63. Collins (1869–1952) was a pioneer in wireless telephony. He wrote widely on scientific and technological subjects.

64. All of these men understood the importance of books and had significant personal libraries and/or established bookstores. As Schomburg's biographer Elinor Des Verney Sinette points out, such bibliophiles "viewed their collecting as another facet of the continuing struggle against social, economic, and cultural prejudice." *Arthur Alfonso Schomburg: Black Bibliophile and Collector* (1989): 76.

65. Aristotle, about 350 BCE, in his works "On the Heavens" and "Metaphysics" makes the argument for a spherical Earth.

66. Passed in 1922. See note 14 in this section for the Colonial Restriction Act.

67. Roland Lecavelé (pen name Roland Dorgelès, 1885–1973) was a French novelist and a member of the Académie Goncourt. He is best known for his novel *Les Croix de Bois* (Wooden Crosses, 1919), a study of World War 1. The novel was the winner of the Prix Femina Award.

68. Or piastre, a unit of currency used in various locations, especially in the Middle East. The term comes from Italian and means "a thin metal plate."

69. American slang of the 1920s for small, inexpensive cars.

70. Arnold (1875–1946) was a China expert and was the United States Consul to the country in 1914. He then accepted the post of commercial attaché to China through the Commerce Department until 1940.

71. Also Timbuktu, a city in what is now the West African country of Mali. Although it was a center for trade and a seat of learning and Islamic culture from the 12th to the 17th centuries, it is now largely thought of in popular Western culture as an obscure, almost mythical location.

72. A term coined by English philosopher Herbert Spencer in *Principles of Biology* (1864). Spencer adapted the term to concepts contained in Charles Darwin's Writings on natural selection.

73. Sir Henry (Harry) Johnston (1858–1927) was a British explorer who visited most of Africa and wrote about his experiences in such books as *The Colonization of Africa* (1899), *The Opening Up of Africa* (1911), and *The Backwards Peoples and Our Relations with Them* (1920).

74. The front seats near the pulpit, usually reserved for fervent followers.

75. Horace Henry Powers (1835–1913) served as United States Representative from Vermont from 1891 until 1901.

76. Dutch name to describe the Khoikhoi peoples in South Africa. It is now generally considered to be a derogatory term (as it applied to Sarah Baartman, the 19th century woman displayed in sideshows and in caricatures for her protruding buttocks).

77. The Library at Alexandria was one of the most extensive in the ancient world. The library was created by the Greek general Ptolemy, who was the successor of Alexander the Great in the 3rd century BC. It was destroyed during the Roman conquest of Egypt about 48 BCE.

78. Taken from the patriotic British song, "Rule, Britannia." The words to the song were from James Thomson's poem "Rule, Britannia" in the masque *Alfred* and put to music by Thomas Arne in 1740. Thomson used only one "never" in his line.

79. Julius Caesar invaded Britain in 55 BCE and again in 54 BCE. The real conquest of the island came under Emperor Claudius in 43 AD and lasted over 350 years. See Peter Salway, *A History of Roman Britain* (Oxford Univ. Press, 2001).

80. From "The Marseillaise," adopted as the French national anthem in 1795. It was composed by Claude Joseph Rouget de Lisle in 1792.

81. The UNIA or Pan-African flag adapted by the UNIA in 1920. The red represents the blood that unites people of Black African ancestry, the black their existence as a nation, and the green Africa's abundant natural resources.

82. "The Universal Ethiopian Anthem," also called "Ethiopia, Thou Land of Our Fathers," was co-authored by Benjamin E. Burrell (1892–1959) and Arnold Josiah Ford (1877–1935). Burrell, a Jamaican, was a poet, journalist, and political activist. Ford, a native of Barbados, "was affiliated with his own synagogue, Beth B'nai Abraham, and with the Commandment Keepers congregation." *Marcus Garvey: Life and Lessons, A Centennial Companion to The Marcus Garvey and Universal Negro Improvement Association Papers*, ed. Robert A. Hill and Barbara Bair (1987): 383.

83. Some leaders such as Du Bois believed that through racial mixing (miscegenation) Blacks would be gradually absorbed into American society.

84. Hymn #23 from *A Selection of Anti-Slavery Hymns* (1834).

85. Also Rif, a mountainous region of northern Morocco.

86. Gabriele D'Annunzio (1863–1938), Italian poet, soldier, and politician. His nationalistic views would impact Benito Mussolini.

87. Abolitionist William Lloyd Garrison (1805–1879): "To the Public," *The Liberator* (January 1, 1831).

88. Chiang Kai-shek assumed the leadership of the Kuomintang Party in 1926. He was a Chinese nationalist who did not have strong connections with the West and tried to unify China, particularly in the Northern Expedition in 1927. At this time, anti-Western factions attacked the consulates of the United States, the United Kingdom, and Japan. Chiang's government also became engaged in a bloody power struggle with the Chinese Communist Party beginning in 1927.

89. Arthur Brisbane (1864–1936) was a leading American journalist and newspaper editor.

90. This is an excerpt from a poem by George Wells Parker (1882–1931) with this title written in 1923. Parker, an African American who supported Garvey, co-founded the nationalistic Hamitic League of the World in 1917 and wrote the pamphlet *Children of the Sun* (1918).

The title *When Africa Awakes* was used for a collection of essays by Hubert H. Harrison (1883–1927) published in 1920. Harrison was at one time a managing editor of the *Negro World*. He had a profound influence on Garvey before Harrison turned to socialism. For more on their relationship, see Jeffrey B. Perry, *Hubert Harrison: The Voice of Harlem Radicalism, 1883–1918* (2009).

91. From "The Universal Ethiopian Anthem." See note on page 227 for more on the song. See also note 82, part 2.

92. An adaptation of the words from the Book of Mark (16:15): "Go ye into all the world and preach the gospel to every creature."

93. W. A. Domingo (1889–1968) was an editor of the *Negro World* (1918–1919) before breaking with Garvey. Domingo, a boyhood friend of Garvey's, was a socialist and member of the African Blood Brotherhood. He wrote several essays critical of Garvey. When he heard of Garvey's conviction, Domingo wrote a telegram to the Prosecutor, Maxwell S. Mattuck, congratulating him on "Bagging the Tiger."

94. "Something is rotten in the state of Denmark," Shakespeare, *Hamlet* (Act 1, Scene 4).

95. A popular Garveyite song composed by Arnold Ford.

96. For more on Garvey and propaganda, see Tony Martin, *Race First*, 89–109.

97. Ernest "Sunshine Sammy" Morrison and Allen "Farina" Hoskins. See Jacques Garvey's essay "A Black Star" in this anthology.

98. Du Bois stated that Black theater must be "by us, for us, about us, and near us." *Crisis* 32.3 (1926): 134–6.

99. Garvey paid a price for not heavily advertising such products, "[b]ut, in keeping with its philosophy of race pride, the *Negro World* refused to carry adverts for hair-straightening and skin-lightening products, or any other 'advertisement that would in any way libel the race'" (Colin Grant, *Negro with a Hat*, 139). However, particularly in later years, as the need for revenue increased, this policy was loosened. For example, in the Oct. 16, 1926 issue, there were ads for Nelson's Hair Dressing, promoting "smooth, straight and glossy" hair, and another product that promised to "reduce protruding, prominent, thick unshapely lips to normal." Both ads depicted women with Caucasian features. See Winston James (150) for other examples of such advertisements. Beauty product manufacturer Madam C. J. Walker, a supporter of the UNIA, had numerous ads in the *Negro World*. As Barbara Bair observes, some of the ads promoted female entrepreneurship, which would be in keeping with the UNIA message of Black self-sufficiency ("Our Women" 119–20).

100. "The earth is the LORD's, and the fullness thereof, the world, and they that dwell therein" (Psalms 24:1).Interestingly, in Jacques Garvey's phrasing, Blacks are now rulers.

101. "So God created man in his own image" (Genesis 1:27).

102. The passage is slightly paraphrased from American author Pearl S. Buck's first novel *East Wind: West Wind, The Saga of a Chinese Family* (1930). Since this novel was published after Jacques Garvey's article, it seems as if Amy is quoting from an earlier excerpt or version of the book.

103. The article is the famous "The Negro Artist and the Racial Mountain." It became a seminal manifesto of the Harlem Renaissance, advancing the position that the Black artist should not be concerned about what Whites or middle-class Blacks think. Though Hughes is celebrating Black pride, he, of course, would have bristled at the restrictive propagandistic view of art advocated by Garveyites.

104. German-born American artist (1886–1953). He provided illustrations for Alain Locke's *The New Negro* (1925). One of his illustrations is of Langston Hughes.

105. Also crosier (a stylized staff in the shape of a shepherd's crook) and flail, also flabellum (which had a short handle with three beaded strands attached to it); these were important parts of royal regalia in ancient Egypt.

106. The scarab beetle was worshipped by ancient Egyptians who manufactured amulets in its image.

107. Victor Francis Calverton (born George Goetz, 1900–1940), a radical intellectual, founded the *Modern Quarterly* in 1923. He was an influential Marxist literary and political critic who had a close relationship with many Black intellectuals in the 1920s and 1930s. He edited an *Anthology of American Negro Literature* in 1929.

108. The leading organization advocating Prohibition. See note 63, part 1.

109. "Theirs but to do and die," from Alfred, Lord Tennyson's poem, "The Charge of the Light Brigade" (1854).

110. The Kuomintang, who fought the Communists from 1927 to 1948 before eventually being defeated. See note 88 in this section.

PART 3: POST-WOMAN'S PAGE EDITORIALS

1. Jacques Garvey is referring to the Conference of Berlin (1884–1885), conducted by German Chancellor Otto von Bismarck, where Africa was divided among the 14 nations, including Germany, France, Portugal, and Britain. As a result, only Liberia and Ethiopia were left as independent African states.

2. The Cape of Good Hope off the southwestern coast of South Africa.

3. Jacques Garvey likely intends three hundred million.

4. The system of apartheid in South Africa and other racist measures in states such as Rhodesia demonstrate that a small number of Whites were able to maintain control over a much larger group of Blacks for decades.

5. William Ormsby-Gore, 4th Baron Harlech (1885–1964). He was a member of Parliament from 1910 until 1938 and served as Under-Secretary of State for the Colonies from 1922 until 1929. He eventually became a member of the House of Lords and was appointed High Commissioner of South Africa, serving from 1941–1944.

6. Garvey generally supported capitalism and distrusted Communism. See, for example, "The Negro, Communism, Trade Unionism and His (?) Friend" in *Philosophy and Opinions* (1925). For more, sometimes conflicting, views on this complex subject, see Tony Martin, *Race First*, 220–72; Rupert Lewis, *Marcus*

Garvey: Anti-Colonial Champion (Africa World Press, 1988): 125–52; William Z. Foster, "The Garvey Movement: A Marxist View," *Marcus Garvey and the Vision of Africa*, ed. John Henrik Clarke (Vintage, 1974): 414–20. Though he initially found aspects of Mussolini's nationalistic agenda appealing, Garvey condemned him after the Italians invaded Ethiopia in 1935. He satirized the leader in such poems as "Mussolini—Scourge of God" (1935), "The Fascist Brute" (1935), and "The Devil in Mussolini" (1936). See *The Poetical Works of Marcus Garvey*, ed. Tony Martin (Majority Press, 1983). For more on Garvey and Fascism, see Mark Christian Thompson's *Black Fascisms: African American Literature & Culture between the Wars* (Univ. of Virginia Press, 2007), and Tony Martin, *Race First*, 58–62.

7. The well-known British author of such novels as *The Time Machine* (1895), *The Invisible Man* (1897), and *The War of the Worlds* (1898). Wells (1866–1946) was a socialist and praised Blacks in *The Future in America* (1906) and *The Outline of History* (1919–1920).

8. Free thinkers took the philosophical position that thought should be based not on authority or tradition but rather on logic and reason. Since the existence of God could not be proven by empirical evidence, free thinkers tended to be atheists.

9. Hearst (1863–1951) was the major American newspaper publisher of his time. The competition between Hurst and fellow newspaper owner Joseph Pulitzer for sensational news stories with dubious credibility led to the creation of what is known as yellow journalism.

10. Worked for the British South Africa Company for over thirty years.

11. William Johnson Sollas (1849–1936) was a British geologist and anthropologist who taught for many years at the University of Oxford.

12. Derived from the Arabic word *kafir*, a non-believer or infidel, one who does not follow Islam. It was used in South Africa to refer derogatorily to a Black person.

PART 4: SPEECHES

1. The UNIA petitioned for the right to land in Africa for settlers to start an independent Black nation. The appeal was denied.

Works Cited

Adler, Karen S. "'Always Leading Our Men in Service and Sacrifice': Amy Jacques Garvey, Feminist Black Nationalist." *Gender and Society* 6.3 (1992): 346–75. Print.

Bair, Barbara. "'Our Women and What They Think': Amy Jacques Garvey, Negro Womanhood, and the Woman's Page of the *Negro World*." *Feminist Forerunners: New Womanism and Feminism in the Early Twentieth Century*. Ed. Ann Heilmann. London: Pandora Press, 2003. 101–22. Print.

———. "True Women, Real Men: Gender, Ideology, and Social Roles in the Garvey Movement." *Gendered Domains: Rethinking Public and Private in Women's History: Essays from the Seventh Berkshire Conference on the History of Women*. Eds. Dorothy O. Helly and Susan M. Reverby. Ithaca, NY: Cornell Univ. Press, 1992. 154–66. Print.

Benjamin, Keisha N. "'Mr. Black Man, Watch Your Step! Ethiopia's Queens Will Reign Again: Women in the Universal Negro Improvement Association." *Columbia Undergraduate Journal of History* 1.2 (2008): 67–98. Print.

Blain [Benjamin], Keisha. "How Did Rank and File Women in the Universal Negro Improvement Association Use the Woman's Page of *Negro World* to Define the New Negro Woman?" *Women and Social Movements in the United States 1600–2000* (Sept. 2008): 1–10. Print.

Broussard, Jinx Coleman. *Giving a Voice to the Voiceless: Four Pioneering Black Women Journalists*. New York: Routledge, 2004. Print.

Collier-Thomas, Bettye. "Amy Jacques Garvey." *Notable Black American Women, Book II*. Ed. Jessie Carney Smith. Detroit: Gale Research, 1996. 246–9. Print.

Dossett, Kate. *Bridging Race Divides: Black Nationalism, Feminism, and Integration in the United States, 1896–1935*. Gainesville, FL: Univ. Press of Florida, 2008. Print.

Ewing, Adam. *The Age of Garvey: How a Jamaican Activist Created a Mass Movement and Changed Global Black Politics*. Princeton: Princeton Univ. Press, 2014. Print.

Ford-Smith, Honor. "Women and the Garvey Movement in Jamaica." *Garvey: His Work and Impact*. Eds. Rupert Lewis and Patrick Bryan. Trenton, NJ: Africa World Press, 1991. 73–83. Print.

Goldthree, Reena N. "Amy Jacques Garvey, Theodore Bilbo, and the Paradoxes of Black Nationalism." *Global Circuits of Blackness: Interrogating the African Diaspora*. Eds. Jean Muteba Rahier, Percy C. Hintzen and Felipe Smith. Urbana, IL: Univ. of Illinois Press, 2010. 152–73. Print.

Grant, Colin. *Negro With a Hat: The Rise and Fall of Marcus Garvey*. Oxford: Oxford Univ. Press, 2008. Print.

Jacques Garvey, Amy. *Garvey and Garveyism*. New York: Collier Books, 1970. Print.

James, Winston. *Holding Aloft the Banner of Ethiopia: Caribbean Radicalism in Early Twentieth-Century America*. London: Verso, 1998. Print.

Kornweibel, Theodore, Jr. *"Seeing Red": Federal Campaigns against Black Militancy, 1919–1925*. Bloomington, IN: Indiana Univ. Press, 1998. Print.

Lewis, Ida. "Mrs. Marcus Garvey Talks with Ida Lewis." *Encore* (May 1973): 66–8. Print.

Marshall, Paule. "Black Immigrant Women in Brown Girl, Brownstones." *Caribbean Life in New York City: Sociocultural Dimensions*. Eds. Constance R. Sutton and Elsa M. Chaney. New York: Center for Migration Studies of New York, 1994. 81–5. Print.

Martin, Tony. *Race First: The Ideological and Organizational Struggles of Marcus Garvey and the Universal Negro Improvement Association*. Dover, MA: Majority Press, 1976. Print.

Matthews, Mark D. "'Our Women and What They Think': Amy Jacques Garvey and 'The Negro World.'" *Black Scholar* 10.8/9 (1979): 2–13. Print.

McDuffie, Erik S. "'[She] devoted twenty minutes condemning all other forms of government but the Soviet': Black Women Radicals in the Garvey Movement and in the Left during the 1920s." *Diasporic Africa: A Reader*. Ed. Michael A. Gomez. New York: New York Univ. Press, 2006. 219–50. Print.

Reed, Beverley. "Amy Jacques Garvey: Black, Beautiful & Free." *Ebony* (June 1971): 45–54. Print.

Satter, Beryl. "Marcus Garvey, Father Divine and the Gender Politics of Race Difference and Race Neutrality." *American Quarterly* 48.1 (1996): 43–76. Print.

Taylor, Ula Y. "'Negro Women Are Great Thinkers as Well as Doers': Amy Jacques-Garvey and Community Feminism in the United States, 1924–1927." *Journal of Women's History* 12.2 (2000): 104–27. Print.

———. *The Veiled Garvey: The Life & Times of Amy Jacques Garvey*. Chapel Hill: Univ. of North Carolina Press, 2002. Print.

Watkins-Owens, Irma. "Earliest Twentieth-Century Caribbean Women: Migration and Social Networks in New York City." *Islands in the City: West Indian Migration to New York*. Ed. Nancy Foner. Berkeley: Univ. of California Press, 2001. 25–51. Print.

White, E. Frances. "Africa on My Mind: Gender, Counter Discourse and African-American Nationalism." *Journal of Women's History* 2.1 (1990): 73–97. Print.

Zackodnik, Teresa. "Recirculation and Feminist Black Internationalism in Jessie Fauset's 'The Looking Glass' and Amy Jacques Garvey's 'Our Women and What They Think.'" *Modernism/Modernity* 19.3 (Sept. 2012): 437–59. Print.

Index

www.ingramcontent.com/pod-product-compliance
Lightning Source LLC
Chambersburg PA
CBHW030621310726
48979CB00003B/828